CRITICAL ISSUES

FOR FUTURE SOCIAL WORK PRACTICE

WITH AGING PERSONS

D1189554

CRITICAL ISSUES

for Future Social Work Practice with Aging Persons

Edited by

SHEILA M. NEYSMITH

COLUMBIA

UNIVERSITY PRESS

NEW YORK

COLUMBIA UNIVERSITY PRESS
Publishers Since 1893
New York   Chichester, West Sussex

Copyright © 1999 by Columbia University Press
All rights reserved
Library of Congress Cataloging-in-Publication Data
Critical issues for future social work practice with aging persons /
   edited by Sheila M. Neysmith.
      p.   cm.
   Includes bibliographical references.
   ISBN 0-231-11338-2 (cloth : alk. paper). — ISBN 0-231-11339-0
   (paper : alk. paper)
      1. Social work with the aged—North America. 2. Social case work
   with the aged—Research—North America. 3. Aged—Care—Research—
   North America. 4. North America—Social policy.   I. Neysmith,
   Sheila M.
   HV1478.N7C75   1999
   362.6—dc21   99-22409

Casebound editions of Columbia University Press books are printed on
permanent and durable acid-free paper.
Printed in the United States of America

c 10 9 8 7 6 5 4 3 2 1
p 10 9 8 7 6 5 4 3 2 1

To Ben and Hilda Katz,
whose commitment to improving the care of older people
paved the way for this book

Contents

Acknowledgments

The last section of chapter 1 outlines some of the specific events that resulted in this book. Such, of course, was only part of the story. Inviting people to participate in a project is the first step. Once an invitation is taken up, the process takes on a life of its own.

The book would not have been possible without the efforts of my colleague, and coauthor of chapter 1, Margaret MacAdam. When we initially discussed the idea of a series of seminars that would start to develop a research agenda for the Ben and Hilda Katz Centre, the latter was still on the drawing board. It was Margaret, supported by the social work department of Baycrest, who put in place the resources and organizational structure that resulted in the rich monthly discussions actually happening. If I appropriately thanked each person, I would soon be listing half the social work department. Suffice to say that month after month their debates contributed to the wealth of ideas of what a gerontological social work research center could do to enrich our understanding of aging.

All the authors in the book have responded over and over to requests for changes in their manuscripts and met what I can only assume seemed like impossible deadlines for sending me materials—and they were all so unfailingly gracious about it! I thank each one of you and hope you will be proud of the final product.

For each seminar the Faculty of Social Work at the University of Toronto and the Baycrest Centre for Geriatric Care reached out through their networks to solicit participation from various community groups. These activists, service providers, and community residents have many demands made on their time.

I am sure that defining a research agenda was not particularly pressing for any of them! However, they responded to our plea for relevance and thus made possible what I hope is an analysis that reflects some of their priorities.

A special word of thanks is due to John Michel, executive editor at Columbia University Press, who for over a year pushed me to put forward a prospectus that outlined what a book on critical issues for social work practice with aging persons might look like. He and the staff at CUP have been extraordinarily helpful throughout.

In this, and other work that I have undertaken over the years, my partner Michael Milner has been an inexhaustible source of warmth and support. Any statement of thanks will always be inadequate.

Finally, this book is dedicated to Ben and Hilda Katz as a concrete way of thanking them for the trust and commitment that the center embodies. May it further your vision as it grows through the decades of the twenty-first century.

CRITICAL ISSUES

FOR FUTURE SOCIAL WORK PRACTICE

WITH AGING PERSONS

Controversial Concepts

SHEILA NEYSMITH AND MARGARET MACADAM

As we enter the twenty-first century, social work is caught up in a vortex of institutional changes related to the restructuring of health and welfare programs. Social policies are changing in virtually all Western societies as responsibility for the support and assistance of those in need is increasingly consigned to the family and market spheres. The establishment of mixed economies of care, and the separation of funders from service providers that accompanies this model, together are changing both the organization of social work practice and its representation in language and theorizing. These processes of restructuring are presented usually as adaptations to international economic pressures, often seen as inevitable and apolitical (Cohen 1996). As various sectors of the population try to cope with the effects of change, restructuring is offered as the explanation rather than examined as a response to market pressures in an increasingly globalized economy. Ultimately ignored in restructuring discussions is the fact that effects do not fall equally on all sectors of the population. It is the less privileged sectors of the population, however, that social workers encounter. One of the arenas where the results of restructuring are being felt most sharply is the field of aging, particularly in long-term care services.[1]

The above changes have been occurring since the early 1980s but in a piecemeal fashion. Within the Canadian context the process has been described as a "politics of stealth," resulting in the "hollowing out" of the welfare state (Jessop 1993). This phrase captures how many decisions have been implemented through changing program regulations rather than legislation, which would open up public debate. Social policies may thus appear un-

changed on the surface, but once the cover of legislation is lifted the fragmented and weakened program structures which have been eaten away over
time are revealed. As we live this particular historical moment, the speed and
scope of these changes can seem overwhelming. In addition, the ability of the
profession of social work to respond is hampered by the dominance of a market discourse that excludes a social justice framework, the foundation of
post–World War II welfare state programs in which social work reformers
played an active part.

    This book starts from the location of services to elderly people, locations
where social workers are players but do not set policy priorities; where social
workers are charged with meeting need but seldom determine how resources
are allocated. In their various practice settings social workers are immersed in
a restructuring discourse that is reprivatizing much of the caring work which
had been entering the public domain insofar as services such as home care
were considered a welfare state provision. Originally, these services were con-
ceived of as meeting the needs of older persons based on assessments of their
functional capacities. Today such assessments also include evaluating potential help by kin. Indeed, many community care programs have policy goals explicitly stating that they seek to support carers as well as those who are elderly. At one level this can be viewed as a holistic approach to the situation.
However, within the above-noted neoliberal context of privatization, entitlements of an old person to services based on need are too easily displaced in
favor of a model wherein the old person–kin carer dyad becomes the focus for
assessment, thereby reinforcing the socially created dependency of the elderly
person (Holstein 1998; Orme 1998). This shift, occurring across countries
such as Canada, New Zealand, and the United States (to name but those
countries represented in this book), reflects the changing values and public expectations over who is responsible for meeting need. Neoliberal social policies, and the programs that flow from them, mark a change in what it means
to be a citizen and the entitlements that traditionally have been associated
with it.

    As health care is restructured there is an underlying unease that what so-
cial work defines as professional knowledge, skill, and ethical behavior may
have very little bearing on future services (Jarman-Rohde et al. 1997; May &
Buck 1998). Nevertheless, it is a premise of this book that social workers are
implicated in these changes and thus are players in the contested terrain of
defining old people's needs and determining how they are to be met, by
whom and under what material conditions. Admittedly, the social work profession is seldom an institutional force in defining public policy resource al-

locations even though individuals, and at times representatives from some arms of the profession, may enjoy the temporary privilege of walking the corridors of power. However, for those social workers grappling with the inequities that riddle our society, such environments are unlikely to be the arenas from which research and practice theory will emerge that can transform the lives of people who experience gender, class, and race inequities as they age. Consequently, if they are to influence the issues that affect vulnerable groups of people as they age, social workers will probably need to use analytical tools and practice strategies that other groups at the margins have found useful. These include taking into account our limitations, strategically using the profession's sources of power, and building the coalitions that are so necessary if alternatives are to be pursued.

The chapters in this book focus on long-term care areas which affect vulnerable groups, in particular women, as they age. Financially secure and well elderly people are not the center of attention. The analysis concentrates on the social conditions within which people age and the organizational contexts within which services are delivered. In making the decision to emphasize context, we are not turning away from the specifics of social workers' daily practice with aging individuals and their families. On the contrary, we argue that it is in just such situations that the contradictions in old people's lives are visible and thus are accessible for retheorizing. Social work research to inform practice theory is more than testing the effectiveness of intervention models on given client groups, or using context as a background, a set of "givens" that define the parameters of practice. Rather the situations that social workers encounter are sites for formulating theory about the interaction of the personal and the political, articulating questions that will open up new research directions, and reordering assumed professional priorities. It is in this sense that we use the term *critical practice*. As discussed later in this chapter, the phrase is employed to capture a practice orientation which seeks to see aging women in a different way than the prevailing explanations offer. The aim of the book is to challenge current social arrangements and those explanations that reinforce privilege, while opening up alternatives that might allow people to have fuller, more satisfying lives. Thus the reader will find few clearly specified guidelines for practice. Our experience with social change endeavours suggests that such guidelines not only become quickly outdated but can too easily become an analytical crutch, a substitute for that ongoing engagement with the changing political processes that marks the ethical practitioner (Hugman & Smith 1996). The rationale for this position is developed in the next section.

A Feminist Analysis of the Needs of Aging Women

The health care system is an ever-present force in the lives of most aging women. The medicalization of old age in the late twentieth century means that the administrative practices of long-term care policy are important influences on the quality of life of women. The restructuring of health care which has relegated services and costs into home care services and onto families has been borne primarily by women whether they are positioned in the discourse as care providers, receivers, or female kin. In the long-term care field much attention is devoted to predicting health care use patterns and their projected costs. Thus, we know that service use is associated with what are called predisposing factors (e.g., gender, age, race, education), enabling conditions (income, transportation, and availability of kin), and need (operationalized in terms of health status, functional impairment) (Beland & Shapiro 1995; Diwan, Berger, & Manns 1997). Such utilization models are useful to health planners insofar as they point to issues in the organization and delivery of services. They have little relevance, however, to the problems of actually managing the activities of daily living with meager resources that face old people and their families. More importantly, when such variables are used to delineate subgroups of elderly persons deemed at risk, they distract attention from the fact that these are indicators of social conditions that oppress certain groups of elderly people. An emphasis on risk factors can quickly turn old people, rather than the social conditions in which they live, into the problem.

Provider-generated definitions of health care problems such as inappropriate service use, duplication of service, or gaps in service do filter down, however, to the micro level of health care practitioners, social workers, old people, and informal carers—and have consequences! These images and categories may, at one level, be seen as social constructions, but they have a reality in terms of their power to effect service funding and delivery. The resultant tensions get embedded into the work of frontline practitioners in the form of how practice and its possibilities are defined. It becomes the job of the individual worker to negotiate a workable plan within the resources available. The tools for getting the job done may take the form, for instance, of assessment criteria that repackage needs so they fit available services rather than vice versa. In effect, then, frontline workers are engaged in a resource negotiation relationship with old people and their families that is inherently conflictual. Because these conflicts occur at the level of face-to-face interactions and in the context of individually focused problems and strains, it is very difficult to reframe them as institutional and political issues. Thus, while understanding individual circumstances and negotiating relational aspects of the work among daily players are important social work skills, they cannot be practiced in a political vacuum. Social work practice theory needs to be articulated in a way that will not result in elders, family caregivers, and individual practitioners seeing each other as the problem (Aronson & Neysmith 1997; Ungerson 1995). It is all too easy to blame the victim if the analytic gaze focuses too strongly on individuals struggling to survive under very oppressive conditions. Thus, how the context, social conditions, and the social location of the parties involved gets articulated in the specifics of everyday practice are recurring themes throughout the book.

By focusing on women's entanglement in the long-term care system, we are necessarily engaging with a very large body of health care literature. The shape and ingredients of this literature reflect the presence of funders, professions, and organizations, all of which have been powerful players, and thus definers, of knowledge about aging and those aspects of the health care system that serve old people. The financial and human resources involved in health care are vast (from 10 to 14 percent of Gross Domestic Product [GDP], depending on the country), very visible, and the focus of ongoing public debate. High costs are often attributed to the demographic profile of an aging population. Elderly people, and old women in particular because of their higher morbidity and longevity rates, are depicted as a caring problem (Gibson 1996), a problem that will get worse and will be costly to address. Research that puts the lie to this claim (e.g., Barer, Evans, & Hertzman 1995; Robertson 1991, 1997) is routinely ignored as correlations between health care costs and utilization data are proclaimed as "obvious." The power of the demographic crisis discourse remains quite unabated and seems to reappear in a new guise as soon as one form is discredited.

Critical threads in both gerontology (Dressel, Minkler & Yen 1997; Laws 1995; Minkler & Estes 1991, 1999; Phillipson & Walker 1986) and social work literature (e.g., Galambos 1997; Hooyman & Gonyea 1995) have developed oppositional discursive processes and documented the manifestations of apocalyptic demography, in particular its consequences for older women. Many of the points raised in the following pages will resonate with such works. However, at the time of writing these critical voices were being drowned in an oratorio of market rhetoric. The human and financial costs of caring are underlined, but the fact that it is women who do most of the actual caring, and that at any moment in time a relatively small proportion of the population of old women require care, just fades from view. It is here that social workers face ethical choices. Over the last few decades there has been an expansion of ethics that posits the health care encounter as something that must be negotiated

with as much ethical as technical acuity. Traditionally, professional ethical behavior was assumed to rest on proper conduct by the practitioner. As long as
she or he was seen as exercising appropriate moral agency according to parameters set down by professional codes, then ethical requirements were satisfied.
The position of the other partner (client, consumer, patient) was of limited
ethical interest in that the latter was characterized as a passive receiver of benefits rather than an independent agent (Shildrick 1997:7). The active-passive
dichotomy (several of which are discussed later in the chapter) was epitomized
in the medical model, but it essentially informed most professional codes of
ethics—including those of social workers. Positioning the old person as a consumer or customer does not challenge this traditional ethical model. Situating
them as a partner, as an active subject rather than a passive object of intervention can potentially change what is viewed as ethical practice.

Choosing to put the word *critical* in the title of this book signals what
the chapters strive to do. Like many of the concepts discussed in the pages
ahead, the word *critical* has been co-opted into everyday language. This being so, it is important to return to its original meaning. "A critical theory
wants to explain a social order in such a way that it becomes itself the cata-
lyst which leads to the transformation of the social order" (Fay 1987:27). The
latter part of the definition implies that the theory be absorbed by those who
are involved—sometimes referred to as consciousness-raising. Social workers
may have limited power to effect this process, but they do have the responsibility to ensure that their practice theory reflects the existence of the inter-
locking oppressions that characterize our society—oppressions that are not
stable (i.e., where the specifics will vary with time and place), but the effects
of which are real and affect the quality of old people's lives. In order for
change of the magnitude suggested by definitions of critical theory to occur,
people's lives would need to be in a state of crisis. The groups of old women
who are the paradigmatic focus in this book might be seen to be living lives
that are at the point of crisis.

Our focus is primarily on women who are most likely to enter the orbit
of long-term care policy in vulnerable positions, specifically, those with low
incomes, those who might have some degree of disability, and those who are
members of ethno-racial communities. The point to be made is that we are
not talking about *THE* elderly, that homogenizing concept that is so broad as
to be analytically useless. Each chapter is about aging women whether the primary focus is on old women themselves, the consequences for men and women as spouses when aging theory is gender neutral, or the professionals and
paraprofessionals who supplement the informal female caring labor which

constitute the de facto community care programs in most countries. Ever lurking in the background is a health care system that concurrently refuses to recognize this labor as work, excludes it as a health care cost, and undervalues the skills of the caring professions and paraprofessionals involved in frontline service delivery. How theory and research interrogates the lives of women, and the practice models that are built on this theory and research, are extremely important for shaping the options that women have available today *and* the quality of life they enjoy as they care for elderly kin and age themselves. We know from surveys that both men and women rely on women for social support, but the demands of these relationships can leave women with little time and energy to provide for their own old age in a market economy where employment histories are linked to retirement income (McDaniel & McKinnon 1993), and/or where coverage for health services such as dental care and drugs are either provided through employer benefits or they are not available (Lillard, Rogowski & Kington 1997). It is against this backdrop that women assume the lion's share of caring responsibilities.

Gerontology, as an area of scholarship, affects the quality of life of elderly people because it defines needs. In fact, we argue that how concepts are used in gerontology can benefit or harm old people in general, and some groups of women in particular. As programs based on universal entitlement shrink under the mixed economy of care, expert definitions of need become the basis for social allocation.

Programs targeted to certain groups exclude those who do not meet categorical definitions. Thus, we are starting this critical inquiry by selecting several concepts that are part of current aging discourse. In the pages that follow, we scrutinize them in a more systematic way than is possible under the pressure of daily practice demands as social workers borrow words to convey an idea, portray a need, or describe a situation. Some of these concepts are *frailty, autonomy, community, need,* and *managed care.* The choice of concepts and the analytical dimensions used to interrogate them are drawn from antioppression theories as these have been developed in feminist, antiracist, lesbian, and community living literatures.

Frailty or a Devalued Body?

Our concern with the quality of life of women as they age is not based solely on the fact that old women outnumber old men—although as Anne Martin-Matthews shows in chapter 2 they do, and the implications are considerable.

Aging is a gendered process and thus women experience old age differently than do men. One of these differences is that old women inhabit an aging body in a culture where the universalized ideal body ("the gold standard of hegemonic social discourse": Haraway 1989:355) is young, white, able, and male. To be old, nonwhite, disabled, or female is not only to be different but also to be inferior. The implications of this for the well-being of old women has not been a strong theme in gerontology. Certainly, much has been written about the state of the aging female body. Unfortunately, a good deal of it reflects a continuation of the tradition wherein the female body is a site for regulation and control (for feminist assessments of this literature, see Jaggar and Bordo 1989, Nicholson 1990, Sherwin 1998, and Shildrick 1997; for a recent anthology of key pieces, see Weitz 1998). In the field of aging, what is seen as the deteriorating condition of the body has been fueled by professional concerns over the service and resource implications of physical and mental incompetence. That is, the effects of frailty on one's ability to perform certain tasks related to the activities of daily living are less a threat to identity or an indicator of need than they are warning signs of potential demands on service budgets. Ironically, research has consistently demonstrated that these are in fact poor predictors of service use; that it is the presence or absence of informal carers that is most critical.

The social construction of aging as a problem of physical deterioration to be treated by medical practitioners has been a thread in the political economy critique mentioned earlier (see Estes & Binney 1991; Estes & Linkins 1997; Katz 1996). Also, since the early 1980s the humanities have established a presence in gerontology which has challenged dominant medical and social science explanations. This scholarship has expanded and added much-needed diversity to the meaning of growing old. However, as Katz (1996:6) notes, even in these discussions agency is frequently lacking. This idea is taken up in some detail in the next section and is evident in the research reported in chapters by Jane Aronson and Deborah O'Connor where old people, as care-receivers and spouses, respectively, are actors. It is important to emphasize that currently these are oppositional voices, they are not powerful. The medical-market discourse dominates today and seems to be even more firmly entrenched than it was in the 1980s when the policy implications of these challenges were enjoying a bit of prominence. What becomes obscured in the present discourse on scarce health resources is that so-called frailty does not occur in a degendered, universal body. The body being scrutinized *is* old, but frequently it belongs to other devalued social categories as well—that is, it is often female, poor, or visibly ethno-racial. This being said, there are several threads in the oppositional aging literature that provide some space for options. One draws on feminist theory, another on postmodern ideas of subjectivity, and a third might be called the politics of identity and social movements.

During the 1980s there was a reemergence of analyses of the body as black, women's, and gay and lesbian politics coalesced around new understandings of subjectivity of which the body is a part. Such analyses were centrally concerned with exposing how dominant discourses were social constructions that privileged the physical characteristics of some while devaluing those of other groups. At the same time, scholars were grappling with the implications of writings by postmodern theorists such as Michel Foucault. In the process, considerable attention was focused on the body as a terrain for multiple possible interpretations. Foucault's writings documented how the body is fundamental to political, economic, and professional regimes (Katz 1996:21). In this sense the body is socially constructed. However, as feminist philosophers such as Sherwin (1998) and Shildrick (1997) and advocates such as Morris (1993) from the disability movement emphasize, the body has also a real material presence. On the one hand, too much emphasis on social construction can result in policies that downplay how not having certain capabilities affects one's life. On the other hand, while assessments of functional abilities may help determine assistance needed to carry on with the tasks of daily living, they miss the cultural significance and affronts to identity that these incapacities entail in a society where the devalued status of being old and female is best captured in negative labels or the forces that drive a multimillion dollar cosmetics industry. It is this wider cultural terrain that shapes how the physical signs that their bodies are aging affect the quality of life of women.

The major challenges to dominant images of ability, and the social construction of dependency associated with such images, have come from the disability movement. It is important to remember, however, that this movement found its leaders primarily among younger persons with disabilities who were concerned with issues of independent living. Old women will express a different set of priorities. In chapter 5 Amy Horowitz speaks to some of these. In particular, she points to the dearth of rehabilitation programs and the treatment of depression—two conditions affecting many older women. It is a moot point, however, if this lack of attention reflects stereotypes about the "old" or the "disabled" body. With this proviso in mind, the disability movement analysis is important in that it was not generated by health care actors and so it challenges the dominant discourse of frailty and definitions of competence that are operationalized in terms of activities of daily living (ADL) but are interpreted as signs of deterioration, incompetence, or indicators of service use. In deconstructing disability, authors such as Oliver (1990), Morris (1993), and Price (1996) argue that people with disabilities are a threat to the able-bodied because they signify the vulnerability of the latter. We would agree with Shildrick (1997:49) that disability in old age is overdetermined by the demographic fact that it is primarily old women who are being discussed.

The presence of an aged body is a reminder to the observer of what the future holds if one lives to an old age. In an age-phobic society negative reactions are modified only by an awareness that the alternatives are even less welcome! Thus, as Anne Opie demonstrates in chapter 8, an old woman with physical and/or cognitive disabilities faces multiple inscriptions of who she is in her final years—and younger women see the future in front of them. Julia Twigg (1997) captures some of the cultural specifics in her description of what she aptly terms "the social bath." Bathing is both bodily pleasure and functional necessity. However, the former is obscured in health routines where the activity is described in terms of the "bean counting" of minutes per bath and establishing minimum training standards for safely performing the activity. This construction of a bath ensures maximum vulnerability for the old person, yet an old person's recalcitrance to a bath regime is interpreted as resistance. Indeed it well might be, but the resistance may not be to cleanliness so much as to the objectification that permeates the procedure. Thus, routine home care procedures are potentially powerful sites for reproducing gender, race, and class devaluations among old women and those attending to them.

What Do We Mean by Autonomy and Agency?

The concepts of *agency* and *autonomy* are seeing increased emphasis in gerontological literature. However, like the other concepts discussed in this chapter, they come with their own set of troublesome features. Both tend to appear with their opposites, the inevitable dichotomies that are characteristic of modern Western thought. This is a serious situation if one sees words/concepts as social constructions rather than some kind of an objective account of what is "out there." In dichotomies, meaning on one side automatically invokes an opposite. In this case, the opposites are *victimization* and *dependency*. The latter words are considered negative, suggestive of incompetence and not valued. Feminist scholarship is again useful for releasing these definitions from their masculinist anchors.

In classic liberal thought an individual is assumed to act autonomously if she or he is competent—in other words, is rational, has adequate information and understanding about available choices, and is free from explicit coercion toward or away from any of these options. Indeed a primary function of the state from this perspective is to clear away impediments to the exercise of choice through enacting laws and regulations. The validity of these assumptions about freedom and choice in the lives of women is highly questionable. What can go unnoticed when professionals focus on helping individuals exercise choice is the lack of choice in a system that promotes kin-based care. For example, when services are meager and tightly rationed, what other choices are there that are preferable to remaining in a situation where kin care may be cursory, bordering on neglectful, but is at least predictable? This is the exercise of rational choice—given the circumstances. The language of choice can act as a screen and effectively hide conditions of social neglect and isolation, even as we lament the dependency of old women. When practice decisions are constantly being made within a rhetoric of scarce resources, definitions of autonomy are all too often stripped from the full context of older women's lives. The depiction of an old woman as a victim makes it difficult to see her as a survivor, an active agent struggling with limited options. Once in place, such a label hides acts of resistance and struggle for control that elderly women receiving care, as well as their caregivers, engage in on a daily basis (Barry 1995; also see Aronson, this volume, and O'Connor, this volume). Agency does not mean acting for oneself under conditions of oppression. It means being without oppression (Mahoney 1994:65). Individual old women can resist, but they need advocates and partners to build coalitions that can combat oppression.

If conditions are to change, and choice exercised, some important questions to ask are: If an old woman does not want to be labeled as being dependent or a problem, how would services have to be organized so that she is not perceived this way as she, for example, exercises the choice of refusal or puts conditions on the receipt of home care, such as having her meal late in the evening? What service guidelines would need to be in place for a spouse to utilize day care for a lifelong partner without feeling like she or he is betraying the trust of a lifetime? Visions of consumer choice operationalized through programs such as those discussed by Sharon Keigher in chapter 7 do not begin to address these types of concerns.

Moral agency involves being held responsible or accountable for one's actions when these are freely chosen. However, the conditions that shape both options available and choices made are never irrelevant. A critical perspective, unlike the liberal stance noted above, cannot eliminate barriers that impede the ability of individuals to exercise choice, but it can theorize these as important social conditions that must be part of assessments. For instance, the autonomy of most women is conditional upon their access to income. Thus, marital status continues to be an important determinant of the quality of women's lives because it is still the route to resources in old age for most women. The consequences of widowhood, divorce, and separation evident in the statistics presented by Anne Martin-Matthews (chapter 2) affect old women in ways that they do not old men. Women's poor retirement benefits reflect the fact that these are tied to paid work that is done in addition to the many hours of unpaid work (Statistics Canada 1997, 1998:23–34) that affect labor market choices. Long-term care policies compound the inequality when they contain assumptions about the availability of women to do caregiving, work that may be honored in rhetoric but is seldom acknowledged in terms of benefits and rights. Thus the theoretical challenge is not limited only to valuing unpaid work. Equally pressing is the necessity to make very explicit the link between paid and unpaid work. Documenting the effects of the paid-unpaid work connection is critical if old women are to be seen as productive and thus entitled to health and social benefits. Theory that maintains the schism of these separate spheres hides this link and thus reinforces rather than challenges a powerful source of oppression in women's lives. Women are not helpless victims or powerful agents; agency is not the opposite of victimization; victims are not failed agents who lack the skills to act. Gerontology literature that discusses caring decisions without embedding these within a critique of the social conditions under which choices are made reproduces the conditions that deny women autonomy.

In summary, a person does not operate outside of relationships; nor does she or he exercise rational choice based on a calculation of self-interest. To argue that women choose to care is not so much wrong as it is analytically barren. One does not stand back and calculate the costs and benefits of a particular choice. Rather, decisions are made within a web of social relations and options that are shaped by the material conditions available to all parties (Baines, Evans & Neysmith 1998; Clement 1996). Social workers, old women, and female kin who provide informal care will inevitably interpret identity and needs differently (Fraser 1989:153). Ideally, assessments would take these differences into account; in reality, community-based care is too narrowly framed to allow this to happen. In order to do their job, social workers who are involved in assessments have a narrow range of maneuverability. This theme is picked up again in the next section.

Community—Full of Sound and Fury, Signifying . . . ?

One of the most used, yet ephemeral, current program concepts is that of community. The term will probably always be ambiguous, but the challenge is to determine how the idea is being employed today in long-term care policy and how this affects the lives of women as they age. The original referent was to a policy of deinstitutionalization wherein living in the community was invoked as the far more desirable opposite. It is a sobering reminder to gerontologists that today the mental health field is littered with human tragedies that are testimony to what happens when community is assumed rather than examined and built. Few elderly persons were ever actually deinstitutionalized; rather, the phrase "community-based care" is used as a synonym for services delivered in people's homes. Unfortunately, receiving services in one's own home does not mean that one is part of a community, or that the services are developed by or in a community, yet the use of the term carries both these overtones. In addition, a community-based policy implies at least the opportunity for social participation. However, the limited research that is available from elderly service users documents isolation as a persistent and pervasive condition. One could conclude from this research that projects that get people out of the house and in contact with others should be a program priority. Yet, ironically, as funds are cut, so-called social outings are considered expendable and are the first to go as transportation services, always precarious, are rationed to only cover medical appointments (Older Women's Network 1998). Consequently, we suggest that social workers think of community as a discursive strategy, a term used by different constituencies to give meaning to their actions (Giddens 1984). It is part of a vocabulary used by long-term care professionals to convey a shared commitment to not delivering services within an institution; beyond that, however, the concept is deployed in very different ways by social actors for whom it has very different meanings. We now consider several of these.

At the descriptive level, the concept of community invokes a principle of cohesion that can have political and administrative significance. The term is frequently connected to some kind of territory, such as a nation, a neighborhood, or the land claims of aboriginal peoples. However, community is also invoked to refer to interests or rights based on shared characteristics, or a commonly held value (e.g., sisterhood). Here the emphasis is on participation in actions of common rather than individual interest. One's identity may be expressed individually, but it is informed by a sense of collective purpose and benefit. It is this sense of the word that is summoned up in calls for ethnic specific services for some seniors. This sense of relationship of oneself to others offers meaning to members' lives. Thus, an emphasis on community has the potential to dilute some of the individualism and privatization that permeates policies and programs, while serving as a basis for meaningful engagement in society.

Community is frequently used in another way, a way that is probably closer to what public policy tries to convey. One can think of an active community, a constituency that seeks to develop its strengths and capacities. In this case, however, whoever has the power to define the community and claims to represent its interests, also claims authority in terms of defining and meeting a community's needs (Husband 1996:37). Community-based services can also refer to different ways of planning, organizing, or practicing interventions, but within each of these domains different and often opposing meanings can be invoked to justify a wide variety of strategies (White 1993:34). For instance, one way that policy allows for local variation is to institute a decentralized planning process. Planning, however, is more than ensuring that consultations are held with various stakeholders (Aronson 1993; Shemmings & Shemmings 1995). Participation covers social relations within the planning body and the extent to which that body represents the diversity within a community. At the time of writing, across countries, there has been a move to separate funding from the delivery of service. Putting aside for the moment the cost-saving agenda behind such policies, local organizations are presented as the embodiment of civil society. Local organizations it is argued, best know local needs. Yet most service organizations are synthetic, with few consumers having the time and resources to participate at more than a token level. Furthermore, consumer participation is inconsistent with the hierarchical professional structures that lie behind individualized service plans and case management. Critical social work practice means working with consumers so that they can resist being oppressed by the very programs that were designed to benefit them. Ethically, social workers are challenged not to reproduce inequities.

Finally, one can consider community as a component of daily long-term care practice—that is, it could serve as an image for understanding relations between practitioners and service users. Models of practice within community-based systems differ profoundly. Twigg (1993), for example, argues that caregivers are variously seen as clients, partners, and consumers. All, however, are professional models, designed by professionals for professionals. We really do not know what old women or their female kin carers would put into a model they designed. Whether using an empowerment discourse or not (see Anne Opie, chapter 8), professional models assume a position of protection and control toward service users. For example, in partnership models aging individuals and their families and friends are routinely assumed to have primary responsibility for meeting needs, with formal care providers supporting, supplementing, and occasionally substituting for family-based care. The chapters in this book suggest that if all partners had an equal say in negotiating service models, they would look quite different from what exists today. To further equity and democracy, a politics of representation and participation in which practitioners work not only with individual service users but also with advocacy groups and user-led organizations are essential practice ingredients (Davis & Ellis 1996:151).

Needs talk takes many forms. How it is picked up by competing discourses is important. The aging women who are the subjects of this book do not have an abundance of financial, social, and family resources. What is given now is given with considerable difficulty and cost for all concerned. Possibilities of empowerment and choice are thus constrained. These "consumers" cannot exit from the market. Social workers have to manage this considerable difference in power between providers and consumers. The question is, on what basis do we make decisions of where and how to exercise our power in a way that is meaningful to service users?

Case Management, Managed Care, or Managerialism?

Community care policy can cover a variety of organization and service delivery strategies that may share little in common except for the population of potential users. Nevertheless, it is this pool of services that makes up the ingredients in the mixed economy of care. The phrase "the mixed economy of care" was coined in the 1980s to capture changes in the way services were funded and delivered. We use the term in lieu of others, such as the funder/provider split model or welfare pluralism, because it captures more graphically some of the dilemmas in community care service models; in particular, the phrase signals the mixed public, voluntary, and for-profit auspices of care providers that are potentially a source of considerable conflict. The expression also points to the fact that we are talking about economics, that there are different types of funding approaches, that care is what is being discussed, and perhaps most importantly, that all three are linked. Only implied in the expression, unfortunately, is the existence of different sets of players. Nevertheless, in this book we do ask who is located where and investigate the consequences for different long-term care players of being in a particular location. The restructuring process referred to in the opening paragraphs of this chapter is driven by changing economic pressures. Organizations struggle with change in order to survive, costs are re-arranged, families are expected to assume more and more. The elderly women who people the chapters in this book are those for whom the mixed economy is supposedly being reorganized to serve better. As dollars are shuffled between different columns in the long-term care ledger, these are the actors who are the most vulnerable and thus they will bear the highest costs.

There is a health care literature on health maintenance organizations (HMOs), diagnostic-related groups (DRGs), and managed care that attempts to track these costs. This literature is particularly well-developed in the Unit-ed States where private health care purchasers are interested in controlling ris-ing medical care costs. The two large public programs in that country, Medicare and Medicaid, have followed suit, tendering contracts for service provision. This market-based approach places a premium on controlling growth in the price and use of services (Thorpe 1997; Wallace & Villa 1999:247). Although the United States faces a particular policy dilemma around its 41 million citizens who are not insured, the contract approach rais-es quality control dilemmas for all countries where bid-based service con-tracts are signed centrally but implemented locally (Kettner & Martin 1996; Kramer 1994).

Different populations use services differently, but it remains a moot point as to how allocation decisions are made by providers. For instance, in Mani-toba, one Canadian province where costs can be compared, persons with cog-nitive impairment have different service use patterns than those with a de-mentia—two groups that are often thrown into one program category. While these variations raise important questions for service rationing, the authors conclude that the bottom line is that most costs fall on female kin (Shapiro & Tate 1997:678). The persistence of this pattern calls for social workers to re-visit how they juxtapose the needs of various family members. In attempting to do this, social workers will be grappling with the classic dichotomy of the separate private/public spheres. The concept is problematic because caring la-bor flows across the divide. The very idea of separate spheres impedes our abil-ity to think differently about how women's lives can be organized. Many fem-inists argue that the elimination of this dichotomy is essential if we are to carve out a domain of the social that is not bound by the categories of pri-vate/family/female and public/"paid work"/male (Nicholson 1990; Smith 1990). Such a theoretical orientation encourages social workers to examine in-stitutional practices in programs such as home care that link public policy into the private lives of old women and their kin carers. Research is needed that documents how what some writers refer to as "the relations of ruling"

(Smith 1990) are concretized in the specifics of program and practice which then become powerful shapers of the lives of women as they age.

The language that pervades the literature on managed care is one area where the power of discourse can be seen clearly enough to begin to tease out its implications for the welfare of the groups who are the focus of this book. The organizational practices that undergird managed care come directly out of the business restructuring literature: effective and efficient organizations need to be able to adapt to constant change, be decentralized, and remain flexible. For example, health and social service multidisciplinary teams are a central feature of the new world of managed care. This has given rise to the differentiation of care management (planning and coordination) from care production (doing the hands-on work). This split, although apparently effective for the efficient use of more and less expensive personnel, does necessitate communication work that, to use the words of Schweikhart & Smith-Daniels (1996:26), is not "value added" and creates time-lags between care decisions and actions. Different team structures are and will increasingly be assessed in terms of their ability to reinforce operational restructuring objectives. Their consequences for how changes in the provision and delivery of services affect the quality of old women's lives is not part of the managed care discourse.

Metaphors like managed care, the mixed economy of care, partnerships, and so on are never neutral. They, like social problem definition, emphasize a certain set of "truths" which serve to suppress others. Discourse analysis is an important route for uncovering these phenomena, but there are also other routes for resistance such as developing empirical counterknowledge and reading research as well as countertheory and policy for what is absent (Gerlach 1996:433). Sharon Keigher, in chapter 7, provides empirical evidence to challenge some of the assumptions in consumer-directed care, while discourse analysis was used to reveal what is absent in the design of services in chapter 8 by Anne Opie and chapter 4 by Deborah O'Connor.

What Is Critical Practice?

The foregoing concepts have been interrogated because of their high profile in gerontology and long-term care policy discourse today. They are used by all stakeholders, but the meanings attached to each term can vary considerably. In this chapter, we have used them to raise questions about what is happening to women as they age, to provide entry points for analyzing the contested terrain of needs interpretation. These controversies are reflected in theory and research concerned with age, gender, and long-term care. As noted earlier, the humanities have added a richness to gerontological theory that was not there in earlier years when medical, health, and social psychology paradigms dominated and resulted in a description of old people that cast them as passive recipients of care. Indeed, the interpretive school of social research has added new meaning to the experience of aging, while helping to give the old person as subject some agency (see, for example, *Canadian Journal on Aging* 1995; Gubrium & Sankar 1994; *Research on Aging* 1995). These influences are permeating theory and opening up social work practice approaches.

In addition, aging theory has benefited from a strong political economy thread that is rooted in critical theory. Theory and policies from this tradition were never as prominent in North American as in European or, for that matter, Third World literature. Granted, the original political economy perspective was oriented to class differences and was, at times, overly deterministic. Nevertheless, it did shine a much-needed spotlight on those economic and medical forces that are so powerful in the lives of old women. In recent years it has widened its focus to encompass analyses of not only class but gender and race—a widening buttressed by feminist and antiracist literatures. These influences are challenging dominant renditions of aging; multiple aging scenarios, both good and bad, are now foreseen.

There is thus a richness, a flux, in aging research today that can be energizing and progressive but—given the political environment and the way language is being used—there is considerable cause for concern (Phillipson 1996). The new language that accompanies new ideas can easily be picked up and used in ways that are quite contradictory. For instance, images such as productive aging (Gerson & Patterson 1997) can just as easily contribute to, as they can challenge, the devaluing of old age. Similarly, the market assumptions that underlie the mixed economy of care do not see the work that is involved in care-receiving or the varied relational work done by care providers as productive. Thus, feminists find themselves faced with the irony of witnessing the labor and costs of caring finally being put on the public discussion agenda only to have them taken up in ways that render invisible the labor of those groups of women who actually bear most of the costs and who do the work! A meaningful old age in the twenty-first century cannot be proclaimed. Events such as the 1995 White House Conference on Aging, or the Beijing UN Conference on Women in September 1995, are important in that they signal public policy milestones, but it is in the everyday world of practice where the meaning of old age is best observed and strategies for change developed.

It is perhaps strategic to think of concepts as having multidimensional but not consistent lives; different aspects are exposed according to who uses them and for what purpose. Discussions of agency and oppression, choice and entitlement, community and identity are neither about opposites nor synonyms. Similarly, promoting group advocacy and individual empowerment are not inherently contradictory professional activities, but they do focus on different sites for change and thus reflect the practice model of the practitioner. The quest in developing critical practice theory is not to weave all the threads together into a new theoretical tapestry, a new metatheory of aging. Rather the goal is to recognize that there are competing explanations of the situations of people as they age, but these different understandings will frequently employ vocabularies that sound very similar.

Given the above, it is imperative that social workers articulate models of practice that do not further oppress women—good intentions are not enough. To this end, developing practice theory that offers ways of understanding aging that support women will be crucial. Developing mechanisms for doing this requires alternative analytical tools. We use the phrase *critical practice theory* to capture this orientation with some hesitancy, aware that like caring and empowerment, critical is a term that is suggestive and promises more than it can deliver. However, the word designates an analytical stance wherein practice is rooted in a knowledge base that takes account of power differentials embedded in the structures and relations of long-term care services. Critical practice entails promoting consciousness-raising, empowerment, and emancipation. Unfortunately, social work practice theory too often stops at the level of understanding and does not get translated into interventions that embody critical analyses (for examples of how this might be done, see Jack 1995). Or, as discussed in the section on autonomy and agency, ideas are taken up by the profession only at the level of micro practice with individuals and families. Critical practice theory would provide guidelines for interventions with individuals and their families which challenge assumptions that result in the problem being seen as one due to the behavior or attitudes of those who daily come together in the lives of old women. Such practice theory would highlight rather than gloss over the contradictions facing workers and aging women when assessments of need are in fact assessments of service availability; where the presence of kin for doing the ongoing caring work becomes part of the equation for deciding on competing claims for scarce services. In a politics of scarcity, social workers as well as elderly people and their families confront limited options and must make difficult decisions that involve complex consequences and costs for them all. Recognizing that these costs are unequally distributed, and that the mixed economy of care offers few meaningful options, is essential if discussions of old women as clients, consumers, or citizens are not to ring hollow.

Critical social work practice in aging cannot be delineated in terms of a collection of competencies. Antioppressive work and empowerment are not captured by competencies. In fact, competency criteria can exclude people who belong to oppressed groups. Service providers, minimally, need to be aware of oppressive stereotypes that can undermine their ability to recognize people as being competent and rational. When considering if an old woman is making an informed decision, it is difficult to know the background conditions that may have accumulated over the years which make it nigh impossible to exercise seemingly available options. Typical case information that is available, and the questions asked in assessment interviews, are those that are deemed relevant to decisions that service providers must make. There is no reason to believe that such information is relevant to the issues facing old women and those who are providing informal care. In fact, it is extremely difficult to assess realistic options when there is a direct link between oppression and need (Sherwin 1998). Thus, Guberman and Maheu document in chapter 6 how culture can become a gloss for disregarding economic disparities. Similarly, the language of choice and consumer sovereignty fits with discussions of a mixed economy of care and case management but remains silent on the power disparities among the players. As Sharon Keigher demonstrates in chapter 7, there is an array of social and economic costs that fall unequally upon the "partners" in the gray market of care.

Working with the notion of antioppressive or critical practice can provide practitioners with an orientation from which to address the inequities they encounter as they mediate between providers and groups that have little power. The dilemma facing social workers is how to (1) work with complex, and probably incompatible, needs of users and carers, and (2) resist demands to reduce the complex needs identified in caring relationships to resource-led needs criteria (Davis & Ellis 1996:148). In their studies, Davis and Ellis (1996) confirm Anne Opie's findings in chapter 8 that while social workers showed some resistance to standardization of needs recording, they were caught up in the exigencies of rationing, not the least of which was workers' time, which compromised the objectivity, creativity, and breadth of assessment. For instance, workers believed that the unskilled task of information-gathering had to be distinguished from the skilled interpretation of this information—a distinction that may on the surface appear to efficiently use professional time but suggests a lack of understanding that what information is collected becomes the reality. It provides the ingredients for constructing the problem. A socially constructed problem is always "real" in that sense. Because formalized as-sessment criteria are as much about excluding as giving access, critical prac-tice would exert counterbalances, such as reinforcing in the less powerful a sense of their entitlement to help and providing the knowledge and support with which they can exercise their rights.

The Origin and Scope of the Book

This book constantly situates, as it interrogates, prevailing knowledge about ag-ing. The questions explored, the frameworks used, the discourses employed by and available to different constituencies are the focus of the analysis. Five chap-ters in the book were first drafted as presentations designed to begin developing a research agenda for a new social work research center and endowed chair shared by the Baycrest Centre for Geriatric Care, Toronto, Canada, and the Fac-ulty of Social Work, University of Toronto. This initiative presented us with an opportunity to approach several scholars in the field of aging who were seen as engaged in programs of research that were raising questions important for fu-ture social work practice and social policy in aging. Presenters were instructed to address issues of theory and research that their work raised, being particular-ly sensitive to what is excluded in dominant renditions of issues. They were also asked to reflect on the troublesome concept of community. Seminars were re-stricted to thirty participants invited from a range of aging constituencies. Par-ticipants were selected for their diversity and encouraged to specify how issues were arising in their various locations. Half the seminar time was devoted to this discussion. Since participants included graduate students, researchers, social work managers, and staff from a range of services, as well as consumers and ad-vocates, a rich dialogue ensued. With the permission of all present, the seminars were taped. These discussions helped in delineating the issues covered in this in-troductory chapter and in the questions that authors were asked to address as they transformed presentations into book chapters. Perhaps most striking was the reappearance in multiple ways of the themes addressed in this chapter. Thus we have spent some time in this introduction explicating concepts routinely used in social work practice in the field of gerontology. It is important that lan-guage not become a gloss that blunts the edge of critical analysis.

The chapters that follow are written by scholars who reside in three differ-ent countries. However, the focus of their analysis is not on international com-parisons but rather on those social conditions experienced by aging women liv-ing under conditions of social inequity in three wealthy Western societies.

Each author hooks the specifics of the area she is examining to the daily lives of women and various threads of the long-term care discourse. One of the advantages of using a feminist lens for looking at social work practice in the field of aging is that the lessons of the women's movement, and its academic version, Women's Studies, can be drawn upon to inform the framework. Thus an analysis of power relations, or "the relations of ruling" (Smith 1990), permeates each chapter in the book. Despite the current popularity of practice approaches which claim that their goal is to empower clients, such is of secondary concern in these pages. Rather the emphasis here is on explicating how power works to define the problem, interpret its meaning, and then prescribe the range of legitimate alternatives for addressing it. This process of peeling back multiple layers of meaning to expose how an issue gets to be defined as a problem has been termed *deconstruction*. The purpose is not to falsify current explanations so much as to interrogate the grounds upon which they claim so much authority while alternative explanations get so little attention. It is hoped that the persons involved will be empowered in the process, but we suspect that the odds are not favorable that this will happen in most cases.

It is tempting to make "New Millennium Resolutions" as the year 2000 arrives. Although we know that there is nothing magical about a date (there will be much "business as usual"), we do think that the year 2000 can be used as a metaphor for marking the end of an old gerontology that was focused on age as a major category delimiter. Research in the last decade or so of the twentieth century has highlighted that people age in ways that not only reflect their personal biographies; the quality of their individual experiences is marked by the social locations of these histories. They share more commonalities with younger members of these various groupings than they do with those who happen to be of the same chronological age. Although we are reluctant to engage in forecasting, we would suggest that this breaking apart of the age center of gerontology is a moment of opportunity for envisioning alternatives for what aging can mean in the years ahead. What social workers can do is to open up rather than foreclose possibilities because social workers are strategically located to witness the inequities that affect peoples lives on a daily basis. Frail old women and their overextended female kin are not well positioned to contest prevailing definitions of needs, priority hierarchies, or what social issues are worthy of public debate. Nevertheless, like other marginalized groups, aging women (and their formal and informal supporters) will need to do the job themselves; power is not given away, but it can be appropriated. Our hope is that social workers will be enduring partners in such a transformative agenda.

Note

1. Many of the ideas in this chapter reflect the debate that took place over four years as part of a network of feminist scholars (which the first author coordinated), sponsored by the Social Sciences and Humanities Research Council of Canada— Strategic Grants: Women and Change, Grant #816–94–0003, on "Understanding and Facilitating Changes in the Conditions That Shape Caring Labour."

References

Aronson, Jane. 1993. Giving consumers a say in policy development: Influencing policy or just being heard? *Canadian Public Policy* 19(4): 367–78.

Aronson, Jane and Sheila Neysmith. 1997. The retreat of the state and long-term care provision: Implications for frail elderly people, unpaid family carers, and paid home care workers. *Studies in Political Economy* 53: 37–66.

Baines, Carol, Pat Evans, and Sheila Neysmith. 1998. Women's caring: Work expanding, state contracting. In C. Baines, P. Evans, and S. Neysmith (eds.), *Women's caring: Feminist perspectives on social welfare*, 3–22. 2d ed. Toronto: Oxford University Press.

Barer, Morris L., Robert G. Evans, Clyde Hertzman. 1995. Avalanche or glacier? Health care and the demographic rhetoric. *Canadian Journal on Aging* 14(2): 193–224.

Barry, Jackie. 1995. Care-need and care-receivers: Views from the margins. *Women's Studies International Forum* 18(3): 361–74.

Beland, Francois and Evelyn Shapiro. 1995 (editorial). Policy issues in care for the elderly in Canada. *Canadian Journal on Aging* 14(2): 153–58.

Browne, C. V. 1995. Empowerment in social work practice with older women. *Social Work* 40(3): 358–64.

Canadian Journal on Aging. 1995 (Special Supplement: vol.14). Methodological diversity (supplement 1).

Clement, Grace. 1996. *Care, autonomy, and justice: Feminism and the ethic of care.* Boulder, Colo.: Westview.

Cohen, Marjorie. 1996. Democracy and trade agreements: Challenges for disadvantaged women, minorities, and states. In R. Boyer and D. Drache (eds.), *Markets against states: The limits of globalization.* London: Routledge.

Davis, Ann and Kathryn Ellis. 1996. Enforced altruism in community care. In R. Hugman and D. Smith (eds.), *Ethical issues in social work*, 136–54.

Diwan, Sadhna, Cathie Berger, and Edith Kelly Manns. 1997. Composition of the home care service package: Predictors of type, volume, and mix of services provided to poor and frail older people. *The Gerontologist* 37(2): 169–81.

Dressel, Paula, Meredith Minkler, and Irene Yen. 1997. Gender, race, class, and aging: Advances and opportunities. *International Journal of Health Services* 27(4): 579–600.

Estes, Carroll and Elizabeth Binney. 1991. The biomedicalization of aging: Dangers and dilemmas. In M. Minkler and C. Estes (eds.), *Critical perspectives on aging*, 117–34.

Estes, Carroll and Karen Linkins. 1997. Devolution and aging policy: Racing to the bottom in long-term care. *International Journal of Health Services* 27(3): 427–42.

Fay, Brian. 1987. *Critical social science.* Ithaca, N.Y.: Cornell University Press.

Fraser, Nancy. 1989. *Unruly practices: Power, discourse, and gender in contemporary social theory.* Minneapolis: University of Minnesota Press.

Galambos, Colleen M. 1997. Quality of life for the elder: A reality or an illusion? *Journal of Gerontological Social Work* 27(3): 27–44.

Gerlach, Neil. 1996 (review article). The business restructuring genre: Some questions for critical analyses. *Organization: Interdisciplinary Journal of Organization, Theory, and Society* 3(3): 425–53.

Gerson, David and Gina Patterson. 1997. Productive aging: 1995 White House Conference on Aging—Challenges for Public Policy and Social Work Pracice. *Journal of Gerontological Social Work* 27(3): 9–25.

Gibson, D. 1996. Broken down by age and gender: The "problem of old women" redefined. *Gender and Society* 10(4): 433–48.

Giddens, Anthony. 1984. *The constitution of society: Outline of the theory of structuration.* Berkeley: University of California Press.

Gubrium, Jaber and Andrea Sankar (eds.). 1994. *Qualitative methods in aging research.* Thousand Oaks, Calif.: Sage.

Haraway, Donna. 1989. *Primate visions: Gender, race, and nature in the world of modern science.* New York: Routledge.

Holstein, Martha. 1998. Opening new spaces: Aging and the millennium. *Journal of Aging and Social Policy* 10(1): 1–11.

Hooyman, Nancy R. and Judith Gonyea. 1995. *Feminist perspectives on family care: Policies for gender justice.* Thousand Oaks, Calif.: Sage.

Hugman, R. and D. Smith. 1996. *Ethical issues in social work.* London and New York: Routledge.

Husband, Charles. 1996. Defining and containing diversity: Community, ethnicity, and citizenship. In Waqar I. U. Ahmad and Karl Atkin (eds.), *"Race" and community care,* 29–48. Buckingham, U.K.: Open University Press.

Jack, R. (ed.). 1995. *Empowerment in Community Care.* London: Chapman and Hall.

Jaggar, Alison and Susan Bordo (eds.). 1989. *Gender/body/knowledge: Feminist reconstructions of being and knowing.* New Brunswick, N.J.: Rutgers University Press.

Jarman-Rohde, Lily, JoAnne McFall, Patricia Kolar, and Gerald Strom. 1997. The changing context of social work practice: Implications and recommendations for social work educators. *Journal of Social Work Education* 33(1): 29–46.

Jessop, R. 1993. Toward a Schumeterian workfare state? Preliminary remarks on post-Fordist political economy. *Studies in Political Eonomy* 40 (spring): 7–39.

Katz, Stephen. 1996. *Disciplining old age: The formation of gerontological knowledge.* Charlottesville: University Press of Virginia.

Kettner, Peter M. and Lawrence L. Martin. 1996. Purchase of service contracting versus government service contracting: The views of state human service administrators. *Journal of Sociology and Social Welfare* 23(2): 107–119.

Kramer, Ralph. 1994. Voluntary agencies and the contract culture: Dream or nightmare? *Social Service Review* 68: 33–60.

Laws, G. 1995. Understanding ageism: Lessons from feminism and postmodernism. *The Gerontologist* 35(1): 112–18.

Lillard, Lee, Jeannette Rogowski, and Raynard Kington. 1997. Long-term care determinants of patterns of health insurance coverage in the Medicare population. *The Gerontologist* 37(3): 314–23.

Mahoney, Martha. 1994. Victimization or oppression? Women's lives, violence, and agency. In M. Fineman and R. Mikitluk (eds.), *The public nature of private violence*, 59–92. New York: Routledge.

May, T. and M. Buck. 1998. Power, professionalism and organisational transformation. *Sociological Research on Line* 3(2): <http://www.socresonline.org.uk/socresonline/3/2/5.html>.

McDaniel, Susan A. and Allison L. McKinnon. 1993. Gender differences in informal support and coping among elders: Findings from Canada's 1985 and 1990 General Social Surveys. *Journal of Women and Aging* 5(2): 79–98.

Minkler, Meredith and Carroll Estes (eds.). 1991. *Critical perspectives on aging: The political and moral economy of growing old*. Amityville, N.Y.: Baywood.

———. 1999. *Critical gerontology: Perspectives from political and moral economy*. Amityville, N.Y.: Baywood.

Morris, Jenny. 1993. Feminism and disability. *Feminist Review* 43: 57–70.

Nicholson, Linda (ed.). 1990. *Feminism/postmodernism*. New York and London: Routledge.

Older Women's Network. 1998. Focus group discussion. Toronto, Ontario. February 23.

Oliver, Michael. 1990. *The politics of disablement*. London: Macmillan.

Orme, Joan. 1998. Community care: Gender issues. *British Journal of Social Work* 28: 615–22.

Phillipson, Chris. 1996. Interpretations of ageing: Perspectives from humanistic gerontology. *Ageing and Society* 16(3): 359–69.

Phillipson, Chris and Alan Walker (eds.). 1986. *Ageing and social policy: A critical assessment*. Aldershot, U.K.: Gower.

Price, Janet. 1996. The marginal politics of our bodies? Women's health, the disability movement, and power. In Beth Humphries (ed.), *Critical perspectives on empowerment*, 35–51. Birmingham, U.K.: Venture Press.

Research on Aging. 1995 (Special Issue: vol. 17, no. 1). Qualitative methodology.

Robertson, Ann. 1991. The politics of Alzheimer's disease: A case study in apocalyptic demography. In M. Minkler and C. Estes (eds.), *Critical perspectives on aging*, 135–50.

———. 1997. Beyond apocalyptic demography: Toward a moral economy of independence. *Ageing and Society* 17(4): 425–46.

Schweikhart, Sharon and Vicki Smith-Daniels. 1996. Reengineering the work of caregivers: Role definition, team structuring, and organizational redesign. *Hospital and Health Services Administration* 41(1): 19–36.

Shapiro, Evelyn and Robert Tate. 1997. The use and cost of community care services by elders with unimpaired cognitive function, with cognitive impairment/no dementia, and with dementia. *Canadian Journal on Aging* 16(4): 665–81.

Shemmings, David and Yvonne Shemmings. 1995. Defining participative practice in health and welfare. In R. Jack (ed.), *Empowerment in community care*, 43–58. London: Chapman and Hall.

Sherwin, Susan. 1998. A relational approach to autonomy in health care. In S. Sherwin (ed.), *The Politics of Women's Health: Exploring Agency and Autonomy*, 19–47. Philadelphia: Temple University Press.

Shildrick, Margrit. 1997. *Leaky bodies and boundaries: Feminism, postmodernism, and (bio)ethics.* London and New York: Routledge.

Smith, Dorothy. 1990. *The conceptual practices of power: A feminist sociology of knowledge.* Toronto: University of Toronto Press.

Statistics Canada. 1997 (The Daily, August 19). *Who cares? Caregiving in the 1990s. 1996. General Social Survey. Cycle II—Social and community support.* Catalogue 11–001E.

——. 1998 (The Daily, March 17). *1996 Census: Labour force activity, occupation and industry, place of work, mode of transportation to work, unpaid work.*

Thorpe, Kenneth. 1997. The health system in transition: Care, cost, and coverage. *Journal of Health Politics, Policy, and Law* 22(2): 339–61.

Twigg, Julia. 1997. Deconstructing the "social bath": Help with bathing at home for older and disabled people. *Journal of Social Policy* 26(2): 211–32.

——. 1993. The interweaving of formal and informal care: Policy models and problems. In A. Evers and G. H. van der Zanden (eds.), *Better care for dependent people: Meeting the new agenda in services for the elderly*, 115–31. Bunnik: Netherlands Institute of Gerontology.

Ungerson, Clare. 1995. Gender, cash, and informal care: European perspectives and dilemmas. *Journal of Social Policy* 24(1): 31–52.

Wallace, Steven P. and Valentine M. Villa. 1999. Caught in hostile cross-fire: Public policy and minority elderly in the United States. In M. Minkler and C. Estes (eds.), *Critical gerontology*, 237–55.

Weitz, Rose (ed.). 1998. *The politics of women's bodies: Sexuality, appearance, and behavior.* New York: Oxford University Press.

White, Deena. 1993. The community-based mental health system: What does it mean? *Canadian Review of Social Policy* 31: 31–61.

2

Widowhood

*Dominant Renditions, Changing Demography,
and Variable Meaning*

ANNE MARTIN-MATTHEWS

Gerontologists generally consider "widowhood and retirement [to be] two of the major role transitions of later life" (Gold 1996:224). Both transitions have traditionally been defined as "exits" from primary adult roles, and each has in fact been characterized as "identities that are nonrelationships" (Matthews 1979:81). Since biblical times, accounts of the plight of the widowed have evoked powerful images of women at their most vulnerable and in greatest need. Widowhood has become an especially seminal concept, reflecting and influencing our thinking about old people in general, and old women in particular. Cultural beliefs, centuries-old traditions, and modern-day empiricism—and the social policies and practices that derive from them—combine to create dominant renditions of widowhood in later life. These dominant renditions in turn serve to reinforce and re-create our understanding of the nature and meaning of becoming and being widowed. On the basis of these dominant renditions, and the assumptions inherent in them, the "status" of being a widowed person becomes a powerful category according to which access to certain benefits and resources is granted or denied.

In the historical development of the welfare state, for example, the penury and generally deprived social circumstances of widowed women emerged early on as matters that were deserving of consideration as "public issues" rather than being left as "personal troubles" (Mills 1959:8). It has been argued that this recognition of public responsibility reflects the awareness that "some of the repercussions of widowhood, such as the poverty experienced by many . . . are, at least in part, socially created" (Connidis 1989:92). This chapter argues that the repercussions of other marital statuses and social conditions in later life are similarly socially created but, standing alongside the dominant renditions of widowhood, fail to emerge as public issues.

However, the experience of widowhood in later life is changing, and its incidence declining, thus fundamentally challenging its role as being virtually synonymous with women's experiences of old age. The inevitability of its association with poverty, need, dependency, and powerlessness is also being called into question. Its defining characteristic, the loss through death of the partner, is becoming increasingly ambiguous in the face of medical advances and longevity. The nature of these changes, and the ways in which they challenge the dominant renditions of the nature of men's and women's experiences of old age, are the focus of this chapter.

Implicit in each of the chapters in this volume is a consideration of what is being excluded in dominant renditions of the issues relevant to gerontological social work. In considering the dominant renditions of widowhood, this chapter highlights the role of a dominant demography and demographic determinism, agency, ambivalent loss, ambiguous statuses, and gender. Each of these concepts challenges some aspect of the "dominant renditions" of what widowhood is and what it means in later life.

Dominant Demography and Demographic Determinism

We speak of dominant discourses and dominant renditions in our fields of inquiry; but there is also a "dominant demography" we must be aware of. Far too often a form of *demographic determinism* has colored the way gerontologists, social work practitioners, and policymakers approach issues. This term (and/or the term *dominant demography*) refers to the fact that our renditions of the "problem" or the "issue" often focus on the demographically most typical or most pressing of situations: the "largest" groups or the "most evident" and so forth. This is one reason why much of the discussion of marital status issues in later life has focused on widowhood.

In acknowledging that the lens of demographic determinism often drives what we attend to, we must come to recognize what is lost, or at least less considered, in the focus of that lens. In the study of marital status in later life, we are becoming increasingly aware of fundamental shifts in the marital statuses people occupy as they enter old age and in the distribution of marital status categories throughout the aged population. Because these patterns represent challenges to the dominant renditions of widowhood in later life, the discussion below uses widowhood as the referent category, even though the status of being married, for example, is far more demographically prevalent, especially in the early years of old age (and profoundly so for men).

These demographic analyses are also intended to be more than mere "context-setting" for subsequent discussions in this chapter as well as elsewhere in this volume. As Matilda White Riley has noted, "Life course research treats structures as if they were merely the 'context' for people's lives. As context, of course, social structures are powerful organizers of people's developmental patterns . . . [and] the strategic interdependence between lives and structures can only be comprehended when structures too are examined in their own right" (1996:256).

Indeed, the guiding principle of studies of "age and structural lag" is that there exists a dynamic interplay between people growing older and society undergoing change (Riley, Kahn & Foner 1994). One of the ways in which society has undergone change is in the increase in the prevalence but a decline in the incidence of widowhood in later life.

Over a period of thirty years (1961 to 1991), census data document this substantial increase in the prevalence of widows and widowers aged sixty-five years and over in both Canada and the United States.[1] In each decade, the growth in numbers of widowed women has been greater than that for men, although this trend is rather more striking in Canada. The number of elderly widows grew by 150 percent in Canada and 80 percent in the United States across the three decades; this compares with 30 percent growth among the population of elderly widowers in Canada and 27 percent in the United States (Statistics Canada 1976, 1982, 1993; U.S. Bureau of the Census 1962, 1972, 1982, 1992).

However, the *rate* of growth for widowhood in both Canada and the United States in recent decades has been lower than for most other marital statuses except singlehood (Martin Matthews 1991; Stone and Frenken 1988), with a notable decline in average annual rates of growth of widowhood among women in particular. One explanation is the reduction in the mortality rates of older men; this reduction is beginning to impact on the incidence of widowhood, especially among women aged sixty-five to sixty-nine but also among women aged seventy-five to seventy-nine (see table 2.1).

Thus, the increased prevalence of widowhood stands in contrast to its declining incidence. The cumulative effect of declining incidence of widowhood in later life is depicted in table 2.1, which compares Canadian data for 1971 and 1991. One of the reasons for the decline in the rate of widowhood in Canada is the increasing incidence of divorce among Canada's elderly population. Table 2.1 depicts this trend as well. While the numbers of

Table 2.1   Widowed and Divorced Populations Aged 65 Years and Over, by Sex
and Age Cohorts, Canada, 1971–1991

Widowed	Men (Percentage of Age Cohort)*		Women (Percentage of Age Cohort)*	
	1971	1991	1971	1991
65–69	7.7	6.8	33.0	28.5
70–74	13.1	10.4	46.1	41.1
75–79	20.4	15.8	57.9	54.4
80–84	31.3	24.2	68.8	67.1
85–89	43.5	35.8	76.1	76.9
90 +	54.8	48.5	79.3	82.3

Divorced	Men (Percentage of Age Cohort)*		Women (Percentage of Age Cohort)*	
	1971	1991	1971	1991
65–69	1.1	3.8	1.1	4.7
70–74	1.0	2.8	0.7	3.2
75–79	0.7	2.2	0.5	2.2
80–84	0.6	1.7	0.4	1.4
85–89	0.5	1.2	0.4	0.9
90+	0.4	1.2	0.3	0.7

SOURCE: * Percentage calculations are from Statistics Canada (1993), *1991 Census of Canada*, Catalogue 93–310, Table 5:
Distribution of the Canadian Population by Marital Status, 1971–1991 (p. 22).

divorced elderly persons are substantially lower than the numbers of widowed elderly, there has nevertheless been a remarkable increase in the prevalence of divorce among old people over a thirty-year period. This is especially true of elderly divorced women, whose proportional increase has been
double that of elderly divorced men in Canada. Overall, the incidence of divorce has increased three to fourfold within most age groups, well into later life. However, this rate does not as such reflect the rate at which elderly
men and women are terminating their marriages; rather, it more accurately
reflects the number of persons entering old age as divorced persons (Stone
& Frenken 1988:39).

Although the Canadian divorce rate has more than doubled since the 1968
federal *Divorce Act*, the current rate of 28 percent of marriages ending in divorce is still considerably lower than the U.S. rate of 44 percent (Vanier Institute of the Family 1994). Since much of the literature which reflects, and in
turn shapes, our dominant renditions of both widowhood and divorce in later life originates in the United States, it is important to note the striking dif-

ferences in the magnitude of the increasing prevalence of divorced older people in the two countries. Over the thirty-year period from 1961 to 1991, the number of divorced elderly women in Canada increased thirty-six times, while in the United States the increase was just over sixfold. Among elderly divorced men, the number increased over seventeen times in the same thirty-year interval, compared to a sixfold increase in the United States. One might argue that divorce has longer been the norm in the United States, and so one could anticipate more stability than change over time. The comparative recency of divorce legislation in Canada could also account for at least some of the difference in the magnitude of increase.

Remarriage trends in Canada suggest a further explanation. The likelihood of remarriage for widows and widowers has declined by more than 40 percent in recent years in Canada. There are several suggested reasons for this pattern. These include societal norms which are increasingly favorable to cohabitation without marriage, and economic disincentives in terms of pensions and survivor benefits which financially punish people who remarry after the age of sixty-five.

Comparative analyses of twenty to thirty years of census data in both Canada and the United States suggest, then, that the structure of the life course in terms of marital status in later life has changed substantially. While it is still the case that the social condition within which most women age is widowhood and the social condition within which most men age is marriage, among both older women and older men proportionally more are married, fewer are widowed, and more are divorced than was the case in the early 1960s. It is projected that, in the future, the incidence of singlehood will increase in later life; those who are single in later life will have come to that circumstance via a wide range of paths, either through divorce, separation, lifelong singlehood, or widowhood.

Dominant renditions of old age have not kept pace with these changing realities. If dominant demographies continue to direct the focus of our lens, then one would expect a shifting of focus to greater consideration of later life marriage and divorce. In this context, one meaning of widowhood—the perception of it as the normative marital status of women's old age—will change. While it is difficult to say whether or not Canada's divorce rate will ever equal that of the United States and thus render widowhood even more nonnormative in later life, it appears that the meaning of widowhood as a defining characteristic of most women's later years will change dramatically in the next twenty years or so. As a category defining access to benefits and services, widowhood may no longer be useful.

Policy Implications of Dominant Renditions:
The Widowed Spouse's Allowance

While the analyses of demographic trends illustrate several of the emerging challenges to dominant renditions of widowhood, one might well ponder their significance. Are the dominant renditions of widowhood reflected in any meaningful way in differential access to resources, benefits, or services for the widowed? Is the acceptance of widowhood as a "public issue," as noted previously by Connidis (1989), reflected in a substantial way in legislation and public policy? The answer in Canada is yes.

There persist important ways in which Canada's public policies and practice fail to consider the changing implications of marital status in later life. The Spouse's Allowance and the Widowed Spouse's Allowance are examples. In 1975, Canada's federal government introduced a Spouse's Allowance program for the purpose of giving financial assistance to low-income, single-earner couples where the earning spouse had retired and the other spouse was not as yet eligible to receive the Old Age Security benefit, which is payable at age sixty-five. Through a series of amendments introduced by various governments between 1975 and 1985, the benefit was extended to all low-income widows and widowers in Canada between the ages of sixty and sixty-four (Income Security Programs 1987). The benefit therefore represents an important milestone in recognizing as a policy issue the financial insecurity of the near-elderly widowed. Neither age of the spouse or income of the spouse at death nor length of time since the death restrict eligibility. The benefit is, however, means-tested for both married and widowed applicants.

Both men and women are eligible under both the Spouse's Allowance and Widowed Spouse's Allowance programs. However, most of those eligible to receive benefits are in fact married or widowed women who have not worked for pay outside the home. Other low-income individuals in the sixty to sixty-four age group who have never married or who are separated or divorced are excluded from the program.

As laudable as the objectives of such a policy are, this is a classic example of social policy framed within the dominant renditions of women's experiences of entry into old age, and thereby failing to keep pace with the realities of changes in marital status among older people in Canada. Sheila Neysmith's introductory chapter calls for a challenge to current arrangements and to those explanations that reinforce "privilege." For the widowed in Canadian society, there is precious little privilege overall, but they do have (as do married people) the privilege of access to this particular social program. Social policy that recognizes the needs of low-income members of two marital status "categories" while denying access to equally "needy" members of other marital status categories is on shaky ground indeed. One Canadian Member of Parliament was especially eloquent in challenging this legislation:

> Women in the 60 to 65 age bracket get a pension or an allowance not because they are persons, not because they are in need. They get a pension on the basis of being able to answer the question: "Have you got a man?" If they do not have a man, dead or alive, by definition of the bill they do not qualify. *(Stanley Knowles,* House of Commons Debates, *1979:462)*

Reflecting this perceived inequity, litigation challenging these programs has been initiated in Canada under the provisions of the *Canadian Charter of Rights and Freedoms*. Individuals and groups such as Single and Divorced Speak Out have been active in initiating litigation because, although they meet income and age criteria for the program, they do not qualify because they never married or their spouse died after the termination of the marriage through divorce (Livingstone 1988). While no legal judgments have as yet been rendered in these cases (even though several have been pending for years), the continued existence of this policy in Canada raises important questions as to the dominant renditions of later life widowhood in the policy domain.

The Issue of Agency

Recognizing Agency

In chapter 1, Sheila Neysmith notes the lack of attention to agency in studies of old age. Typically, elderly persons are portrayed in the gerontological literature as "acted upon" (often as victims in positions of dependency) rather than as "actors" in their own life stories. Dependency is assumed by the very meaning of the word *widowhood*, which derives from the Sanskrit and means "empty" (Caine 1974). Almost by the very nature of their status, widows are assumed to be "acted upon"—first because of the deteriorating health of the partner (thus throwing them into the role of caregiver) and subsequently by his death. Indeed, in the context of the initial bereavement period of widowhood, taking almost any kind of action is discouraged. However, while agency is decidedly lacking in many gerontological discussions of widowhood in gen-

eral, accounts by widowed women themselves as well as those studies which
give voice to the experiences of widowed women speak forcefully of agency,
of being survivors, of action and growth and the exercising of power. Most
such works fall within the interpretive school of social research which, as
Sarah Matthews noted long ago, "helps to give the old person as subject some
agency" (1979:23).

What is striking in the widowhood literature in the accounts of women
as "actors" is the power and intensity of the experience. Based on extensive
research on mutual self-help organizations for the widowed, Silverman
(1987:189) concludes that "in studying the outcome [of widowhood] we
cannot talk about recovery but of transformation." My own extensive interviews with widowed women are replete with accounts of how "I've blos-
somed into my own personality"; "I became a lot more independent, a lot
more my own person"; I never thought I'd be able to cope. It makes you
stronger" (Martin Matthews 1991:28). These images fly in the face of dominant renditions of the widowed which portray them as weak and incapable
(Lopata 1995).

Strengthening Agency

Given the general failure in the gerontological literature to acknowledge the
growth and personal development experienced by many widowed persons in
adapting to loss and change, it is not surprising that the notion of strength-
ening agency similarly stands outside dominant renditions. Social work practitioners have a role to play in elements of this transition. In so doing, the
"dominant renditions" of other related concepts are important to note. For
example, in the area of social support, researchers have been slow to question
assumptions as to the inherently beneficial or at least benign nature of social
support (Gottlieb 1993; Morgan 1989). Within research and practice orientations where social support is "commodified," "more" is assumed to be better.
However, social practice—let alone personal experience—tells us that this is
not necessarily the case. In an earlier study, I concluded that the potential
benefits of support will be offset if there is too much support, if it comes at
the wrong time in the process of adaptation, if it is too intensely focused upon
the widowed person, or if it is offered only by those with one particular set of
attributes (such as only provided by adult children, or only provided by married friends) (Martin Matthews 1991). The dominant renditions of social support are only beginning to reflect the potentially negative implications of support offered in these circumstances.

Indeed, my research suggests that in order for many widowed individuals—and particularly widowed women—to achieve personal growth in widowhood, access to an informal network built on "the strength of weak ties" (Granovetter 1973) may be fundamentally important. Such ties, potentially devoid of vested interests and perceptions based on past history of relationship, can be consequential in providing information which assists the widowed person who is seeking new directions and opportunities in personal development in later life. There is some evidence that a loose rather than a tightly supportive network may in fact be especially beneficial in the reorganization of the social world and social roles in widowhood. "High-density networks" may be less well suited to helping widowed persons "to develop new social roles consonant with their changed status" (Vachon & Stylianos 1988:177). In this context, while appropriate sociocultural support may be of particular benefit to widowed persons, sociocultural constraints may also be a hindrance, and even a threat, to agency.

Resources in Achieving Agency

The role of the widowed woman herself as a resource, her agency reflected in her personal growth, has already been noted. The role of the social work practitioner in recognizing the potentially complex role of family support and sociocultural norms has also been addressed briefly. The power differential between practitioner and elderly client presents a challenge, however, to his or her facilitative role. Even within the context of agency, the best that many widowed persons may achieve is what Sarah Matthews has called "gaining leverage" rather than actually gaining power (1979:124).

Standing well outside dominant renditions of widowhood, however, is another resource identified by widowed women: what Lopata (1979:75) has called the "memory-constructed husband." The role of the deceased spouse in facilitating agency, especially in the initial period of widowhood, is noted in the accounts of many widowed women and in some research (as cited in Martin Matthews 1991:51–52). Enduring and active ties to past relationships are by no means restricted to the former spouse. In a fascinating analysis of the role of social worlds in aging lives, David Unruh (1983:47) observes that "most important for the study of social worlds in aging lives is the idea that social worlds may be meaningful even though they do not exist in any concrete sense." In some clinical contexts these activities may stand so far outside the dominant renditions as to be considered virtually "dysfunctional"; I argue, however, for their place as a source of agency for some widowed women.

Agency and Access to Income

As Neysmith notes in chapter 1, for most women agency and autonomy are conditional upon their access to income. In this context, marital status in later life is important because it continues to be the route by which most women access resources in old age. It is important, therefore, to examine briefly the issue of the socioeconomic consequences of widowhood for women and for men. This examination of socioeconomic "need" is also important in the context of the dominant renditions of widowhood, for traditionally widowhood has been almost exclusively and implicitly associated with need.

For many—although not all—widowed persons, the experience of bereavement precipitates poverty among individuals who have not been poor as a member of a couple (Hurd & Wise 1987; McDonald 1997). For those not yet in old age, most widows are worse off financially two years after widowhood than before, with the drop in total family income beginning in the year *before* widowhood, when an ill spouse is no longer able to continue working (Hudson 1984). Data from the U.S. National Longitudinal Surveys cohort of mature women suggest that 40 percent of widows and over one quarter of divorced women fall into poverty for at least some time during the first five years after the end of a marriage (Morgan 1989).

What, then, if any, are the implications of the decline in widowhood for women's and men's socioeconomic status in later life? One might assume that if the incidence of widowhood in later life is in decline that this will bode well for women's socioeconomic status. Unfortunately, not so. Studies that utilize panel data to follow individual women from marriage into widowhood indicate that the economic consequences of divorce and separation are no less detrimental to women than are those of widowhood (Holden & Smock 1991). This is in spite of the fact that, in contrast to divorce, no decline in economic well-being need necessarily be expected, especially as, after widowhood, there is still only one household and that household is smaller. Cohort analyses by Rosenthal et al. (in press) similarly suggest that future cohorts of "older women, like today's, will not be financially secure in later life unless they are married."

In fact, longitudinal studies of the effects of divorce and widowhood indicate that both widowhood and divorce have negative and prolonged consequences for women's economic well-being. This is not the case for men, where marital dissolution often leads to an improved economic standard of living (Burkhauser, Butler & Holden 1991; Holden & Smock 1991; Sorensen 1992).

However, the estimates of change in economic status following separation, divorce, and widowhood are highly variable, ranging from declines of 9 percent to 30 percent among women, with the estimates of increase for men showing approximately the same degree of variation. These variations have been described as "uncomfortably large" and suggest that much yet remains to be known about the degree of change in women's and men's economic status upon the termination of marriage (Sorensen 1992). While the magnitude of change may be open to debate, however, the direction of change (decrease for women; status quo or increase for men) is widely substantiated.

To the extent that declines in widowhood are offset by the increasing likelihood of being married in later life, a substantial proportion of women remain one man away from poverty in old age (McDonald 1997); to the extent that declines in widowhood are offset by the increasing likelihood of being a divorced person in later life, later life continues to "hold substantial economic peril" for older women (Burkhauser, Butler & Holden 1991).

These findings suggest both support for and challenges to dominant renditions of widowhood. In terms of agency defined by access to income, these data suggest genuine limits to the power of many elderly widows to shape their social condition. Dominant renditions of widowhood are largely reaffirmed here. However, in terms of the traditional association between widowhood and need expressed as economic need, these analyses indicate that, of course, not all widows are needy; they further confirm that among elderly women, by no means are all the needy widowed.

Analyses of 1991 Canadian census data contribute further to this picture. They confirm that separated women are often *particularly* disadvantaged in socioeconomic terms in later life. However, data documenting this situation are recent and cross-sectional because of the comparative "invisibility" of this marital status group in demographic terms. So far have the separated stood outside dominant renditions of marital status transitions in later life, that Statistics Canada did not even list "separation" as a distinct marital status category until the 1991 census. Previously, "the separated" were subsumed under the classification of "currently married." Yet again, a dominant demography defines the focus of the lens and thereby shapes the research methodologies on which we rely to answer our questions.

Ambivalent Loss

In a commentary on the role of social psychology in the study of the life course of older persons, Linda George has argued that "one of the important, but often neglected, consequences of social change is its impact on the cultural meanings attached to social phenomena" (1996:251–52). Different *meanings* may, over time, come to be attached to the marital statuses and marital transitions experienced in later life.

Because of other changes in society (already documented in the discussion of dominant demography), the potential exists for change in the nature of the emotional and affectional tie lost in widowhood. There are a number of ways in which this could potentially be different in the future from the way it has been, and is today. For many couples in the past for whom divorce was not an option, and for many in the present for whom either the stigma of divorce or religious/cultural proscriptions against divorce remain strong, widowhood is the only source of release from an unhappy union. To this extent there certainly exist cases in which widowhood represents "ambivalent loss." In my research, numbers of individuals spoke of the strain of public expectations of grief and mourning for a spouse who was, in the words of one, "an unusually cruel man," or in the words of another, "a wife whose mean-spiritedness brought me and my children nothing but misery. Her passing was the greatest blessing of my adult life." Dominant renditions of transitions to widowhood rarely acknowledge the conflict inherent in the disjuncture between the societal norms and values attached to widowhood and the personal experience of ambivalent loss when the death of the partner is not experienced as a bereavement.

In terms of the meaning of the social condition of widowhood, one might suppose that, in the future, widowhood would more likely signify the end of an enduring and emotionally valued tie than has been the case even in the recent past. One might expect that those who become widowed would more likely be the "survivors" of enduring relationships. This could be due to changing societal norms and values wherein the options of terminating an unhappy union are more available than they have been for today's elderly, and the social stigma attached to so doing has lessened considerably—if not disappeared entirely, except in relation to certain religious and cultural proscriptions.

However, these issues are extremely complex ones. As the data above indicate, even in the absence of societal proscriptions against separation and divorce, the socioeconomic costs of the transition from married to single (through either widowhood or divorce) are frequently very high indeed. Until such time as separation and divorce are no longer associated with "substantial economic peril" for women in particular, pressures will remain to hold women in unions because doing so is the only economically viable option for them.

Ambiguous Statuses

Dominant renditions of the "problems" of widowhood in later life have typically been characterized by very narrow conceptual definitions of "families" and partnerships. Hazel MacRae (1992) and others have noted the increasing importance of enduring and emotionally and socially supportive ties which may be characterized as "family-like" (in terms of the positive attributes of that phraseology). The term *fictive kin ties* is used in this context. In most social science research, the topic of fictive kin ties (and, therefore also, of fictive kin loss) is rarely acknowledged. Nevertheless, the significance of these ties in the lives of older persons is apparent. In a study of the informal support networks of old people, I found that fully 15 percent of the "family" ties identified by older men and women did not involve ties of blood, marriage, or adoption (Martin Matthews 1993). These close bonds, their place in the lives of older persons, and the implications of their loss stand outside dominant renditions of loss and change in later life.

Similarly, issues of loss and change in gay and lesbian relationships in later life stand outside the dominant renditions of later life bereavement. Although a literature is beginning to emerge in relationship to partner loss in relation to AIDS (Dustan 1998), the field of social gerontology neglects a vast array of issues which confront "never married" or "ever single" persons in later life. Indeed, many of the "statuses" associated with "family life" today are highly ambiguous and therefore often excluded from more "traditional" analyses.

The "ambiguous status" of widowhood also extends to those who have lost a partner in a union never formalized (perhaps even involving different residences) and never sanctioned or even acknowledged by other family members and friends. Especially in light of social policies that deter and even penalize remarriage and new partnerships among those of "pensionable age," these ambiguous statuses are not uncommon among older people today.

Certainly in institutional settings, social work practice involves ongoing involvement with the "ambiguous statuses" (some bordering on widowhood) of later life relationships. Ross, Rosenthal, and Dawson (1997) describe the circumstances of "quasi-widowhood" among women whose husbands have been institutionalized, and whose marital role consists of "visits" to a spouse whose care has now been taken over by a formal care "system." Other examples provided by social workers themselves include circumstances involving institutionalized individuals who, even though continuing to receive regular visits from a spouse, enter into close interpersonal relationships with other residents of the institution, with some of these assuming a marriage-like character of their own.[2] The "experience" and "meaning" of marital status is important in these contexts in shaping the expectations and responses of the "visiting" partner, and in shaping the attitudes and responses of fellow residents (and staff) as they observe developing relationships. Such situations present challenges to social work practice. Many of these illustrations of ambiguous status are without historical precedent. Rarely does social work training prepare practitioners for these "variants" on a widowhood theme.

Standing Outside the Dominant Renditions: Gender

An analysis of what is left out of the dominant renditions of widowhood in later life reveals that *men's* experiences stand largely outside prevailing explanations and accounts. Widowhood research focuses almost exclusively on women not only because women are four times more likely than are men to be widowed, but also because men's issues as widowed persons have not reached the public agenda. Their concerns are not "public issues" as they are for widowed old women. In addition, widowed men are very hard to find in the research that we do and in the support groups that we initiate, so we tend not to ask the questions that would include them.

The paucity of knowledge of the implications for social work practice of men's experiences of widowhood is a perfect illustration of the role of demographic determinism in shaping our research questions and thereby our practice concepts. Because a particular social condition (such as widowhood among men) is not demographically prevalent is not to say that it does not exist. Years go, Lyn Lofland (1975) wrote of the "thereness" of women in the sociology of the family, with women present in every scene as important backdrops to the setting but never quite part of the action. What is striking about issues of gender in the study of marital status in later life is the "thereness" of men, the "lack of visibility of men" in aging families (Bengtson, Rosenthal & Burton 1996:267). Demographic determinism has played a role here . "If social isolation has always been a social problem for unmarried males, for many generations it has been so demographically unusual that it was rarely seen as such. And it is likely that the field of family research, which has focused almost exclusively on either couples or women and children, has probably helped to blind us to the problems that have existed" (Goldscheider 1990:543).

A central issue in this discussion (about which we have few answers) involves the understanding of what gender actually *means* in the context of marital status. For the most part, gender is used an an independent or control variable in many domains of family studies. Academic publishing norms seem to dictate an emphasis on findings of observed gender differences rather than lack of differences. This may lead to some distortion in our understanding of the importance of gender in family life and aging (Bengtson, Rosenthal & Burton 1996:267). It is rare in marital status studies to examine the magnitude of gender differences (many are quite small) or even to recognize that in many areas of investigation, no gender differences are found (Miller & Cafasso 1992).

Instead, a more promising approach is to look further *within* gender. In so doing, we must recognize that the knowledge we have of "widowhood" and "widowed elderly persons" is gendered. What we know of widowhood in later life is of *women's* experiences of widowhood in later life. Similarly, the little we know of later life divorce is of *women's* experiences of later life divorce. There is some suggestion that demographic realities will force a recognition of the ways in which women's and men's experiences of widowhood and divorce are unique. As one example, Goldscheider (1990) argues that there will soon be new cohorts entering old age with a history of family-of-procreation ties that have been impacted by divorce. While past research has focused on women and children as the initial "victims" and sufferers from divorce, the "hazards of older males" may become more visible in this context (Bengtson, Rosenthal & Burton 1996; Goldscheider 1990). As with singlehood among women, the number of old unmarried men is projected to grow dramatically. "In old age, as employment-based resources become less central and as family relationships based on marriage and parenthood grow in importance, it is males who are at risk" (Goldscheider 1990:553). One reason, of course, that family relationships become more salient in old age is because of the increasing importance of "family members" as careproviders in the emerging mixed economy of care.

Certainly, there is mounting evidence of the effects of parental divorce on intergenerational relations throughout the life course (Uhlenberg, Cooney & Boyd 1990). Moreover, divorce does not appear to affect the intergenerational relationships of men and women equally; this transition has been found to be particularly detrimental to the relationships between fathers and their children (Cooney 1989).

How important are these issues in the context of social policy and of social work practice? They become critically important in the context of policy initiatives becoming increasingly focused less on entitlement to social programs but based more on "targeting limited resources to those in greatest need" (Plouffe 1997). This shift involves a moving away from programs broad-ly designed to promote the independence, health, and social well-being of older persons in general; the basis of the principle of "targetting" rests on "se-lection on the basis of need" and "of seniors in situations of risk" (Plouffe 1997). Recent analyses by Statistics Canada, for example, identified the par-ticularly high risk of social isolation among widowed and divorced men aged seventy-five and older—at levels far higher than that experienced by women (Stone 1997). This is an important finding in the context of reshaping our dominant renditions of widowhood, divorce, and gender.

In noting the significance of this finding, however, one must recognize the emergent literature on the social construction of "need" and "risk"—re-ferred to by Neysmith in chapter 1—and of how our understanding of these concepts is often narrowly circumscribed in terms of the dominant theoreti-cal orientations in gerontology and by the limited research methodologies on which our knowledge is based. Nevertheless, this research (Stone 1997) sought specifically to be sensitive to the dominant demography of population aging, and to seek ways to identify groups which—although numerically small—nevertheless bear recognition in terms of their potential "at risk" sta-tus. Our research and practice must do no less. As we know, aging is gen-dered. Men and women experience aging and old age differently and, as these findings illustrate, in ways that are not uniformly "better" for one gender than for the other.

An analysis of thirty years of census data in Canada and a selected compari-son of U.S. data reveal an emerging pattern of decline in the incidence of wid-owhood in later life. If current trends continue, and especially if Canada's di-vorce rate catches up to that of the United States, it is entirely possible that among cohorts of currently married younger women, widowhood could be-come a comparatively nonnormative status in later life. Although the length of marriage in later life is increasing, there is every indication that most women will be single in their old age.

Dominant renditions of widowhood restrict our capacity to as yet fully appreciate the implications of these different paths to singlehood in later life. Socioeconomic analyses suggest that women arriving in old age as divorced persons will, by and large, fare no better than the widowed. This chapter has identified the need for social policy that is responsive to the needs of mem-bers of all marital statuses. How the determination of need will be defined in the absence of marital status per se as a category of eligibility remains to be seen; we know that socioeconomic criteria alone frequently fail to be responsive to the multiple and various social locations of widowed persons. In an era when choice is linked to one's ability to purchase needed services, the prognosis is poor for many who reach old age—either through widowhood, divorce, or separation—as single persons. The challenges facing some men in these circumstances may be far greater than we have previously realized. The challenges for social work policy and practice are complicated by important issues that remain largely outside our dominant renditions of widowhood in later life, notably the lack of recognition of agency, the ambiguous statuses and ambivalent loss which may characterize widowhood, and especially its gendered nature. However, it is important to recognize that we are not merely "acted upon" in the perpetuation of these dominant renditions. We have agency. As social scientists, policymakers, and social work practitioners, we contribute to and determine the nature of the dominant renditions characteristic of our fields of inquiry and practice.

In her introductory chapter, Sheila Neysmith called for a practice orientation that seeks to have people see themselves in a different way than the prevailing explanations account for. However, as a necessary first step, we ourselves (as researchers, policymakers, and social work practitioners) must see people—in the context of this chapter, widowed and divorced old people in particular—in a different way than the dominant renditions account for. In terms of prevailing understandings and explanations involving widowhood in later life, this chapter offers a beginning.

Notes

1. While the focus of this volume is generally on the experiences of older women in relation to issues of social work practice, I have elected—for reasons that will become apparent later in this chapter—to include a discussion of men's experiences of divorce and widowhood in these analyses.

2. The examples in this section were provided to me by social workers participating in a presentation I made to staff of the Baycrest Centre for Geriatric Care, North York, Ontario, in March 1997.

References

Bengtson, V. L., C. J. Rosenthal, and L. Burton. 1996. Paradoxes of families and aging. In R. H. Binstock and L. K. George (eds.), *Handbook of aging and the social sciences*, 253–82. 4th ed. Academic Press.

Burkhauser, R., J. Butler, and K. Holden. 1991. How the death of a spouse affects economic well-being after retirement: A hazard model approach. *Social Science Quarterly* 72(3): 504–519.

Caine, Lynn. 1974. *Widow.* New York: Morrow.

Connidis, Ingrid Arnet. 1989. *Family ties and aging.* Toronto: Butterworths.

Cooney, Theresa M. 1989. Co-residence with adult children: A comparison of divorced and widowed women. *The Gerontologist* 29(6): 779–84.

Dustan, Leigh A. 1998. Bereaved gay men: Responses to loss of partner. Master's thesis, School of Family and Nutritional Sciences, University of British Columbia, Vancouver.

George, Linda K. 1996. Missing links: The case for a social psychology of the life course. *The Gerontologist* 36(2): 248–55.

Gold, Deborah T. 1996. Introduction: Cross-fertilization of the life course and other theoretical paradigms. *The Gerontologist* 36(2): 224–25.

Goldscheider, Frances. 1990. The aging of the gender revolution. *Research on Aging* 12(4): 531–45.

Gottlieb, Benjamin H. 1993. Social support: A relationship process, not a commodity. *Canadian Journal on Aging* 11(4): 306–310.

Granovetter, Mark S. 1973. The strength of weak ties. *American Journal of Sociology* 78(6): 1360–80.

Holden, K. and P. Smock. 1991. The economic costs of marital dissolution: Why do women bear a disproportionate cost? *Annual Review of Sociology* 17: 51–78.

Hudson, C. M. 1984. The transition from wife to widow: Short-term changes in economic well-being and labor force behavior. Ph.D. diss., Department of Sociology, Duke University, Durham, N.C.

Hurd, M. and D. Wise. 1987. *The wealth and poverty of widows: Assets before and after the husband's death.* Washington, D.C.: National Bureau of Economic Research, Working Paper no. 2325.

Income Security Programs. 1987. *Your spouse's allowance.* Ottawa: Minister of Supply and Services.

Knowles, Stanley. 1979. *House of Commons Debates: Official Reports*, October 22. Ottawa: Minister of Supply and Services.

Livingstone, B. 1988. Separated and unequal: Divorcees seek widows' pensions. *Hamilton Spectator.* February 16.

Lofland, Lyn H. 1975. "The 'thereness' of women: A selective review of urban sociology." In Marcia Millman and Rosabeth Moss Kanter (eds.), *Another voice: Feminist perspectives on social lives and social science,* 144–70. New York: Anchor Books.

Lopata, Helena Znaniecka. 1979. *Women as widows: Support systems.* New York: Elsevier.

———. 1995. Feminist perspectives on social gerontology. In Rosemary Bleiszner and Victoria H. Bedford (eds.), *Handbook of aging and the family,* 114–31. Westport, Conn.: Greenwood.

McDonald, Lynn. 1997. *Transitions into retirement: A time for retirement.* Final report, prepared for Human Resources Development Canada, National Welfare Grants Program.

MacRae, Hazel. 1992. Fictive kin as a component of the social networks of older people. *Research on Aging* 14(2): 226–47.

Martin Matthews, Anne. 1991. *Widowhood in later life*. Toronto: Harcourt Brace.

——. 1993. Issues in the study of the caregiving relationship. In Steven Zarit, Leonard I. Pearlin, and K. Warner Schaie (eds.), *Caregiving systems*. Hillsdale, N.J.: Lawrence Erlbaum Associates.

Matthews, Sarah H. 1979. *The social world of old women: Management of self-identity*. Beverly Hills, Calif.: Sage.

Miller, B. and L. Cafasso. 1992. Gender differences in caregiving: Fact or artifact?. *The Gerontologist* 32(4): 498–507.

Mills, C. Wright. 1959. *The sociological imagination*. New York: Grove Press.

Morgan, L. 1989. Economic well-being following marital termination. *Journal of Family Issues* 10(1): 86–101.

Plouffe, Louise. 1997. Seniors at risk: Prediction and policy. Paper presented at the Annual Scientific and Educational Meetings of the Canadian Association on Gerontology, Calgary, Alberta, October.

Riley, Matilda White. 1996. Discussion: What does it all mean? *The Gerontologist* 36(2): 256–58.

Riley, Matilda White, Robert L. Kahn, and Anne Foner. 1994. *Age and structural lag: Society's failure to provide meaningful opportunities in work, family, and leisure*. New York: John Wiley.

Rosenthal, Carolyn, Margaret Denton, Anne Martin-Matthews, and Susan French. In press. Changes in work and family over the life course: Implications for economic security of today's and tomorrow's older women. In Byron Spencer and Frank T. Denton (eds.), *Independence and economic security of an older population*.

Ross, Margaret M., Carolyn J. Rosenthal, and Pamela G. Dawson. 1997. Spousal caregiving in the institutional setting: Task performance. *Canadian Journal on Aging* 16(1): 51–69.

Silverman, Phyllis R. 1987. Widowhood as the next stage in the life course. In Helena Znaniecka Lopata (ed.), *Widows*, vol. 2, *North America*, 170–90. Durham, N.C.: Duke University Press.

Sorensen, A. 1992. Estimating the economic consequences of separation and divorce: A cautionary tale from the United States. In L. J. Weitzman and M. Maclean (eds.), *Economic consequences of divorce: The international perspective*, 263–82. New York: Oxford University Press.

Statistics Canada. 1976. *Population cross-classifications of characteristics: 1971 census of Canada*. Catalogue no. 92–729. Ottawa: Minister of Industry, Trade, and Commerce.

——. 1982. *Population: Age, sex, and marital status—1981 census of Canada*. Catalogue no. 92–901. Ottawa: Minister of Supply and Services.

——. 1993. *The nation: Age, sex, and marital status—1991 census of Canada*. Catalogue no. 93–310. Ottawa: Minister of Supply and Services.

Stone, Leroy. 1997. Preliminary findings of the Seniors-at-Risk Project. Symposium presentation at the Annual Scientific and Educational Meetings of the Canadian Association on Gerontology, Calgary, Alberta, October.

Stone, Leroy O. and H. Frenken. 1988. *Canada's seniors*. Catalogue no. 98–121. Ottawa: Minister of Supply and Services.

Uhlenberg, P., T. Cooney, and R. Boyd. 1990. Divorce for women after mid-life. *Journal of Gerontology: Social Sciences* 45(1): S3–S11.

United States Bureau of the Census. 1962. *Statistical abstract of the United States, 1962 (83rd ed.)*. Washington, D.C.: GPO.

———. 1972. *Statistical abstract of the United States, 1972 (93rd ed.)*. Washington, D.C.: GPO.

———. 1982. *Statistical abstract of the United States, 1982 (103rd ed.)*. Washington, D.C.: GPO.

———. 1992. *Statistical abstract of the United States, 1992 (113th ed.)*. Washington, D.C.: GPO.

Unruh, David R. 1983. *Invisible lives: Social worlds of the aged*. Beverly Hills, Calif.: Sage.

Vachon, M. L. S. and S. K. Stylianos. 1988. The role of social support in bereavement. *Journal of Social Issues* 44(3): 175–90.

Vanier Institute of the Family. 1994. *Profiling Canada's families*. Ottawa: Vanier Institute.

3

Conflicting Images of Older People Receiving Care

Challenges for Reflexive Practice and Research

JANE ARONSON

The systemic ageism embedded in contemporary Western culture and the social practices that generate and sustain the oppression of older people have been
made increasingly visible in recent years (Laws 1995; Macdonald & Rich 1983;
Townsend 1986). Older people with attributes that signal their potential dependency—for example, being ill or disabled, poor, or female—are especially
exposed to these oppressive practices and are, coincidentally, those most likely
to enter the orbit of long-term care and, thus, of social workers. Long-term care
constitutes the array of institutional and home-based services and resources that
are directed to elderly people's needs for health and social care. In the late 1990s
in Canada, as in most Western jurisdictions, these services and resources are
made up of a mixed economy of care—a complex and shifting array of public,
voluntary, and private programs and service organizations. These organizations
and the cumulative practices of service providers within them play critical parts
in both distributing resources and in shaping images and vocabularies about
older citizens' entitlements and the significance of their needs (Fraser 1989).
These images, usually only implied, warrant elaboration: they shape the identities and material possibilities of elderly people in need of care and, of particular
concern in this chapter, they therefore shape the consciousness and work of
those engaged in practice with them.

This chapter's focus on images of older people receiving care is rooted
in postmodern and feminist analyses of the power of language and narrative
as constitutive—not just representative—of social life and identity (Lather
1991:39). Conceptualizations of "narrativity" illuminate how a limited repertoire of public and private "stories" guide us to think and act in certain

ways and not in others (Somers & Gibson 1994:59). These narratives, in which we are located and in which we locate ourselves in shifting and fluid ways, derive from individual sources and biographies as well as from larger social, political, and cultural institutions. They may be well or poorly developed, privileged or suppressed.

To explore the repertoire of narratives and images of elderly people who are frail, disabled, or ill and to consider the positioning of social service providers in that repertoire, I have reviewed a range of conceptual literature, accounts, and analyses of health and social service organizations, my own and others' research, and fictional and autobiographical sources. From this review, three narratives about elderly people in need of assistance are discernible: "being managed," "managing," and "making demands." The first image, "being managed," finds expression in the dominant pattern of managerial talk about public and private service provision. It deepens old people's marginalization by casting them in a very passive role, as little more than bearers of predictable assortments of problems requiring standardized management. In contrast, "managing" captures the possibilities of people actively striving to direct their own particular journeys through old age and the jeopardies it may bring, and to stay in charge of everyday life and its challenges. "Making demands" is a similarly active narrative, though with a more voiced and public emphasis; it finds expression in elderly citizens' demands for resources to overcome collectively experienced obstacles in all areas of their lives.

"Being managed" is the dominant, privileged imagery embodied in the practices of policymakers and health and social service organizations, while the possibilities of "managing" and "making demands" are relatively muted and undeveloped. These three narratives are not material or static categories actually lived out as distinct realities in old people's lives. Rather, they represent conceptually distinguishable sets of vocabularies, symbols, and ideas that may all have a bearing on and shape elderly people's actions, identities, and experiences of needing care. Individual elderly people and the service providers who relate to them may shift their positioning between narratives over time and may draw simultaneously on different narratives—thus knowing intimately the tensions and contradictions among them.

Elaboration of these three narratives illuminates service use and service-giving as sites of disarray and conflict between images that are—more or less—dominant or muted, damaging or enhancing to older people and conducive to progressive or oppressive forms of practice. Just as elderly people themselves are situated and situate themselves in this contested context, so do we locate ourselves as practitioners and researchers. The challenges and possibilities of standing back and locating ourselves and our work more consciously amid these conflicting images and vocabularies are the focus of this chapter. I consider most particularly how social work practice and research can be fashioned wittingly and strategically to counter the damage of the dominant narrative, to amplify less oppressive alternatives, and thus to enhance elderly people's welfare as active, entitled citizens. To this end, the forms and foci of "being managed," "managing" and "making demands" are elaborated below and, within each, the location of social work practice and research is considered. In closing, issues of particular concern for social work in the foreseeable future that emerge from this analysis are discussed.

Elderly People "Being Managed": An Organizational Narrative of Rational Efficiency

The form and language of the dominant public narrative, "being managed," is highly developed; it exists in written and spoken form, is communicated by and embedded in the policies and practices of powerful political, health, and welfare institutions, and is commonplace in media representations of governments' battles with deficits and calls for belt-tightening (Armstrong & Armstrong 1996). In their preoccupation with deficit reduction and limiting social spending, federal and provincial governments in Canada are, increasingly, replacing traditional approaches to the organization of public health and social care with models of corporate management that promise efficiency and cost-saving (Working Group on Health Services Utilization 1994). This trend, mirrored in other comparable jurisdictions, is transforming the culture of health and social services as well as creating new forms of work organization and a new language for the expression of their purposes (Clarke & Newman 1997). Previous talk of commitments to the collective shouldering of health risks and to public administration have been replaced by narrower images of rational management, internal competition, and the efficiencies of the private market. Primacy is given to practical tasks and their standardized organization. Emphasis on outcomes measurable in economic terms and in the terms of the simplest organizational indicators (admissions, discharges, cases open and closed) leads, by design, to less complex and accessible health and social services for patients and to a deterioration in working conditions for employees (Armstrong et al. 1997; Shapiro 1997; Sky 1995).

While there is a considerable academic literature and much public policy and media attention given to this new managerial culture in health and wel-

fare services, our knowledge of the form and language of its unfolding in elderly people's private worlds is, in contrast, quite impoverished. In its expression in some of my own research, it is typically brief and unelaborated; sen-
tences are short and passively contructed and the words are spoken with little
animation. For example, in a study of older women reflecting on their frailties
and concerns (Aronson 1992), participants made these kinds of observations
about their situations in the community: "I've just given up; they [home care]
will do as they will"; "You just have to make do—there's no choice." These
women's bleak utterances were accompanied by allusions to the inevitability of
their situations because of government cuts and resource constraints: "There's
no money for more help anyhow. They tell us all the time. . . . My nurse says
she won't be able to come so much and can't stop long—she's got to get round
to more folk on her list. She's doing her best. I suppose I should be thankful
that she comes at all. There's nothing you can do, dear."

These statements reflect the power of the dominant managerial discourse
on elderly people and long-term care to confine elderly people's sense of their
possibilities. Opie identified the same powerful process in her study of elderly caregivers in New Zealand where, as in Canada, straitened images of public resources prevail (Opie 1995). Elderly caregivers recognized their social
workers' "busyness," understanding it as "a fact of life" rather than a cause for
complaint. Of this understanding, Opie notes: "Within the articulation of a
discourse of 'busyness' are references to scarcity and, further, references to uncertainty about right to access and to what constitutes a legitimate use of services" (1995:208). Similarly, from the U.K., Walker and Warren observed that
elderly service users found their support workers stretched and overextended,
and noted that "neither users nor their carers felt in a position to make demands" (1996:146).

Rendered undemanding by this sense of inevitable scarcity, elderly people's
expectations are lowered, their entitlement undermined, and they are, literally,
more easily managed. Ironically, political decisions to make health and social
services more scarce and meagerly rationed are often accompanied and justified
by talk of enhancing "customer" satisfaction and the choice of service "consumers" (Croft & Beresford 1995; Stricklin 1993). Marketplace notions of consumer choice and empowerment (e.g., of the control and dominance of the pur-
chaser at the supermarket) do not accord with the realities of a service system in
which limited options are dispensed according to providers' assessment and in
which power differentials between users and providers are immense (Aronson
1993; Croft & Beresford 1989, 1995). Nonetheless, the rhetoric of consumer participation associated with the new managerialism serves to shroud the funda-

mental disempowerment of "being managed" (Grace 1991). Of welfare clients positioned in a similarly disempowered fashion in relation to welfare bureaucracies, Ferguson notes: "to be a recipient is also to be a spectator" (1984:146). Positioned as passive and minimally entitled "spectators" in the public arena of long-term care, elderly people must deal with their needs privately—often, research suggests, in privately borne struggles to lessen the potential shame of appearing and feeling needy (Aronson 1990; Barry 1995).

The managerial narrative that reduces elderly people in this passive and disempowered fashion is centrally concerned with solving organizational and financial problems from the standpoint of funders, whether public or private. Elderly people figure quite minimally in this narrative so that, significantly, definitions of their needs go unspoken, obscured by the language of organizational imperatives and scarce resources. Subject to scrutiny, it is clear that elderly people "being managed" are subject to "thin" definitions of need (Fraser 1989:163) determined by professionals through standardized assessment procedures. Hochschild (1995:338) captures this "thinning" process and the reduction in care that it justifies when she notes how, in our language, we reduce "the range of ideas about what a child, wife, husband, aging parent or home 'really needs' to thrive. Indeed, the words 'thrive' and 'happy' go out of fashion, replaced by thinner, more restrictive notions of well-being." These thinner notions of well-being translate into the everyday details and texture of service practices with elderly people—for example, in decisions to cut home care workers' time allotments to allow for only practical definitions of their work and in eliminating supports deemed inessential to all but basic physical survival (Aronson & Neysmith 1996; Twigg 1997). In the dominant narrative, such practices are communicated as necessary and fiscally responsible decisions and are expressed in programmatic and administrative forms (e.g., admission criteria, assessment protocols, service priorities). That they actually represent a reinterpretation and thinning of needs is not made explicit.

Social Work with Elderly People "Being Managed":
Case Management? Solution-focused Practice?

Within this dominant narrative of "being managed," social workers are pressed to focus only on the immediate, the practical, and the surface (Chambon 1994). Writing from the United States, where social service delivery is, for the most part, run on the lines of competitive private industry, Munson notes that "the managed care efficiency movement has produced a shift away from clinical process to therapeutic procedures that are fragmented and of short duration" (1996:246). Observers of the reorganization of community care in the U.K. identify a comparable reshaping of practice so that assessment of elderly persons' situations is driven by service availability rather than by clients' needs. Assessment is, thus, a much simplified process—more a matter of routine administrative judgment than of professional judgment (Biggs 1990–91; Lewis et al. 1997). The more complex and time-consuming work of individual assessment, of understanding elderly people in the context of their individual biographies, and of supporting them emotionally and practically through changes and losses over time is, effectively, squeezed out (Hughes & Mtezuka 1992; Opie 1995). Ruth Silcock (1996:73) captures this image of practice in a poem entitled "The Social Worker":

> *The news for you, the young man said,*
> *Is that you have to find*
> *A nursing home within a week.*
> *I hope that's not unkind.*
> *Our hospital has no more beds,*
> *There's no more room: and so*
> *Your mother with her mended hip,*
> *Unmended mind, must go.*
>
> *I have a list that you can take*
> *With numbers you may ring*
> *And what the cost will be. I think*
> *That covers everything.*
> *It's up to you. I've work to do.*
> *No time to lose. And so*
> *Remember, you have just one week.*
> *Your mother has to go.*

Many observers suggest that—even before the retreat of the state and the reorganization of services of the last ten years—social work with elderly people was a very limited domain of practice, not unlike Silcock's current rendering of it. Seen as relatively low-status work, social services for older people were largely short-term and focused on the practical and did little to challenge received ideas about elderly people's (and especially elderly women's) low social valuation (Bowl 1986; Marshall 1989). Finch and Groves (1985:111) note how easily social service practices confirmed elderly women's confinement to the domestic sphere and to an absence of choices about how they lived in later life:

"To deny them the kind of support that might facilitate such choices means that social workers are colluding with social processes that effectively consign the elderly, most of whom it must be said again are women, to a kind of half life." This "depressing pattern of work" (Bowl 1986:131) was the focus of considerable criticism within social work from the mid-1980s onward. However, its legacy means that practitioners now striving to resist the dominant narrative of elderly people "being managed" have only a slim base of critical analysis and accumulated practice wisdom on which to draw.

Just as the narrative of "being managed"—the managerial discourse—presses social work practice into new and problematic forms, so of course does it shape the conduct and focus of related research. Research within the managerial discourse that focuses at the micro level of practice and experience tends to position elderly people very narrowly. Typically, elderly people are cast as consumers of services rather than as citizens with social entitlements. In long-term care environments in which private providers dominate, evaluation research—more commonly referred to as quality assurance—is clearly a variant of market research and, as such, is concerned to foster multiple and conflicting interests: "Satisfied consumers are loyal customers and the pay-offs translate to referrals, market share, profitability and, most importantly, better outcomes of care" (Stricklin 1993:17). Research within this "being managed" narrative tends to strip elderly people from the wider context of power relationships that shape their experiences of need and their encounters with service-giving institutions. For example, in their study of older patients' hospital discharge experiences, McWilliam et al. (1994) conceptualize and explore patients' "mindsets" and "senses of purpose" as variables that shape their degree of disempowerment in the medical system. Such individualized foci of attention risk making elderly people's psychological dispositions the exclusive focus for explanation and intervention, rather than the organizational structures and the everyday practices of health care providers that foster, even require, the development of subordinate and "managed" identities in elderly people (Latimer 1997; Opie 1998).

A key seam of research within the narrative of "being managed" focuses at the organizational level. Service organizations concerned with cost-efficiency and economic accountability measure outcomes and performance in the narrow terms of their documentary realties (Ng 1990), relying usually on statistical data that are highly standardized and quantified. Knowledge derived from quality assurance and outcome measures based on such material captures, of course, a very particular aspect of organizational life and interests. Of managerialism and this "new knowledge," Lupton (1992:101–102) observes: "The more the complexity of human interaction is simplified, the better it may be seen to 'fit' the requirements of departments subject to external pressures to monitor and measure their performance." She cautions that more critical knowledge-building concerned with the complexity and messiness of human dilemmas and actual practice are deemed to be of little value in such contexts: "It is likely that feminist-inspired research will be seen to deliver the wrong kinds of knowledge, collected in the wrong kinds of way, about the wrong kinds of thing" (1992:102). How to intrude the perspectives and interests of those "being managed" and of practitioners and researchers committed to making them the subjects rather than the objects of service receipt represents a daunting challenge—a challenge that requires us to be very clear about the theoretical and political positioning of our research and, as Chambon (1994) emphasizes, attentive to the language in which we express ourselves and frame our work.

Elderly People "Managing":
An Individual Narrative of Active Self-direction

"Managing" in the face of disability or illness in old age is, in contrast to "being managed," a fairly private and muted narrative. It finds expression in individual older people's accounts of self-assertion and self-direction and is articulated in active language: "I want to manage"; I must manage—it's a struggle"; "I'm managing, don't want to give up" (Aronson 1992). These assertions incorporate activity against odds, engagement in struggle, refusal to yield. "Managing" sometimes takes the form of tenacious and creative endurance. Older women describe, for example, how—against the odds of disability, pain, or discomfort—they use their limited energy judiciously to stay in charge of their everyday lives and to accomplish the activities they value (Aronson 1992; Ford & Sinclair 1987). In her journals, May Sarton (1988, 1996), a U.S writer and poet, chronicles meticulously both joy in the details of everyday life and the tenacity required to survive the confines and frustrations of ill health, weakness, and diminishing social ties. To sustain this kind of determined positioning, old people must often involve others in their efforts: "I pay someone to clean and do the heavy things and the yard work. I couldn't manage here on my own otherwise"; "The homemaker helps me keep going, helps me manage" (Aronson 1992). Even though relying on others, these women still construe themselves as active and engaged.

At the heart of this narrative is people's concern to direct the course of their own aging and, when faced with illness, disability, and the need for assistance, to shape the conditions of broaching or accepting help in ways that are consistent with their own particular biographies. Striving to assert individual definitions of need represents a central feature of "managing." The thin, predetermined definitions implied in "being managed" are resisted and disrupted here. For example, Eliasson (1990) describes a frail elderly woman who relied on a homemaker to do all her shopping. Wanting to ensure that she got the products she most liked, she prepared precise lists and maps of shelf arrangements in stores to simplify and expedite the homemaker's task. In the course of their work, frontline providers can often find themselves asked to individualize and "thicken" official, minimalist definitions of need and need-meeting in this way. Another homemaker reported how the elderly woman whom she helped with cleaning and cooking decided periodically to let the cleaning go in favor of having help with a home permanent; thus, together, they periodically defied official definitions of the homemaker's work and of the elderly woman's entitlement (Aronson & Neysmith 1996).

Resistance to standard definitions of need can also be manifest in older people's active disengagement from those cast as formal helpers. For instance, Mrs. Williams, an elderly woman interviewed in a community study by Parker (1983), refused and dismissed offers of formal service providers who deemed her at risk and sought to protect her. A working-class woman suspicious of all officialdom and its intrusions into her private world, she was committed to managing on her own terms and described a lifetime of doing so.

Social Work with Elderly People "Managing":
Needs-led Practice? Strengths-based Practice?

Within a "managing" narrative, social work practice is attentive to and supportive of the individuality and complexity of old people's efforts to negotiate old age. In contrast to the image of practice implied in the narrative of elderly people "being managed," the importance of longer-term work and of assessment processes that take in both the full context of people's present social circumstances and their life histories is central (Hughes & Mtezuka 1992; Opie 1995). Attention to relationships and process, rather than to short-term tasks and outcomes looms large in this more textured and skilled approach to practice. We have seen that elderly people's "managing" is often accomplished within the context of social relationships—whether the continuous tie with a social worker knowledgeable of their history or the long-standing relationship with a homemaker, friend, nurse, or aide. Ultimately, it is suggested that the well-being of frail elderly people living both at home and in institution-

al settings hinges on such "small-scale solidarities of interpersonal relationships which can be stimulated and encouraged by public policies" (Evers
1993:25). Social work's mandate to attend to the social relations of need-meeting as well as to the coordination of various resources and providers gives
workers special knowledge of these ties. This knowledge can be put to use
both in sustaining them at the local level and in highlighting their importance in broader policy arenas.

Public policies uncommitted to supporting this kind of relational base
for health and social services jeopardize elderly people's efforts at "managing." If they cannot count on care providers to personalize their work as part
of their official job responsibilities, to have time to understand their histories
and, thus, the significance of their current needs, they must either submit to
"being managed" or struggle to manage in other ways, e.g., by relying on the
help of family members/informal caregivers whom, typically, they do not
want to burden (Aronson 1990) or on the discretionary help of paid caregivers. Seeking help through these latter discretionary channels is a complex
process, potentially fraught with tension and inequity for both elderly people and service providers. Elderly people come to their encounters with service providers from a position of subordination in a culture that devalues age
and bodily frailty. If confronted with only thin, meager definitions of their
needs and busy service givers, their sense of devaluation and disentitlement
is deepened and, thus, their efforts to thicken or disrupt expert need interpretations must be undertaken indirectly and with stealth. Indirect and dis-
guised efforts to exert influence are the resort of people whose welfare depends upon groups with superior power; knowing they cannot make direct
claims or demands, they employ indirect means to persuade and coax (Baker Miller 1976; Bartky 1990).

The resources and tactics necessary to negotiate these fundamentally inequitable conditions are not equally available to all elderly people. For example, the elderly women, described earlier, who persuaded their homemakers
to assist them with shopping and personal care in particular ways were successful in influencing how their needs were defined and met. Their success
hinged on the fact that they had the capacity (cognitively, socially) to establish positive relationships with their care providers who, simultaneously, had
the capacity to personalize their work and to extend themselves. In the absence of these conditions, very different scenarios would result. Rather than
being seen in a positive light as tenacious, creative, determined, or apprecia-
tive, clients with similar wishes or needs could easily be deemed manipula-
tive, difficult, demanding, and unrewarding (Ferguson 1984). Encounters be-

tween elderly people and service providers at these frontlines of long-term care are shaped, too, by the complex crosscutting effects of social class and race, which have been the focus of relatively little attention. Elderly people tend to be homogenized in a culture that stereotypes them, so that the legacies of lifetime patterns of privilege and oppression are little explored. Equally, the variations in status and privilege of service providers and their implications for elderly people "managing" are poorly understood (Barry 1995; Neysmith & Aronson 1997).

Social work practice with elderly people who are "managing" requires awareness of these complex power dynamics and of workers' places within them. As noted above, workers' time can represent a crucial resource to elderly service users. Time is required to establish continuous well-informed relationships as a basis for supporting them through changes and losses in health and in social relationships and in making thorough and personalized links with needed resources. In the present economic and political climate, workers' use of time is often the object of stringent managerial surveillance so that practice aimed at supporting elderly people's "managing" may be extremely strained (Chambon 1994; Munson 1996; Rose 1997; Silcock 1996). Workers may resort, like the home care providers mentioned earlier, to working in formally disallowed and discretionary ways (e.g., breaking organizational rules about time limits for keeping cases open, putting in extra time).

In the mixed economy of care, where social workers are often charged simultaneously with need-definition and with managing tightly rationed resources, they may also learn to "work the market" in clients' interests and thus sustain their own professional identities as advocates (Clarke & Newman 1997:102–103). While such discretionary and inventive organizational "tinkering" (Pawlak 1976) on behalf of clients may meet with local success, it is a hidden and unacknowledged form of skill and work. Problematically, such unacknowledged micro-tactics do nothing to open up debate about contested definitions of need and the resources and skills required for practice that supports old people in their "managing." Problematically too, such undercover advocacy does not open up debate about the strain and potential demoralization that such tactics can generate among workers (Hadley & Clough 1996; Riffe & Kondrat 1997). We know relatively little of the costs to practitioners' health and well-being of working in ways that puts them, effectively, at odds with the institutions that employ or fund them—where they uncomfortably straddle narratives of "being managed" and "managing."

Rhoda Hurst Rojiani (1994) offers us an insightful account of another facet of the tensions in the structuring of power between elderly people "managing" and social workers whom they may encounter; she provides a practitioner's perspective on the reserve expressed by elderly people like Mrs. Williams, described earlier. Hurst Rojiani recognized that, for an elderly woman with whom she worked, her very presence as a formal, expert helper represented a form of diminishment and jeopardy to be fended off at all costs: "No matter how much I as a social worker emphasize the client's right to self-determination, how much I think of myself as an advocate and an empowerer, my professional presence in the life of a client indicates that some funding source in society deems her needy and inadequate in some way" (1994:149). This acute observation about the imbalance of power between practitioners located in and legitimated by a professional discourse and elderly people deemed "needy" serves to remind us of the challenges of reflexive practice: of recognizing power differences and finding ways to use them to work with rather than manage older people.

Social work's efforts to address power differences by "empowerment" strategies have been a substantial focus in the practice literature in the last decade. Critics identify the vagueness and rhetorical superficiality of the term and warn of its potential to deceive:

> Unless it [empowerment] is accompanied by a commitment to challenging and combatting injustice and oppression, which shows itself in actions as well as words, this professional Newspeak allows anyone to rewrite accounts of their practice without fundamentally changing the way it is experienced by service users. *(Ward & Mullender 1993:148)*

We have also witnessed a range of initiatives to "involve" users in the service organizations on which they rely—for example, in the structuring of residents' councils, or inclusion of user representatives on organizational committees (Aronson 1993; Church & Reville 1989; Croft & Beresford 1989, 1995). These initiatives are certainly improvements on the hollow marketplace imagery of consumer sovereignty or customer satisfaction, but they require careful and realistic delineation of their intentions and possibilities in practice. Too often, rather large claims to empower and involve translate into important but small-scale processes to, for example, give elderly nursing home residents a say about menus or smoking areas that can frustrate or make skeptical more politicized service users who are located closer to the third narrative ("making demands").

Ford and Sinclair (1987:157) characterize the determined process of older persons' everyday negotiation and engagement in "managing"—whether resisting or accepting others' help—as a fight: "the fight is not unlike a guerrilla war: unannounced, unacknowledged, small scale and relentless." Their insight into this fight and, hence, their ability to acknowledge its existence, is derived from research built on lengthy, open-ended interviews with older women. Most of our knowledge of the "managing" narrative comes from first-person accounts of this kind: autobiographical, fictional, and those generated in qualitative social research committed to giving elderly people some voice. The most critical work of this kind is at pains to emphasize that the work of "managing" for frail elderly people has not only personal but also political significance. In spending time with nursing home residents commonly construed as passive and disengaged, Diamond (1992) discerns instead their work and constant effort and the political significance of both. He reflects on the role of research in this light:

> The research objective here is to start with everyday situations and link them to social policy. . . . This necessarily involves a redefinition of who constitutes the social actors in social policy to include not only those who make policies, but also those who live them out. To include the latter is to conceptualize nursing home patients not just in terms of their sicknesses, but also as social and political beings, and to listen to their world, even its babble, for its social and political significance.
>
> *(Diamond 1992:52–53)*

On a similar point, Ford and Sinclair note that while many of the older women they interviewed expressed little interest in politics or consciousness of ageism and saw their struggles in very individual terms: "It would be a mistake to assume that this lack of critique or political involvement implies a lack of response" (1987:156). Building knowledge about this response—this "managing" and its political significance—is underpinned theoretically by analyses of the politics of everyday experience, contested notions of need, and the material and discursive contradictions of the state's institutions and practices (Fraser 1989; Smith 1990). Research within a "managing" narrative makes particular methodological demands. Recognizing "managing" as a story about resistance to the dominant organizational imagery of elderly people in need of help, research located here seeks to enable older people to find their own words for their struggle not to "be managed." Methodologically, then, researchers must find ways to hear this suppressed, alternative account. Hurst Rojiani (1994:143) reflects on exactly this challenge as she notes the inappropriateness of the traditional tool box of methods for hearing older people on their own terms: "If I had used a questionnaire or structured interview or had insisted on using the bureaucratic language of long-term care, I would never have captured Miss K's views: she would simply have been coerced into translating her experience into the prevailing research paradigm—giving me what she thought I wanted." This body of critical work that grapples with the theory, methodology, and methods of social work—related research in a "managing" narrative is, as yet, fairly small. Because it does not fit into the dominant managerial discourse, it is typically seen as policy-irrelevant—a politically rooted misperception that will require constant challenge (Finch 1986; Lupton 1992).

Elderly People "Making Demands":
A Collective Narrative of Politicized Resistance

Unlike "being managed" and "managing," "making demands" is a narrative located in the domain of public politics, largely outside the purview of the service-giving and professional discourse. "Making demands" finds expression in positions taken by senior citizens' advocacy organizations. For example, in voicing their concerns about cuts and reorganization in health care and social services, Canadian Pensioners Concerned speak of older people's entitlement to care and support when needed—an entitlement based on citizenship and on the social settlement established earlier in their lives that promised economic and social security in old age (Canadian Pensioners Concerned 1995). One of their members articulated this in an interview in more personal terms: "My husband paid taxes all our lives, he joined up and fought in the war, I did my bit, we raised our kids. . . . Now, we expect to be helped when we need it. . . . It's our right, surely."

"Making demands" coincides with Fraser's (1989:171) identification of oppositional needs discourses and the articulation of runaway needs that unsettle and expand the confines of expert discourses and that resist being reprivatized by the institutional machinery of the state. Elderly people positioned here might call attention to their needs not just for health and social care but for better housing, adequate incomes, and the ability to participate in the broader public culture. For example, in defining the focus of the Gray Panthers, Maggie Kuhn (1986) typically identified three priority areas: enduring peace in the world, health, and housing. This construction of elderly people's interests resists confining definitions of functional need and looks, rather, at what all people—including elderly people—might need to thrive.

The disability rights movement has done much to resist this circumscribed positioning of people with disabilities as only service users "being kept clean . . . in the contained environment of their own home" (Morris 1993:161). The Independent Living Movement has, rather, set its sights on much broader social change, concerning itself not only with better services and more influence in their design but also with more fundamental questions of civil rights and equal opportunities (Croft & Beresford 1995; Morris 1991, 1993; Priestley 1995). This focus brings to the foreground the connection between individual needs for support and care and systemic barriers to the participation of people with disabilities as a collectivity.

The development of a narrative about elderly people "making demands" and striving to develop a comparably politicized language and consciousness about the injustices old people encounter as a collectivity faces some particular challenges. Specifically, the intersection of systemic ageism and ableism, together with the particular devaluation of older women (the majority of the older population) in contemporary culture, suppress this narrative significantly. For many of the current generation of older women who did not work outside the home during their lives, this suppression is especially easily accomplished. Younger women with disabilities and public identities may more readily protest the way health and social services reduce them to nothing but their physical impairments. The observation of an older woman representing a seniors' organization at a conference illustrates this contrast; she noted how she felt overlooked and reduced by virtue of her age and her lifetime of unpaid work at home: "It's as if I've never been anything."

Social Work with Elderly People "Making Demands":
Advocacy? Antioppressive Practice?

While "making demands" is located outside formally defined professional territory, social work can certainly contribute to its amplification and to challenging the ageist, ableist, and sexist social forces that suppress it. In her effort to reconceptualize empowerment in social work with and on behalf of older women, Browne (1995) offers us some valuable direction. Her characterization and valuing of "connection and relatedness" as key sources of power and strength for older women contrasts starkly with the isolated realities of many older women receiving home-based care. Ironically, the rhetorical invocation of "community" care is often bereft of community connection and means, rather, that older people simply survive in private households with "consumer of service" as the only identity available to them. As noted at the beginning of this chapter, critics of this pattern of so-called community care observe how this narrowed identity and thin definition of need can be enforced by seemingly small-scale service and resource decisions to, for instance, provide transportation in order to keep medical appointments but not in order to sustain cultural/social connections. Browne's analysis requires us to revisit ideas long-held in gerontology and social work about the character and possibilities of connection, social solidarity, and participation for women in later life. In particular, she calls for a revaluing of ties of friendship. The reality that friendships among women are, throughout life, cast as secondary to ties of marriage and family (Friedman 1993) has especial irony in later life when—because of patterns in life expectancy—marriage relations are the exception and the company of predominantly women is to be expected (Martin-Matthews, this volume).

The possibilities of practice that recognize and seek to foster the potential strength in such connections and wider interventions that challenge the political and economic roots of older, disabled women's marginality are finding their way into the social work literature. Writing of the possibilities of antidiscriminatory social work with older people, Hughes and Mtezuka observe that "the development of radical policy and practice is a difficult and lonely task for the individual practitioner. The struggle, in our view, is one in which a corporate or collective approach is essential. Forming alliances with older people and their organizations is one element in this collective strategy" (1992:238). Similarly, Marshall underscores the potential of energetic advocacy and stresses "the need to stand alongside the old person against the forces of ageism, and insist that they deserve and must have at least as much as other people. A simmering anger characterizes the best social workers in this field" (1989:117).

Social workers endeavoring to "stand alongside" in this fashion and to focus on the well-being of elderly people as a collectivity can learn from other areas where quests for justice and inclusion have been more actively politicized (e.g., the disability rights movement, the organized movement of psychiatric survivors). Besides learning from actual strategies, community and organizational practices, and the like, others' reflections on the complexity of disrupting the power relations between professionals and those who seek or must accept their services are also illuminating. For example, in her analysis of the participation of politicized psychiatric survivors in a community mental health system, Church observes:

> "Consumer participation" has the potential to call mental health professionals to account not just for how we do our work but for who we are. We should expect this process to be painful and conflictual. . . . In pain

and conflict, we encounter our deepest investments in the status quo and the strongest possibilities for divesting ourselves of them. *(1995:74)*

Transferring Church's observations to social work with older people, social workers should—in other words—expect to find elderly people "making demands" of them unsettling and, by implication, deeply disruptive of the kind of professional identities associated with images of elderly people "being managed" and "managing." Anticipating this and understanding our reactions in political rather than just personal terms will be important if social workers really are to contribute to elderly people's capacities to "make demands" and if practice for "empowerment" is to have any reality.

Research and writing specifically concerned about social work's engagement in forming political alliances with older people "making demands" is relatively slim and, for the most part, confined to visions and intentions (Bornat, Phillipson & Ward 1985; Hughes & Mtezuka 1992). Efforts to fashion new forms of antioppressive practice can, however, build upon the insights of activists like Anne Bishop (1994), who writes about "how to become an ally" of oppressed groups and of those engaged in alliances with other marginalized populations (e.g., Church 1995; Cosis Brown 1992; Walmsley 1991).

Working Reflexively in the Future

This chapter's elaboration of three narratives, discernible in contemporary culture, about elderly people who are frail, disabled, or ill reveals how each shapes their journeys and identities in old age. Within each, we have seen how social work is structured and identified and have considered how the tensions between narratives find expression in social work practice and research.

Social workers practicing with elderly people will require an ongoing critique of their own positioning among these conflicting discourses about older people, professional service-giving, and the role of the state. Just as we use language, so it uses us (Lather 1991:8), and thus the language of social work's professional claims requires constant scrutiny. Chambon (1994:67) notes how social work "imports a terminology," borrowing from other professional and lay vocabularies while, at the same time, being subject to the corporate language now so dominant in all areas of public service and social welfare. Subject to these various forces and with only a fragile hold on professional status, social work tends to express its purposes in expert and technical terms. For example, the three narratives could be readily transposed out of the terms of elderly people's realities and into the terms of social work technologies; instead of "being managed," "managing," and "making demands," we could read "case management," "needs-led practice," and "advocacy." Each of these expressions implies very different things about need interpretation and power relations between service providers and older people and, in so doing, structures our thinking and our actions. Being conscious of these different ways of structuring, rather than letting them go without saying, means they can be subject to questioning and that, as a result, "new horizons of understanding and action" can be opened up (Chambon 1994:72).

Consciousness of differences in the structuring of research in the three narratives will also be important in the future. We have seen how research framed by a managerial discourse focuses implicitly on organizational interests and, if elderly people's accounts are sought, positions them in narrow terms as consumers of organizational outputs or as inputs to be better adjusted to standardized service delivery. In contrast, knowledge-building about elderly people "managing" and "making demands" attempts to understand their realities from *their* vantage points, to make their typically invisible experiences visible and comprehensible to themselves and to others and to link individual experiences with wider social forces and power relations. Schram (1995:39–40) characterizes these contrasting approaches to research as "top-down" and "bottom-up," respectively. It will be important to strive for clarity about the positioning of social work research in the context of these contrasting political and epistemological approaches to knowledge-building. Debate about research practices is too often reduced to discussion of research methods—in particular, to the apparent opposition between qualitative and quantitative methods. While "top-down" research is often associated with quantitative methods and "bottom-up" with qualitative, the equation of research purpose and political positioning with methods and techniques is oversimplifying (Schram 1995). For example, ethnographic methods can be used to explore elderly people's adjustment to managerial care regimes, just as such methods can be used to make visible their quests for self-determination and political participation. Equally, quantitative methods can be used in the service of managerial efficiency, just as they can be employed to describe and challenge race- and class-based inequities in service distribution. Looking beyond the research "tool box" to clarify more fundamental questions about the purposes that research is intended to serve, about its epistemological foundations, and about its discursive construction is the challenge that lies ahead.

The discursive analysis developed in this chapter has, intentionally, put elderly people's perspectives at its center—ironically, not a common practice in the dominant managerial discourse about societal responses to older persons. Extracting from each narrative how old people's needs and entitlements are constructed and, thus, keeping the focus first on *their* identities rather than on organizational or professional objectives or technologies has been instructive. The as yet relatively weak narrative about "making demands" aims explicitly to ensure that older persons are well-supported in the face of health and social needs and, thus, are enabled and entitled to participate socially, economically, culturally, and politically in worlds and ways of their choosing. The "managing" narrative aims explicitly, but mutedly, to ensure that individual older persons are helped to fashion their own paths through the jeopardies and changes of ill health and social losses. And the privileged narrative about "being managed" is concerned with organizing minimal responses to old people's problems in ways that make as few demands as possible on public resources. These contrasting foci and purposes imply a progressive thinning of needs, a simplification of practice, and a heightening of the power differential between older persons and ostensibly helpful professionals.

Arguably, social work is well positioned to see these discursive processes and to expose their consequences for elderly people's identities and material welfare. Social workers tend to be engaged at crucial intersections between elderly people and the various faces of the state—between institution and community, medical and social, market and government, public and private. At these intersections, the impacts of the dominant managerial discourse and the restructuring of social welfare that is characterizing the late twentieth century unfold in problematic frontline service practices explored in this chapter. The challenge for social work will be to stay alert and analytical about its own position in this contested and shifting ground and to counter the managerial discourse by amplifying practices associated with the less oppressive and marginalizing images of elderly people: by supporting frail elderly people "managing" on their own terms, and in allying with and buttressing those "making demands" for collectively assured entitlements to health and social security in old age.

Acknowledgments

The work reported here was supported in part by a Social Sciences and Humanities Research Council of Canada research network grant on the changing conditions of women's caring labor (816–94–0003). I am grateful for network members' stimulation and sustenance.

References

Armstrong, P. and H. Armstrong. 1996. *Wasting away: The undermining of Canadian health care.* Toronto: Oxford University Press.

Armstrong, P., H. Armstrong, J. Choiniere, E. Mykhalovskiy, and J. P. White. 1997. *Medical alert: New work organizations in health care.* Toronto: Garamond.

Aronson, J. 1990. Older women's experiences of needing care: Choice or compulsion? *Canadian Journal on Aging* 9(3): 234–47.

——. 1992. Are we really listening? Beyond the official discourse on needs of old people. *Canadian Social Work Review* 9(1): 73–87.

—— 1993. Giving consumers a say in policy development: Influencing policy or just being heard? *Canadian Public Policy* 19(4): 367–78.

Aronson, J. and S. M. Neysmith. 1996. "You're not just in there to do the work": Depersonalizing policies and the exploitation of home care workers' labour. *Gender and Society* 10(1): 59–77.

Baker Miller, J. 1976. *Toward a new psychology of women.* Boston: Beacon Press.

Barry, J. 1995. Care-need and care-receivers: Views from the margins. *Women's Studies International Forum* 18(3): 361–74.

Bartky, S. L. 1990. *Femininity and domination: Studies in the phenomenology of oppression.* New York: Routledge.

Biggs, S. 1990–91. Consumers, case management, and inspection: Obscuring social deprivation and need? *Critical Social Policy* 10(3): 23–38.

Bishop, A. 1994. *Becoming an ally: Breaking the cycle of oppression.* Halifax, Can.: Fernwood.

Bornat, J., C. Phillipson, and S. Ward. 1985. *A manifesto for old age.* London: Pluto Press.

Bowl, R. 1986. Social work with old people. In C. Phillipson and A. Walker (eds.), *Ageing and social policy: A critical assessment,* 128–45. Aldershot, U.K.: Gower.

Browne, C. V. 1995. Empowerment in social work practice with older women. *Social Work* 40(3): 358–64.

Canadian Pensioners Concerned. 1995. *Seniors Viewpoint* 21(5): 7–8.

Chambon, A. S. 1994. Postmodernity and social work discourse(s): Notes on the changing language of a profession. In A. S. Chambon and A. Irving (eds.), *Essays on postmodernism and social work,* 63–72. Toronto: Canadian Scholars Press.

Church, K. 1995. *Forbidden narratives: Critical autobiography as social science.* Luxembourg: Gordon and Breach.

Church, K. and D. Reville. 1989. User involvement in the mental health field in Canada. *Canada's Mental Health* 37(2): 22–25.

Clarke, J. and J. Newman. 1997. *The managerial state.* London: Sage.

Cosis Brown, H. 1992. Lesbians, the state, and social work practice. In M. Langan and L. Day (eds.), *Women, oppression, and social work,* 201–219.

Croft, S. and P. Beresford. 1989. User involvement, citizenship, and social policy. *Critical Social Policy* 9(2): 5–18.

——. 1995. Whose empowerment? Equalizing the competing discourses in community care. In R. Jack (ed.), *Empowerment in community care*, 59–76. London: Chapman and Hall.

Diamond, T. 1992. *Making gray gold: Narratives of nursing home care*. Chicago: University of Chicago Press.

Eliasson, R. 1990. Perspectives and outlooks on social science research. In A. Elzinga, J. Nolin, R. Pranger, and S. Sunesson (eds.), *In science we trust?* Lund, Sweden: Lund University Press.

Evers, A. 1993. The welfare mix approach: Understanding the pluralism of welfare systems. In A. Evers and I. Svetlik (eds.), *Balancing pluralism: New welfare mixes in care for the elderly*, 3–32. Aldershot, U.K.: Avebury.

Ferguson, K. E. 1984. *The feminist case against bureaucracy*. Philadelphia: Temple University Press.

Finch, J. 1986. *Research and policy: The uses of qualitative methods in social and educational research*. London: Falmer Press.

Finch, J. and D. Groves. 1985. Old girl, old boy: Gender divisions in social work. In E. Brook and A. Davis (eds.), *Women, the family, and social work*, 92–111. London: Tavistock.

Ford, J. and R. Sinclair. 1987. *Sixty years on: Women talk about old age*. London: Women's Press.

Fraser, N. 1989. *Unruly practices: Power, discourse, and gender in contemporary social theory*. Minneapolis: University of Minnesota Press.

Friedman, M. 1993. *What are friends for? Feminist perspectives on personal relationships and moral theory*. Ithaca, N.Y.: Cornell University Press.

Grace, V. M. 1991. The marketing of empowerment and the construction of the health consumer: A critique of health promotion. *International Journal of Health Services* 21(2): 329–43.

Hadley, R. and R. Clough. 1996. *Care in chaos: Frustration and challenge in community care*. London: Cassell.

Hochschild, A. R. 1995. The culture of politics: Traditional, post-modern, cold-modern and warm-modern ideals of care. *Social Politics* 2(3): 331–46.

Hughes, B. and M. Mtezuka. 1992. Social work and older women: Where have older women gone? In M. Langan and L. Day (eds.), *Women, oppression, and social work*, 220–41.

Hurst Rojiani, R. 1994. Disparities in the social construction of long-term care. In C. Kohler Riessman (ed.), *Qualitative studies in social work research*, 139–52. Thousand Oaks, Calif.: Sage.

Kuhn, M. 1986. Prologue: Social and political goals for an ageing society. In C. Phillipson, M. Bernard, and P. A. Strang (eds.), *Dependency and interdependency in old age*. London: Croom Helm.

Langan, M. and L. Day (eds.), *Women, oppression, and social work: Issues in anti-discriminatory practice*. London: Routledge.

Lather, P. 1991. *Getting smart: Feminist research and pedagogy with/in the postmodern.* New York: Routledge.

Latimer, J. 1997. Figuring identities: Older people, medicine, and time. In A. Jamieson, S. Harper, and C. Victor (eds.), *Critical approaches to ageing and later life,* 143–59. Buckingham, U.K.: Open University Press.

Laws, G. 1995. Understanding ageism: Lessons for feminism and postmodernism. *The Gerontologist* 35(1): 112–18.

Lewis, J. with P. Bernstock, V. Bovell, and F. Wookey. 1997. Implementing care management: Issues in relation to the new community care. *British Journal of Social Work* 27(5): 5–24.

Lupton, C. 1992. Feminism, managerialism, and performance measurement. In M. Langan and L. Day (eds.), *Women, oppression, and social work,* 92–111.

Macdonald, B. with C. Rich. 1983. *Look me in the eye: Old women, aging, and ageism.* San Francisco: Spinsters/Aunt Lute.

Marshall, M. 1989. The sound of silence: Who cares about the quality of social work with older people? In C. Rojek, G. Peacock, and S. Collins (eds.), *The haunt of misery: Critical essays in social work and helping,* 109–122. London: Routledge.

McWilliam, C. L., J. Belle Brown, J. L. Carmichael, and J. M. Lehman. 1994. A new perspective on threatened autonomy in elderly persons: The disempowering process. *Social Science and Medicine* 38(2): 327–38.

Morris, J. 1991. *Pride against prejudice: Transforming attitudes to disability.* Philadelphia: New Society.

——. 1993. *Independent lives: Community care and disabled people.* London: Macmillan.

Munson, C. E. 1996. Autonomy and managed care in clinical social work practice. *Smith College Studies in Social Work* 66(3): 241–60.

Neysmith, S. M. and J. Aronson. 1997. Working conditions in home care: Negotiating race and class boundaries in gendered work. *International Journal of Health Services* 27(3): 479–99.

Ng, R. 1990. State funding to a community employment centre: Implications for working with immigrant women. In R. Ng, G. Walker, and J. Muller (eds.), *Community organization and the Canadian state,* 165–83. Toronto: Garamond.

Opie, A. 1995. *Beyond good intentions: Support work with older people.* Wellington: Institute of Policy Studies, Victoria University of Wellington.

——. 1998. "Nobody's asked for my view": Users' empowerment by multidisciplinary health teams. *Qualitative Health Research* 8(2): 188–206.

Parker, T. 1983. "Some bloody do-gooding cow." In B. Davey, A. Gray, and C. Seale (eds.), *Health and disease,* 119–23. 2d ed. Buckingham, U.K.: Open University Press.

Pawlak, E. J. 1976. Organizational tinkering. *Social Work* 21(5): 376–80.

Priestley, Mark. 1995. Dropping 'E's: The missing link in quality assurance for disabled people." *Critical Social Policy* 15(2–3): 7–21.

Riffe, H. A. and M. E. Kondrat. 1997. Social worker alienation and disempowerment in a managed care setting. *Journal of Progressive Human Services* 8(1): 41–56.

Rose, S. M. 1997. Considering managed care. *Journal of Progressive Human Services* 8(1): 57–65.

Sarton, M. 1988. *After the stroke.* New York: Norton.

———. 1996. *At eighty-two.* London: Women's Press.

Schram, S. F. 1995. *Words of welfare: The poverty of social science and the social science of poverty.* Minneapolis: University of Minnesota Press.

Shapiro, E. 1997. *The cost of privatization: A case study of home care in Manitoba.* Winnipeg: Canadian Centre for Policy Alternatives.

Silcock, R. 1996. *A wonderful view of the sea.* London: Anvil Press.

Sky, L. 1995. *Lean and mean health care: The creation of the generic worker and the deregulation of health care.* Toronto: Ontario Federation of Labour.

Smith, D. E. 1990. *The conceptual practices of power: A feminist sociology of knowledge.* Toronto: University of Toronto Press.

Somers, M. R. and G. D. Gibson. 1994. Reclaiming the epistemological "other": Narrative and the social construction of identity. In C. Calhoun (ed.), *Social theory and the politics of identity*, 37–99. Oxford: Blackwell.

Stricklin, M. L. 1993. Home care consumers speak out on quality. *Home Healthcare Nurse* 11(6): 10–17.

Townsend, P. 1986. Ageism and social policy. In C. Phillipson and A. Walker (eds.), *Ageing and social policy: A critical assessment*, 15–44. Aldershot, U.K.: Gower.

Twigg, J. 1997. Deconstructing the "social bath": Help with bathing at home for older and disabled people. *Journal of Social Policy* 26(2): 211–32.

Walker, A. and L. Warren. 1996. *Changing services for older people.* Buckingham, U.K.: Open University Press.

Walmsley, J. 1991. Talking to top people: Some issues relating to citizenship of people with learning difficulties. *Disability, Handicap, and Society* 6(3): 219–31.

Ward, D. and A. Mullender. 1993. Empowerment and oppression: An indissoluble pairing for contemporary social work. In J. Walmsley, J. Reynolds, P. Shakespeare, and R. Woolfe (eds.), *Health, welfare, and practice: Reflecting on roles and relationships*, 147–54. London: Sage.

Working Group on Health Services Utilization. 1994. *When less is better: Using Canada's hospitals efficiently.* Conference of Federal / Provincial / Territorial Deputy Ministers of Health.

4

Constructing Community Care

(Re)storying Support

DEBORAH O'CONNOR

In community care policy, family caregivers are positioned as the corner-stones. Since it is estimated that between 85 to 90 percent of care and support to seniors in the community is provided by the family (National Advisory Council on Aging 1989), it is not surprising that the involvement of a family member, particularly a spouse, has been identified as one of the strongest guards against institutionalization (Carriere & Pelletier 1995; Hanley et al. 1990; Shapiro & Tate 1988). That providing this care can be stressful, at least for some, is also well documented (Lieberman & Fisher 1995; Zarit 1989), with research suggesting that spouses are particularly vulnerable to the physical and/or emotional problems associated with this stress (Barnes, Given & Given 1992; Biegel, Sales & Schulz 1991; George & Gwyther 1986; Noelker 1990).

The value and the risks associated with the caregiving role are recognized and explicitly sanctioned in policy directives and program developments. It is at this juncture that the private experience of living with a frail or ill family member intersects with the public provision of support; it is at this juncture that ideals of "community care" are generally operationalized.

This intersection is problematic. The majority of family caregivers do not utilize formal support services (Caserta et al. 1987), and spouses have been identified as the least likely of all family members to do so (Gonyea & Silverstein 1991; Tennstedt et al. 1990; Wenger 1990). This raises questions: If support services are so "supportive," then why are family members, particularly wives, not using them? If there is a commitment to community care, why are these persons not buying into it?

The purpose of this chapter is to examine these questions using data from a study that examined the interface between the private experience of living with a memory-impaired partner and the use of formal support services. In this study, fourteen spouses (eight husbands and six wives), were interviewed up to three times using an unstructured interview format; I purposely sought out individuals who had refused available formal support services. Using discourse analytic strategies, the personal experiences of these individuals were examined as reflective of prevailing sociopolitical understandings of gendered family caregiving. I intend to use the findings of this project to problematize the presumption that there is something wrong with spouses who are "resistant" to support services. Instead, the focus will be on deconstructing the assumptions grounding the provision of formal support to demonstrate how they sabotage ideals of community care. Practical approaches to assist in "restorying" support will then be suggested.

Positioning the Project: A Conceptual Context

Traditional ways of researching and understanding the interface between family "caregiving" and formal support have, to date, proved inadequate. Specifically, the conventional focus on stress that dominates the caregiving literature fails to adequately capture the complexity associated with this experience. This body of research assumes the preeminence of stress and/or burden as a defining feature of the experience (Abel 1990; Biegel, Sales & Schulz 1991; Faran et al. 1991). Formal support is then framed as a stress-reducer for the "caregiver" whose raison d'être is visible only as a functional support for the ill relative. This is what Fraser (1990) references as a "thin" conceptualization of need; it assumes a simple, unproblematic, and given interpretation of need. By failing to tease out the complexity, this focus effectively individualizes the failure to utilize services as the personal issue of the "resistant caregiver" and allows the provision of formal support services to remain unchallenged. In contrast, once the complexity of the experience is recognized, and the politics of need-interpretation problematized (Fraser 1990), the possibility emerges that there could be good reasons why individuals may choose not to use available formal support services.

Ideas associated with feminist poststructuralism (Gavey 1997) introduce a way to challenge the simplistic conceptualization of caregiver need. Poststructuralism, alternately referenced by some as postmodernism (Burman & Parker 1993; Gavey 1997), is used here to describe an intellectual movement that rejects the idea that the world can be understood in terms of grand theories or metanarratives. It shifts the focus from a notion of preexisting stable reality and instead recognizes the importance of language for constructing reality. The following key ideas associated with feminist poststructuralism provided the grounding for this study.

To begin, this worldview positions individual experience within a broader context; this suggests that individual interpretation of the experience of living with a memory-impaired spouse can only be fully understood when contextualized within the sociopolitical environment that produced it. Given this, I wanted to listen beyond the individual experience of living with a memory-impaired spouse in order to uncover implicit assumptions that were being used to make meaning. This meant acknowledging the importance of language for constructing reality and then shifting the focus from the individual to the discourses that were being used to frame personal experiences. Discourses refer to sets of assumptions or beliefs that are socially shared and often unconsciously reflected in language (Gavey 1997); they provide the abstract storylines upon which individuals draw to make sense of the world and hence one's personal experience (Burr 1995; Davies & Harre 1990). In this study, I was interested in uncovering the systems of beliefs, assumptions, and values that spouses were relying upon to assign meaning to the use of formal support services.

This understanding challenges the notion that individuals are the coherent, fixed, and rational subjects that more traditional psychological theories, including a stress/burden conceptualization, make them out to be. Rather, such a subject is "de-centered" (Gavey 1997; Lather 1991) and "refashioned as a site of disarray and conflict inscribed by multiple contestatory discourses" (Lather 1991:5). Specifically, there are many discourses available through which one can make sense of the world, but these are not necessarily compatible. Moreover, not all discourses carry the same influence. Some, referenced as dominant discourses and representing the taken-for-granted sets of assumptions and beliefs that often remain unarticulated (and hence unchallenged), are more powerful. These discourses are not neutral but represent political interests that are constantly vying for status and power (Gavey 1997; Weedon 1987). This means that individuals may have multiple, sometimes contradictory and covert, storylines influencing how they make sense of their personal experiences. These competing discourses can cause tension as each struggles to exert power over an individual's sense-making. However, such tensions also open up the possibility of change. While individual experience is constructed from available discourses, people also have the power to con-

struct alternative discourses. Oppressive discourses can be challenged and replaced with more compatible storylines.

These ideas influenced my research process in two ways. First, by challenging ideas that the individual is a coherent fixed entity, the possibilities of
contradiction, change, and intersubjectivity are introduced. This means that
tuning into contradictions and inconsistencies associated with the experience
of living with a memory-impaired partner—rather than attempting to subli-
mate them—became a critical focus in this project. Methodologically, I struggled to find ways to incorporate the complexity and contradictions associated
with each person's experience while simultaneously recognizing that my ren-
dition would always be partial and incomplete.

Second, the focus on language directs attention to the importance of the
stories that research participants tell about their experiences and positions
these stories as a broader reflection of sociopolitical reality. Specifically, there
is growing recognition that people organize and interpret the world through
their stories, and these personal stories rely on available discourses, or storylines, for providing a frame. Taken a step further, culture—used broadly here
to reference societal values and beliefs—is seen as "speaking itself" through an
individual's story (Riessman 1993; Rosenwald & Ochberg 1992). Methodologically, this meant creating the space in which participants had freedom to
"story" their experience; I relied upon open-ended, unstructured interviews to
generate data. The intent of analysis was then on understanding these personal stories as reflective of the storylines available for constructing this experience; particular attention focused on uncovering and naming oppressive discourses. In this project, intensive discourse analytic strategies were used to
contextualize the experience and read beyond the content.

(Re)Cognizing the Experience

Naming is a powerful act (Aronson 1988; Brown 1994). Through the process
of naming, social workers can become aware of hidden assumptions and expectations that they hold regarding how caring is structured within our society. "Unless social workers are aware of the embeddedness of their views
and how they participate in discursive practices, they are unlikely to be
open to alternatives that are being obscured" (Hare-Mustin 1994:33). The
first step, then, is to begin to articulate the underlying assumptions associated with the experience of living with a memory-impaired spouse in order
to situate spouses' responses to their particular experiences. Attending to the

care needs of the ill partner unsurprisingly emerges as a critical aspect of these experiences.

In the following section, I will make explicit how attending to the care needs of a memory-impaired partner is constructed as a private domestic responsibility crosscut by gendered expectations about competence. The intent is to develop the ideas of other feminist researchers by using these participants' stories to expose sets of assumptions grounding both personal interpretation and the provision of formal support. The focus will be on explicating how these sets of assumptions sabotage ideals of community care and evoke pejorative connotations associated with the use of formal support services. Strategies for recognizing and promoting storylines that are more conducive to the use of formal support, and hence support the notion of "community care," will then be examined.

The Dominant Discourse: "In sickness and in health"

All participants assumed "naturally" and "automatically" some responsibility for attending to the personal care needs of their ill partner. The activities associated with attending to these needs ranged from supervising physically active but forgetful spouses to providing total care. Two storylines competed to provide the frame for making sense of one's responsibility for these activities.

The dominant storyline ground the provision of this care as a logical extension of the marital relationship ("It's what a wife does," noted one woman). This expectation for most participants was contextualized by a reference to the "in sickness and in health" part of the wedding vows and carried with it a sense of inevitability. The belief was, unsurprisingly, so strong that it generally went without question; only one participant queried his responsibility, and he acknowledged that should he refuse the responsibility he would "cease to have sons" and be seen as having "played a pretty dirty deal." Another husband captures the lack of real choice:

> So what you have to become used to is the fact that you are watching someone slowly disintegrate before your eyes. They call it the living death, and actually it's the living death of two people really. It's not just for one. Because *you're tied to each other irretrievably and unless you're quite callous*—and some people are—and quite prepared to say "to hell with it, I'm going to put her in a home," you're stuck with it [emphasis added by husband].

It was made clear that attending to the care needs of one's partner was essential if one wished to maintain the status of a "good" husband or wife.

This storyline recognizes the spouse as not simply the most obvious but also the most qualified care provider. Given the intimacy of the relationship, several participants referenced what one husband described as a "sort of mental telepathy" that allowed them to be acutely sensitive to their partner's needs. But there was a cost.

> I have this terrible, I guess you could almost call it egotistical feeling that I can cope with her best. And that I don't trust other people to look after her. . . . And that's my biggest problem . . . because by doing so I'm making myself a prisoner.

This emotional connection assured higher quality care but also had the effect of imprisoning one in the caregiving role.

Except for one participant, the importance of this emotional connection superseded and/or replaced attention to other qualities that would conceivably be associated with suitability; for example, references to qualities such as personal disposition, knowledge, and skill were notably absent. In other words, it was the relational connection that defined quality care; care without this relational connection was necessarily inferior. This had the important function of asserting the spouse's special expertise in this situation: she/he had the knowledge to insure a contextualized, holistic understanding of the ill partner. However, it also had the impact of insuring that providing care remained solidly on the shoulders of the well spouse; two men acknowledged that they had become a "prisoner" in the situation, and several others described their own lives as being "on hold" because, as one woman noted, "caregiving consumes your life."

This dominant storyline positioned service use with only pejorative connotations. First, nonfamily care—that is, care assumed to be lacking an emotional connection—is necessarily construed as inferior. Second, by equating the provision of hands-on care with one's emotional connection to one's spouse, utilizing services had the potential to raise questions about the latter. Specifically, service use was generally linked to institutionalization, which was always subjectively perceived as abandonment. Finally, because providing care is assumed to be "natural" and "logical," by default utilizing services can be interpreted as a sign that one is "unnatural" and therefore deficient; several participants associated the use of services as indicative of whether or not "I was having a problem." This is significant because it implies personal failure in the situation. Ultimately then, the meaning associated with service use, when constructed using the dominant storyline, leaves no space for the sanctioned use of formal support. There is no suggestion within this storyline that caring for a memory-impaired partner is a "community" affair.

Complicating Storylines: Gendering Competence

Gendered storylines about personal competence introduced alternative understandings that could potentially complicate the messages being conveyed by the above storyline. Specifically, the personal narratives of the husbands and wives held gendered interpretations of personal competence which could either strengthen, or challenge, the dominant storyline that located caring activities as a logical extension of the marital relationship and hence a private issue.

For women, the dominant storyline available for defining personal competence supported the privatization of caring activities. Reflecting feminist psychological development theories (i.e., Greenspan 1993; Kaschak 1992; Miller 1986), the stories of the women in this study spoke to the importance of quality relational connections as a source for making sense of their own personal competence. All the women expressed a sense of personal deficiency and shame, at least initially, when confronted with evidence that this connection was deteriorating. In particular, a husband's emotional distress was interpreted as a personal failure. Preserving the relational connection with their partner provided a grounding to many of the wives' day-to-day care practices that was not heard in the stories of the men.

At a practical level, protecting one's husband's sense of self emerged as a guiding principle used by all the women to make sense of their general experience. As described by one woman, this meant "taking on more and more while trying to keep him from noticing . . . as if he was, well, still in control I guess." Ironically, this meant women had the extra work of attending to the partner's care needs while simultaneously insuring that her activities remained invisible. Within this storyline, because of the potential to distress the ill partner, services could be interpreted as threatening the relational bond: "How do you tell someone that somebody is coming to *baby-sit* you?" explained one woman (emphasis in original).

With its focus on the relational connection then, the dominant storyline about women's personal competence developed and supported many of the same ideals and assumptions promoted by the dominant discourse on caring. To feel good about oneself as both a wife and a woman, one must concentrate on selflessly attending to the care needs of one's spouse. This understanding provided the strongest, most consistent framework for constructing the personal experience of living with a memory-impaired husband.

In contrast to the women, this "relational" storyline did not appear to exert particular influence in the men's personal narratives. This is not to suggest that the relationship with one's wife was unimportant, nor to infer that husbands did not grieve the loss of their relationship with their wives. Rather, the importance of maintaining a relational context with their wife did not emerge as a critical facet for defining husbands' sense of personal competence. Instead, an alternative storyline, reflecting Westernized beliefs in the value of individualism and autonomy exerted a powerful influence in the personal stories of all of the husbands, but only a muted influence within the women's stories. This storyline was about being "independent," "in control" and "staying on top of things."

> I don't think there is any way that anybody who has never looked after a patient with this type of illness can understand it. The complete helplessness that you feel for yourself because you can't do anything about it. . . . The only thing that's beaten me in my whole life is [my wife's] Alzheimer's because there's no cure for it and it's got me beat, you know, it is winning, there's no question about it.

This storyline promoted an expectation of individual control over the situation. This expectation was talked about in a variety of ways, including querying personal blame for causing the disease process; adhering to schedules and routines as a way of infusing control; and "taking on" the disease. When a sense of control over the situation was undermined or challenged, a sense of personal failure permeated the men's personal narratives.

In propagating the production of an independent, autonomous self, this storyline provided a language for establishing boundaries on one's caring activities and legitimized attention to personal needs. On the positive side, it afforded the words to challenge expectations of self-sacrifice and limitless caring; there was a general recognition that one *should* look after one's self. However, it also created tension at the individual level because it introduced conflicting expectations and assumptions. How could one have personal needs and be selfless?

> I realize that once you start this journey with accepting their services that uh, the road is coming to an end. It's, you get the feeling that . . . when you're accepting them then, you're at their mercy. That's a very broad

term of course. I, we've, lost some of our independence, now we're dependent on a certain program.

Moreover, by equating personal competence with control over the situation, formal support services were set up as indicative of personal failure and loss of independence.

A Contestatory Discourse: Caring as a Social Contribution

Every participant to some degree used the dominant storyline to make sense of her/his responsibilities vis-à-vis their partner. Gender cut across the construction of meaning in this position: the dominant discourse around personal competence for men and women differed, and these gendered discourses had the power to either foster or challenge assumptions associated with the dominant storyline. A fourth storyline challenged the dominant privatized understanding of the caring activities. It broadened responsibility for an individual's care to a societal responsibility and recognized the caring activities as a social contribution. Arguably, this is the storyline most commonly used to frame ideas about "community care."

This storyline existed simultaneously with the first storyline and contradicted some of the assumptions about private responsibility and personal relationships. For some, the moments of tension introduced by attempting to locate personal experience within two competing storylines were relatively brief because the dominant storyline exerted so much influence. For others, however, the conflict engendered by these competing storylines could be discerned clearly and consistently as they tried to make sense of their experience. This meant that for many of the participants there was considerable conflict and ambiguity surrounding the meaning associated with involving formal support services.

The influence of this storyline on the personal narratives of participants could be recognized in a number of ways. Most obvious, when using this storyline to frame their experience, participants constructed a personal identity that transcended the marital relationship. Specifically, not all participants personally identified with the label "caregiver." Rather, those individuals whose personal narrative was more firmly grounded within the private storyline tended to use more relationally based self-references such as "husband" or "wife." In contrast, participants who used this alternative storyline to construct their personal narratives labeled themselves as a "caregiver" rather than, or in addition to, the more relationally based self-references.

For most, this affiliation with the caregiver label meant that they were no longer an isolated "I"; their experiences were positioned within the context of an "us" or "we." Within this context, difficulties in carrying out the tasks of caregiving were no longer interpreted as individual failures but could be seen as situational and shared by others. The work of caregiving was named and the Herculean expectations of the role became visible. Commented one wife:

> I'm a co-ordinator here. I'm the manager. I'm an administrator and I provide hands-on nursing care, on top of assuming the responsibility of spouse; if I had children I would be mother. I have to do the cooking, the cleaning, the errands; I do the banking, I take care of the car. I'm one person. I have to take care of the gardening, and the snow removal, I have to do the repairs, I've learned to do minor repairs around the house to save money.

A level of expertise was assumed: "I've become the expert," noted one man, while another woman made it clear "I am a professional." Once this insight occurred, the well partner's caring activities could be recognized as performing a valuable public service. As one husband stated:

> The doctors tell me she should probably be in a nursing home and I say, I'm not going to do it. If I'm prepared to keep her here, and they all admit that she's probably getting better care here than she would in a nursing home, I feel that the government should try to pay something or contribute something toward it, in some way.

As productive members of our society, caregivers could then voice the right to recognition for their efforts and to receive assistance with their tasks. Placed within this alternative storyline, service use took on new meaning. It could be perceived as a right; caregivers were productive members of society who were entitled to recognition of their efforts. As one wife noted:

> I wear so many hats throughout the day but no one takes account of that. And we [caregivers] are saving the taxpayers an awful lot of money. We provide a valiant service to our society but they don't see us. We are the pillars of the long-term reform. We are the ones who will make it or break it. It's our willingness. But the government sees us as invisible. . . . What they don't take into account is that I provide an institution. And I do the

work here! And I work but it doesn't count as work and I don't get paid
for it. . . . I *have needs too!* (emphasis in original)

Producing Resistance

Theoretically, the contestatory storyline introduces a language that should foster the use of formal support as an assumed right. It challenges the dichotomy
between family and formal care and truly supports a vision of community care.
With this vision comes an expectation of formal support to family caregivers.

While a number of participants relied upon this storyline to help construct their subjective experience, the anger expressed by these participants
clearly positioned it as a storyline that was accorded only limited credibility
for guiding the actual provision of support services. These participants made
visible different ways that the current delivery of services propagated the first
privatized storyline over the second.

First, utilizing formal support services clearly resulted in a challenge to
their expertise and special relationship with their partner. With few excep-
tions, participants used words such as feeling "patronized," "invisible," "discounted" to describe their interactions with the formal support system; they
felt they were not being given "any marks for intelligence, that they [service
providers] know best."

> And I've had some nurses thinking that they know more than I do—but
> they don't know my husband! It would help a lot if the medical profes-
> sionals, starting with the doctors, and the people who work with us, didn't
> consider us inferior.

The message here was clear. Through the act of going public, expertise regarding one's partner would be discounted and the well partner risked feeling
undermined and invalidated.

Second, although the first storyline suggests the importance of the relational connection as a critical ingredient to quality care, participants made
clear that little attention was given to fostering any relationship with formal
service providers. One wife notes the difficulty she had in arranging to meet
the home-support worker prior to leaving her husband alone with her:

> Well, what I wanted was to see the girls, I wanted to know who it was go-
> ing to be. And they said well, they didn't have that policy. I said well,

that's unfortunate because I'm not going to leave my husband with somebody that I don't know anything about or have never seen. So, they said
well, okay, we've never done it but we'll send her for an hour . . . but I
was charged for that too.

Several other participants also discussed program policies that actively
blocked the well spouse's attempt to formally meet prospective home care
providers before leaving their partner unattended with this stranger. Similarly, and not unexpectedly, the revolving door of service providers was repeatedly identified as problematic. If it is the emotional connection that defines
quality care—as assumed by the dominant discourse on providing care—this
means that the well partner has no hope of supplementing his/her efforts with
a viable substitute.

Third, in contrast to the entitlement to support suggested in the alternative discourse, the provision of the actual support fostered a sense of disentitlement. One way that this was communicated was through the expectation
that the well spouse pay for support services. Most participants at some point
in their personal narrative objected—on principle—to the expectation that
she/he pay for formal support. One husband succinctly clarified his perspective by pointing out that this practice penalized him for requiring personal
time instead of applauding the support that he was providing; he identified
the "double standards" and "rhetoric" being given regarding the legitimacy of
having one's own needs.

Furthermore, assuming that the well spouse has a legitimate right to support, one could expect a foundation of services that addressed some "normative" levels of support. Participants' disparagement regarding the current service situation demonstrated clearly that this was not the case. Although all
lived in relatively service-rich areas, almost all the participants voiced disgust
regarding the availability of appropriate services. One husband declared:

Oh, the government and a few others simply haven't any comprehension
of what it really is, what it's like. They haven't the foggiest idea. . . . You
know, they don't seem to want to have enough respite so people have a
decent break. They say "oh well, people should stay in their homes." But
they seem to have completely ignored the fact that it isn't just one person, it's two people. And um, the caregiver—in some ways they're just
shooting them down. Not giving them a break at all. . . . They say "oh
well, we'll send somebody in with meals on wheels." They [caregivers]
DON'T WANT meals on wheels! [voice becomes louder]. Nothing to do

with it. *THIS IS NOT A MEALS ON WHEELS SITUATION—THIS IS A 24-HOUR SITUATION!* (emphasis in original)

Generally inadequate services offered at inopportune times could be perceived as more burdensome than helpful. Despite these inadequacies, however, the underlying assumption surfaced repeatedly that one "should" feel grateful for whatever one got. For example, participants not infrequently followed up their complaints of the system by quickly asserting their desire not to be seen as "complaining" or "a bother." One woman observed that "making demands" resulted in one earning the designation of "B-I-T-C-H." Ultimately then, although the storyline that recognized the societal value of spouses' caregiving activities seemed to offer the promise of validation, in practice it was perceived as carrying little weight in the actual provision of services. The structural organization of providing support to these spouses clearly reproduced the dominant storyline.

Implications for Practice: Re-storying Support

This study begins to make visible the beliefs, values, and practices that may be sabotaging ideals of a community partnership. My intention has been to position the refusal of formal support as an expected response that is well grounded in the storylines currently being used to construct the ideals of family and community care. If there is a commitment to "community care," the goal becomes to re-story support services in order to promote storylines that are more conducive to a partnership. In the following section I will highlight some of the ideas for practice that emerged through this study.[1]

In order to develop a storyline that truly fosters a community partnership, re-storying is required at two levels. At the individual level, it is important to begin to explicitly challenge the storyline that positions caring as a "natural" and hence private extension of the marital relationship, requiring the limitless hands-on provision of care. The task is to begin to question some aspects of this storyline in order to create the space for difficulties to be interpreted as situational rather than indicative of individual deficiencies. In the following section I will discuss issues that surfaced in my conversations with the participants which seemed to provide points of entry for this re-storying.

However, in recognizing the anger expressed by those participants who had developed an alternative framework for making sense of their experience, the futility of promoting a different individual storyline when the societal storyline does not change becomes apparent. Therefore, a second critical task of social work intervention is to advocate for services which in fact demonstrate the assumptions underlying the storyline that caring for a frail or ill individual is a societal responsibility (Neysmith 1998). In other words, although I am focusing specifically on micro-level issues here, it is recognized that these strategies must be linked to structural changes.

Excavating the Site:
Questioning Underlying Assumptions of Care

I came away from the interview with the only participant who openly queried the assumption that he assume responsibility for his increasingly vulnerable wife feeling appalled and angry. Reflecting upon my response, I became aware of just how ingrained my own assumptions were about the sanctity of marriage. This was frightening to me; at a more intellectual level these ideas were certainly open to question. It was at this point in the process that my focus explicitly shifted to examining the hidden, taken-for-granted assumptions that were guiding my practice and the provision of services.

Fook highlights the need for this examination of our personal systems of beliefs and values, suggesting that it is through this process that social workers can begin to examine the ways that they contribute to social control by "subtly holding clients in powerless positions and reinforcing identities ascribed to them by the dominant order" (1993:60). For me, several questions surface here. For example, is it our expectation that because of a marital commitment to another individual, the well partner should be expected to quietly sacrifice his/her life when one partner becomes ill? This is currently the implicit expectation associated with dominant views on marriage. This assumption guarantees that individual's believing in this story about marriage will feel deficient, guilty, and inadequate should the responsibilities of coping with an ill partner move beyond his or her capability. There is some recognition that there "should" be limits. For example, a Canadian federal policy paper notes that "at a certain point, family responsibility becomes society's responsibility, and caregivers need to be assured that they will not be expected to shoulder limitless burden" (Health and Welfare Canada 1988:17). Social workers need to examine their own attitudes and underlying assumptions to determine where that "limit" is. Repeated research findings which highlight the significance of caregiver health as the primary determinant of placement (e.g., Cohen et al. 1993) would suggest that the only legitimate exit from the responsibility of caring for one's partner is when one is visibly ill oneself.

Moreover, is there a right *not* to be the primary caregiver? The current emphasis on "supporting the caregiver" allows no recognition that it may not always be support—even practical support—that family members want. Croft (1986) argues that current policies do not offer carers a real choice as to whether they want to remain primary carers or not; services are to prop them up rather than to take the brunt of responsibility from them. At its most obvious level, this means that the assumption that all spouses are in fact in the best position to provide care requires conscious questioning. In my study, three husbands acknowledged some form of physical aggression against their ill wife and in a fourth case it was highly suspected although not confirmed. Of these individuals, at least two would have willingly relinquished their role as primary care provider to their spouse had there been a legitimate alternative to take on this role. It also means recognizing that spouses who may have the requisite skill to care may in fact not want to care. Women, for example, who have traditionally been assumed to possess "caring skills" should not be excluded from this consideration.

A first step, then, in undermining the storyline that caring is a natural extension of the marital relationship is to become consciously aware of it. This requires that social workers begin to deconstruct the assumptions associated with this storyline. This requires naming the taken-for-granted assumptions and questioning their implications.

Pouring the Foundation: Acknowledging Expertise

Collaboration is the foundation of a true community partnership. Collaboration implies a reciprocal relationship in which all partners work cooperatively together. Ideally, it requires acknowledging that each partner brings unique knowledge and skill to the relationship which, when combined, promotes a better "product"—in this case, higher quality care. The word *collaboration* conjures up images of respect, recognition, and mutuality. Although there were examples where participants' described this kind of relational quality with individual service providers, the general perception of the participants in this study suggest that this was not the norm. Rather, participants described feelings of being patronized and discounted. This suggests the need to redefine the relationship between service providers and the well spouse.

Perhaps a first step in establishing this "collaborative relationship" is to begin to itemize what each partner actually brings to the relationship. In this study, the importance of the well spouse for preserving the personhood of the ill partner as that person became increasingly unable to independently do so surfaced repeatedly. For example, participants talked about the intimate connection that enabled them to anticipate their partner's needs; they provided the history to contextualize their partner's actions and interpreted the behaviors of even the most seemingly uncommunicative dementia victims in a way that maintained the ill partner's humanity. In principle, the contributions that a close kin can make as a result of his or her unique knowledge of the impaired person's preferences, values, needs, and life history are acknowledged. However, in practice, this study suggests that there is a tendency for service providers to discount this special knowledge, a finding that is consistent with other research (e.g., Hasselkus 1988; Morgan & Zhao 1993; Rutman 1996). Developing a collaborative relationship requires recognizing, validating, and utilizing the unique expertise that the well spouse may bring to the situation. Creating a solid foundation for partnership then requires "hearing" the well spouse. Recognizably, this takes time, an increasingly scarce professional "resource"!

Framing the Experience:
"Extra-ordinizing" and Externalizing

In this study, understanding how the well spouse was making sense of the situation offered a critical piece of insight. Three ways of accounting for the ill spouses' behavior were identified. First, behavioral changes were normalized as indicative of the aging process or as exaggerations of long-standing traits ("She always was stubborn," noted one husband as he described his wife's inability to remember his sister). This type of explanation defined the situation as relatively expectable, and there was little space for turning to outside support. It could foster both a sense of personal deficiency related to the inability to change the situation and/or anger at the ill spouse for failing to change his/her behavior. A second way of talking about one's partner was employed by a number of the women but none of the men. Specifically, several women talked about their husband's deterioration as reflective of their own personal inadequacy: "I felt so ashamed," indicated one wife when her husband failed to recognize her. Within this reading, the problematics of the situation are internalized and the wife is clearly deficient should she require assistance. The third way of accounting for changes was to locate an external cause. There are undoubtedly a number of ways that this externalizing could be accomplished. One wife, for example, attributed her husband's disruptive behavior to the stars. However, the most common way to externalize the difficulties was done by framing the problem as a medical issue.

Medicalizing the problem unsettled the situation and introduced an alternative language, the professional language of medicine, for talking about one's experience. Ultimately, it facilitated a change in the relationship between the participant and her/his partner. Specifically, in order to redefine one's role in relation to one's partner, the partner's symptoms had to be recognized as being outside the normative expectations of both the marital relationship and the aging process. In other words, recognizing and accepting that "something was wrong" exposed a previously hidden space for the well partner to develop a sense of self in relation to a partner that transcended the relationship. This emerged as an important step in moving the location of caring activities to a more visible, public arena.

Speaking practically, then, an important social work task would be to assist the well spouse in naming problems as being outside the marital relationship. Currently, the most accessible language for this "extra-ordinizing" is to medicalize the symptoms. Some research has found a tendency for both physicians and caregivers to perceive a diagnosis as futile or having only negative implications (e.g., Miller, Glasser & Rubin 1992). In this study, however, when asked what "words of wisdom" she/he would like to pass on to someone beginning a similar experience, several participants immediately identified the importance of obtaining an accurate diagnosis as quickly as possible. While not necessarily sufficient in and of itself—for example, several participants intellectually identified their partner's problems as caused by dementia but did not use this explanation in general conversation to account for their partner's day-to-day behavior—a diagnosis generally helped the well spouse to depersonalize their partner's problematic behavior and to open for questioning their own responsibilities vis-à-vis their partner's care.

Social workers cannot make a medical diagnosis. However, the diagnostic period emerged as a critical point for introducing formal support. Several participants identified this period as the time when they had been very receptive to formal intervention—most, however, felt that they were left to struggle on their own. The need for assistance in maneuvering the complex diagnostic maze, dealing with seemingly disinterested or unknowledgeable professionals, and obtaining comprehensive, comprehendable information were three areas where need for formal support was identified. Ideally, social workers would be linked to family physicians in order to insure accessibility during this important juncture.

Externalizing the problem by medicalizing it has recognized risks. First, there is the danger of reinforcing the status quo that suggests that the only legitimate entitlement to help is for medical reasons. Second, this depersonal-

ization of the ill partner's symptoms has potential implications for the holistic, humane treatment of the ill partner because it sets the stage for discounting his or her behavior as merely a symptom of disease. The tension, then, is
in both extra-ordinizing the situation while simultaneously preserving the
personhood of the ill spouse. Third, the language of medicine is predicated
upon the "expert" knowledge of the physician and health professionals. As has
already been noted, this positioning of the health professional as the "expert"
effectively discourages collaborative partnerships. Finally, defining the problem in medical terms diminishes the opportunity for the well spouse to effectively intervene in the "life" of the problem. For example, as illustrated by several of the men, attempts to take on a dementia will invariably meet with
failure because the well spouse lacks the power to control the disease process.

While medicalizing effectively extra-ordinizes the problem, there may be
other more constructive ways for externalizing the problem. For example,
naming the problem as "unrealistic expectations (being placed on the well
spouse)" opens up alternative possibilities for action. Drawing on the ideas of
narrative therapy (i.e., White & Epston 1990), an important social work intervention might be to assist the well spouse to construct an understanding of
the "problem" that positions it as both a separate entity but also one that has
immediate relevance to the well spouse and some potential for action. This
can be done through the use of externalizing questions. Externalizing questions make it

> possible for persons to experience an identity that is distinct or separate
> from the problem; the problem is to an extent disempowered as it no
> longer speaks to persons of the truth about who they are as people or
> about the very nature of their relationships. This opens new possibilities
> for action. (White 1995:23)

This process begins by taking the language the person uses to describe the
problem and modifying it so that the problem is objectified. One way to easily begin externalizing an issue is to give it a name and turn it into a noun.
Feeling overwhelmed, for example, can be examined as "overwhelmed feelings"—a simple shift that repositions the problem from a behavior or personal
attribute to a separate entity. Externalizing questions can then focus on identifying the relative influence of "the problem" (White & Epston 1990). For example, how has the issue led the person into difficulties? What effect does the
issue have on the well spouse's life and relationships? Have there been times
when the issue could have taken over but didn't? The goal of this externaliz-

ing conversation is to begin unpacking the storyline being used to construct the experience in order to open the space for alternative understandings. This is an important step in creating a situation that has some potential for change.

In essence, then, an important objective of social work intervention is to assist the well spouse to reposition the difficulties he/she is experiencing as being outside the normal expectations associated with both personal behavior and the marital relationship. Medicalizing is the most common way of accomplishing this, but it has serious drawbacks. The need to discover alternative ways for extra-ordinizing the situation and externalizing the issues continues to be a practice challenge.

Reinforcing the Pillars of Competence

In a variety of ways, all the participants demonstrated that living with a memory-impaired partner resulted in a serious attack on their sense of competence. This was related to both the loss of control over the situation and, particularly for women, the personalization of the deteriorating marital relationship. Participants in this study identified the ease with which this attack on their competence could be interpreted as a personal deficiency. Specifically, the loss of control associated with the process was often perceived as stemming from one's own personal ineptness.

Once the situation has been reframed as extraordinary, issues around retaining control can be normalized as situational rather than a sign of personal weakness or deficiency. For example, this may include reinforcing the ill spouse's deterioration as a symptom of a disease process rather than a response to the well partner's treatment. Similarly, the Herculean nature of the caregiving task can be named. Identifying and labeling the contradictions and impotency inherent in the situation encourages difficulties to be normalized rather than internalized as personal failure. This then opens up psychological space to begin acknowledging and validating personal efforts while simultaneously recognizing limitations.

Because so many of the participants either explicitly expressed or implicitly alluded to the loss of control associated with the use of services, it would seem that this is a topic that requires direct exploration with the well spouse. This could include discussing concerns about losing control and verbally repositioning service use as a means for retaining control. However, in addition to verbally reframing the use of service, concrete opportunities for exercising control must be made. For example, insuring that the well partner has necessary information regarding what services are available and is therefore in a position to determine which services can most adequately respond to his or her needs would seem important. Similarly, efforts could be taken to accommodate the well partner's schedule. Perhaps most importantly, participants in this study identified the need for control in selecting who would be providing assistance. Other studies have reported similar findings (e.g., Caserta et al. 1987; Gwyther 1994; Morris 1994). Depersonalizing concerns around personal competence and then insuring that the well partner exerts control in the decisions surrounding his or her service use have the potential to reinforce the perception of services as a right.

Additionally, social workers need to be attuned to the potential backlash that service use may have in further undermining personal competence. There is a fine line between providing good—but not too good—service! Many of the participants held the expectation that she/he "should" be able to manage a given situation; requiring assistance, or watching another person handle the situation in a more effective manner, could leave him or her feeling deficient and/or unable to live up to established standards. For example, identifying his one criticism regarding his use of a home care service, one husband noted that

> she [the home care worker] was *too good* to my wife. . . . I'd be building up and building up and building up and . . . refusal. What makes it all so bad is that these girls from the [home care agency] do a beautiful job, they're excellent. . . . I fight like hell with [my wife] to try to get her to take it [her medication] and Anne [the home care worker], no problem. It makes me feel like sending her [the wife] to the moon [emphasis added].

This highlighted for me the need for social workers to consciously contextualize both their efforts and those of others such as the home care worker. For example, recognizing that one's response to a particular situation or behavior is colored by the overall situation may be useful to address explicitly; as one wife noted, "Nurses aren't expected to work 60-hour work weeks."

Working Within the "Building" Codes:
Recognizing the Power of the Ill Spouse

For me, one of the most obvious themes to emerge early in this study was the influence of the ill husband in defining the situation. This study clearly challenged the typical construction of the "care-receiver" as passive and dependent: "no more than aggregate bundles of need" (Barry 1995:373). Rather, all the women highlighted the importance of their husband's cooperation in service planning. While husbands did appreciate their ill wives' cooperation, several provided examples to suggest that it was not imperative. In contrast, all the women in this study identified reluctance to utilize services that were not condoned by their partner. Other studies have reported similar findings (Lawton, Brody & Saperstein 1989; Gwyther 1994; Miller 1990; Rudin 1994).

This means that social workers need to develop new ways for working with the impaired partner rather than focusing solely on the well spouse for decisions. Recognizing the deteriorating capacity for decision-making associated with a dementia, this task is formidable and time-consuming. It requires searching for ways to frame support with the ill spouse that assume his or her dignity and will be perceived as nonthreatening. One wife, for example, found that when she presented the use of service as something her husband could do for her, as opposed to focusing on her husband's deficits, her husband responded more favorably to the use of services. Listening to the women's stories alerted me to the physical dangers associated with ignoring the significant power wielded by the husband. Four of the six women in this study expressed fear of physical aggression, and two experienced physical assaults. This potential for physical violence directed at wife caregivers is beginning to be supported by other research (i.e., Bartlett 1994). Service providers must be sensitive to power issues, especially with wives. There is an implicit assumption that women can, and should, assume control over the decisions affecting their memory-impaired husbands. This presumption ignores both the historical and physical sources of power within the marital relationship. This is a critical omission. Instead, issues of power must be explicitly addressed. This, for example, would include exploring possible threats to the wife's safety when dealing with a husband who suffers from a dementia. Similarly, the potential impact on a wife's sense of self when placed in the position of defying her husband with her decisions is an issue that warrants attention. Failure to recognize power issues could result in service providers inadvertently placing women in a no-win and potentially dangerous situation where they feel caught in the middle, trying to respond to the instructions of health professionals and still meeting the demands of their partner (Hasselkus 1988).

Building Communities: Breaking the Barriers of Isolation

A pervasive theme in both this study and other research on caregivers is a sense of intense isolation. Research suggests that the intensity of demand made on carers, the loss of time to maintain friendships and interests, and increasing exhaustion can contribute to the growth of mutual dependency and isolation (Abel 1990; Opie 1992). All the participants in this study referenced increasing isolation as a condition of their experience.

In addition to the discomfort that isolation causes, it also prohibits a redefinition of one's activities. The social situations in which one's identity is normally continuously reconstituted simply disappear when one is isolated (Rossiter 1988:244). Isolation prevents an alternative storyline from emerging because there is no opportunity for new or different understandings to be raised or explored since meaning always emerges from social interaction (Deaux 1991). Without a social context, the perception of one's activities will remain grounded in the private.

An important step, then, is to begin to attack barriers of isolation in order to create a space to question. One means toward this is through the relationship between the social worker and the well spouse. The social worker can provide a valuable external source of recognition of the work that the well partner is doing and assist in renaming the experience. This relationship can provide a social context within which the well partner can reconstitute his or her identity.

However, more importantly, connecting with other caregivers was highlighted by several participants as critical. This connection helped them to realize that they were not alone and that the issues and problems they were dealing with were not individually owned but rather a shared experience and thus situational. Traditionally, the primary way of fostering contact with other caregivers has been through the use of support groups. The difficulty with this approach is that it presupposes some degree of motivation to attend a group; some recognition of the possibility of sameness/similarity with other caregivers is both a prerequisite and an outcome. Furthermore, the group must be seen as having sufficient potential to warrant the probable amount of work and energy that it would take to get oneself to it. In other words, even prior to attending, the potential rewards of doing so must be visible.

This has several implications for practice. First, although theoretically support groups may offer a valuable opportunity for constructing a new storyline because of the possibility of developing a collective identity, actually connecting to a group may require a "getting ready" stage. Simply providing the information about group meetings seems inadequate. Second, alternative ways of connecting which may be less threatening and less dependent upon individual motivation require exploration. One participant, for example, was involved in an informal telephone network. Finally, different types of groups may be more useful at different stages for challenging the dominant storyline.

For example, a primary focus on education and information may be useful initially as a means toward extra-ordinizing the issues. However, if the power of the group rests in its possibilities for promoting a coalition, then a shift from education to recognizing similarities would be required. Currently, the thrust is toward time-limited, educationally focused group interventions (Lavoie 1995), which may respond to the first set of needs but not the latter. In fact, this type of support group may sabotage the development of a collective identity by reinforcing a narrowly defined, problem-centered focus to one's situation. There is a recognized tension associated with promoting this coalition with other "caregivers." Specifically, the more firmly an individual is positioned as "caregiver" the easier it becomes to see him or her only within this context. A challenge to social workers, especially in the current context of massive restructuring and fiscal constraints, is to find ways of insuring that the individual fulfilling the caregiving function remains visible as a unique, multidimensional individual.

The massive body of literature about "the caregiver" could lead to the conclusion that there exists a strong foundation for grounding social work practice in models of community care with possible family members as appropriate carers of relatives. In this chapter I have tried to demonstrate that this body of knowledge is misleading and problematic—it is based on a "thin," reductionist understanding of the experience. By implementing a research strategy that assumed complexity and contradiction, I have tried to broaden understanding by examining personal experience as reflective of prevailing sociopolitical discourses.

This perspective problematizes the presumption that formal support is necessarily perceived as supportive by spousal "caregivers." Rather, once the storylines available for making sense of the personal experience of living with a memory-impaired partner are identified and deconstructed, the assumptions prevalent in the dominant discourses that actually sabotage ideals of community care become visible. The storylines most accessible to women are especially oppressive.

While individual experience is constructed by available storylines, this does not mean that oppressive and negative storylines cannot be challenged and re-storied. To this end, I have outlined some points of entry and ideas for beginning to construct a storyline more consistent with the ideals of community care, and I identify social work interventions that might usefully assist in this re-storying. Recognizably, to be effective these micro-level interventions must take place within a context that is committed to building collaborative communities.

Note

1. These ideas are not intended to serve as a "recipe" for guaranteeing that all spouses living with a memory-impaired partner will, or should, utilize available services. This expectation would undermine the complexity of this issue and could be used to once again position the well spouse as problematic instead of recognizing the limitations of this understanding. For example, this study does not consider how storylines associated with race, culture, sexual orientation, and/or ability would undoubtedly implicate service use.

References

Abel, E. 1990. Informal care for the disabled elderly: A critique of recent literature. *Research on Aging* 12(2): 139–57.

Aronson, J. 1988. Women's experience in giving and receiving care: Pathways to social change. Ph.D. diss., University of Toronto.

Barnes, C., B. Given, and C. Given. 1992. Caregivers of elderly relatives: Spouses and adult children. *Health and Social Work* 17(4): 282–88.

Barry, J. 1995. Care-need and care-receivers: Views from the margins. *Women's Studies International Forum* 18(3): 361–74.

Bartlett, M. C. 1994. Married widows: The wives of men in long-term care. *Journal of Women and Aging* 6(1–2): 91–106.

Biegel, D. E., E. Sales, and R. Schulz (eds.). 1991. *Family caregiving in chronic illness.* Newbury Park, Calif.: Sage.

Brown, L. S. 1994. *Subversive dialogues: Theory in feminist therapy.* New York: Basic Books.

Burman, E. and I. Parker (eds.). 1993. *Discourse analytic research.* New York: Routledge.

Burr, V. 1995. *An introduction to social constructionism.* New York: Routledge.

Carriere, Y. and L. Pelletier. 1995. Factors underlying the institutionalization of elderly persons in Canada. *Journal of Gerontology: Social Sciences* 50B(3): S164–S172

Caserta, M., D. Lund, S. D. Wright, and D. Redburn. 1987. Caregivers to dementia patients: The utilization of community services. *The Gerontologist* 27(2): 209–214.

Cohen, C., D. Gold, K. Shulman, J. Wortley, G. McDonald, and M. Wargon. 1993. Factors determining the decision to institutionalize dementing individuals: A prospective study. *The Gerontologist* 33(6): 714–20.

Croft, S. 1986. Women, caring, and the recasting of need—a feminist reappraisal. *Critical Social Policy* 16(1): 23–39.

Davies, B. and R. Harre. 1990. Positioning: The discursive production of selves. *Journal for the Theory of Social Behaviour* 20(1): 43–63.

Deaux, K. 1991. *Social identities: Thoughts on structure and change.* In R. C. Curtis (ed.), *The relational self.* New York: Guilford.

Faran, C., E. Keane-Hagarty, S. Salloway, S. Kupferer, and C. Wilken. 1991. Finding meaning: An alternative paradigm for Alzheimer's disease family caregivers. *The Gerontologist* 31(4): 483–89.

Fook, J. 1993. *Radical casework.* St. Leonards, N.S.W. (Australia): Allen and Unwin.

Fraser, N. 1990. Struggle over needs: Outline of a socialist-feminist critical theory of late-capitalist political change. In L. Gordon (ed.), *Women, the state, and welfare.* Madison: University of Wisconsin Press.

Gavey, N. 1997. Feminist poststructuralism and discourse analysis. In M. M. Gerber and S. N. Davis (eds.), *Toward a new psychology of gender.* New York: Routledge.

George, L. and L. P. Gwyther. 1986. Caregiver well-being: A multidimensional examination of family caregivers of demented adults. *The Gerontologist* 26(3): 253–59.

Gonyea, J. G. and N. M. Silverstein. 1991. The role of Alzheimer's disease support groups in families' utilization of community services. *Journal of Gerontological Social Work* 16(3–4): 43–55.

Greenspan, M. 1993/1983. *A new approach to women and therapy.* 2d ed. Blue Ridge Summit, Penn.: Tab Books.

Gwyther, L. 1994. Service delivery and utilization: Research directions and clinical implications. In E. Light, G. Niederehe, and B. Lebowitz (eds.), *Stress effects on family caregivers of Alzheimer's patients.* New York: Springer.

Hanley, R. J., L. M. B. Alexcih, J. M. Wiener, and D. L. Kennell. 1990. Predicting elderly nursing home admissions. *Research on Aging* 12(2): 199–228.

Hare-Mustin, R. T. 1994. Discourses in the mirrored room: A postmodern analysis of therapy. *Family Process* 33(1): 19–35

Hasselkus, B. R. 1988. Meaning in family caregiving: Perspectives on caregiver/professional relationships. *The Gerontologist* 28(5): 686–91.

Health and Welfare Canada. 1988. *Mental health for Canadians: Striking a balance.* Ottawa: Minister of Supply and Services.

Kaschak, E. 1992. *Engendered lives.* Boston: Basic Books.

Lather, Patti. 1991. *Getting smart: Feminist research and pedagogy with/in the postmodern.* New York: Routledge.

Lawton, M. P., E. Brody, and A. Saperstein. 1989. A controlled study of respite service for caregivers of Alzheimer's patients. *The Gerontologist* 29(1): 3–16.

Lavoie, J-P. 1995. Support groups for informal caregivers don't work! Refocus the group or the evaluations? *Canadian Journal on Aging* 14(3): 580–603.

Lieberman, M. A. and L. Fisher. 1995. The impact of chronic illness on the health and well-being of family members. *The Gerontologist* 35(1): 94–102.

Miller, B. 1990. Gender differences in spouse caregiver strain: Socialization and role explanations. *Journal of Marriage and the Family* 52: 311–21.

Miller, B., M. Glasser, and S. Rubin. 1992. A paradox of medicalization: Physicians, families, and Alzheimer's disease. *Journal of Aging Studies* 6(2): 135–48.

Miller, J. B. 1986. *Toward a new psychology of women.* 2d ed. Boston: Beacon Press.

Morgan, D. L. and P. Z. Zhao. 1993. The doctor-caregiver relationship: Managing the care of family members with Alzheimer's disease. *Qualitative Health Research* 3(2): 133–64.

Morris, J. 1994. Community care or independent living? *Critical Social Policy* 14(1): 24–45

National Advisory Council on Aging. 1989. *1989 and beyond: Challenges of an aging Canadian society.* Ottawa.

Neysmith, S. 1998. From home care to social care: The value of a vision. In C. Baines, P. Evans, and S. Neysmith (eds.), *Women's Caring: Feminist perspectives on social welfare*, 233–49. 2d ed. Toronto: Oxford University Press.

Noelker, L. S. 1990. Family caregivers: A valuable but vulnerable resource. In Z. Harel, P. Ehrlich, and R. Hubbard (eds.), *The vulnerable aged: People, services, and policies*. New York: Springer.

Opie, A. 1992. *There's nobody there.* Philadelphia: University of Pennsylvania Press.

Riessman, C. K. 1993. *Narrative analysis.* Newbury Park, Calif.: Sage.

Rosenwald, G. C. and R. L. Ochberg (eds.). 1992. *Storied lives.* New Haven: Yale University Press.

Rossiter, A. 1988. *From private to public.* Toronto: Women's Press.

Rudin, D. L. 1994. Caregiver attitudes regarding utilization and usefulness of respite services for people with Alzheimer's disease. *Journal of Gerontological Social Work* 23(1–2): 85–107.

Rutman, D. 1996. Caregiving as women's work: Women's experience of powerfulness and powerlessness as caregivers. *Qualitative Health Research* 6(1): 90–111.

Shapiro, E. and R. Tate. 1988. Who is really at risk of institutionalization? *The Gerontologist* 28(2): 237–45.

Tennstedt, S., L. Sullivan, J. McKinlay, and R. D'Agostino. 1990. How important is functional status as a predictor of service use by older people? *Journal of Aging and Health* 2(4): 439–61.

Weedon, C. 1987. *Feminist practice and poststructuralist theory.* New York: Basil Blackwell.

Wenger, G. C. 1990. Elderly carers: The need for appropriate intervention. *Aging and Society* 10: 197–219.

White, M. 1995. Re-authoring lives: Interviews and essays. Adelaide, South Australia: Dulwich Centre Publications.

White, M. and D. Epston. 1990. *Narrative means to therapeutic ends.* New York: Norton.

Zarit, S. 1989. Do we need another "stress and caregiving" study? *The Gerontologist* 29(2): 147–48.

5

Aging and Disability in the New Millennium

Challenges for Social Work Research and Practice

AMY HOROWITZ

The purpose of this chapter is to challenge the gerontological social work community to rethink and broaden current conceptual, empirical, and service delivery approaches to older people with disabilities. Although issues surrounding health care needs and long-term care systems have dominated much of the literature in social gerontology over the past several decades, aging service and research communities have, paradoxically, taken a relatively narrow approach to aging and disability. This approach, which has been referred to as "benevolent ageism" (Sheets, Wray & Torres-Gil 1993), has been based on the assumption of inevitable decline in functional and/or cognitive abilities among older persons coupled with an increasing need for supportive care. Regardless of the increasing emphasis on autonomy and control in the gerontological literature, elders continue to be perceived primarily as passive recipients of care. Concurrently, increasing emphasis is placed on the experienced stresses and needs of family members who act as caregivers to dependent elderly relatives. It is hypothesized that this assumption arises, to a great extent, from the predominant concern in the empirical and practice worlds with the needs of older people suffering from Alzheimer's disease and related cognitive disorders, to the relative exclusion of elders who are experiencing a wide range of chronic physical age-related impairments.

As we enter the new millennium with the aging of the "baby boomers," we must now more than ever confront the changing face of aging and disability. It is a challenge that has interrelated implications for both micro-level (individual and family) quality-of-life issues and macro-level approaches to the organization of social and health care systems for older people with disabilities. Four major themes will be discussed in the following sections, each with unique as well as interrelated paradoxs and tensions with the others. In the first section, trends in disability rates are reviewed, with both "good news" and "bad news" scenarios for coming cohorts of older persons. Complementing this overview of disability trends is a discussion of changing attitudes toward disability on both individual and societal levels. The second section focuses on geriatric rehabilitation as a long-neglected but increasingly critical sector of the long-term care service system for older people. It is argued that rehabilitation for disabling conditions needs to be considered as an option of first choice in addressing disability among older people, and that the arena for delivery of rehabilitation services needs to be expanded from the medical, acute care model to a more comprehensive social health approach for chronic conditions in community-based care. Third, these changing trends, attitudes, and approaches to disability calls for a reconceptualization of the role of the family vis-à-vis older disabled relatives. While not discounting the caregiving support so critically provided by family members, it is argued that we need to go beyond the concept of a unidirectional caregiving relationship to one that considers the elder as an active player as the recipient of care, as well as one that sees the family as a partner in maintaining and maximizing the elder's physical and emotional well-being. The fourth section focuses on quality-of-life concerns among the disabled elders, specifically the emerging evidence regarding the complex reciprocal relationship between depression and disability in later life. Evidence regarding the mediating role played by health care interventions (e.g., rehabilitation) and social supports in the depression-disability relationship will be addressed in this discussion. Throughout this chapter the emphasis is on identifying issues and raising questions for social work researchers and practitioners to address, rather than on providing proscriptions for future practice and service delivery. Examples from the author's research focusing on older persons with chronic vision impairments will be used to illustrate some of the generic challenges of aging and disability that confront us as we move into the twenty-first century.

The Changing Nature of Aging and Disability

Trends in Disability Rates—The Good News Scenario

Gerontological researchers and educators have made substantial progress over the past several years in dispelling the stereotype, prevalent among professionals and the public alike, that aging is synonymous with disability. This has been a major accomplishment, opening up new avenues of research into the aging process and the roles older people continue to play in family and community life.

Yet there is no denying the fact that rates of disability increase dramatically with age. If one lives long enough, it is likely that the experience of disability, in varying degrees and duration, will touch the lives of most older people. Many of the recent professional and political health care debates have focused on the challenges that society currently faces in addressing the needs of disabled elders, and the increased demand on public resources that the aging of the baby boom generation will create in the coming decades.

However, recent evidence regarding trends in disability rates among the older population have provided us with a good, or at least a "better" news scenario. Analyses by Manton, Corder, and Stallard (1997), based on the National Long-Term Care Surveys (NLTCS), indicate that there has been a significant trend toward decline in disability prevalence among older people. Specifically, their analyses indicate that there were 1.2 million *fewer* older people who were disabled in 1994 than would have been expected based on disability rates observed in 1982. That is, based on 1982 rates, with adjustments for the growth in the numbers of older people and the aging of the elderly, it was estimated that in 1994, 8.3 million elders in the United States would be disabled. However, the actual number of disabled elders in 1994 was 7.1 million. These declines were evidenced in all age groups, even the oldest-old. Furthermore, there was an acceleration of this trend toward decline in disability, an acceleration first observed in the 1980s (Manton, Corder & Stallard 1993). In terms of actual proportions of the older persons who were disabled, the percentage of those who were disabled in IADL or ADL tasks (see following paragraph) decreased between the years 1982 and 1994 from 14 to 11.5 percent among persons sixty-five to seventy-four. Among those aged seventy-five to eighty-four, the disabled decreased from 32 to 27 percent. And even among those eighty-five and older, these investigators reported a decline from 65 percent in 1982 to 60 percent in 1994.

This "good news" scenario has been tempered a bit by other investigators who question a clear trend in the reduced prevalence of disability. For example, Crimmins, Saito, and Reynolds (1997) conducted similar analyses utilizing the Longitudinal Survey on Aging (LSOA) and the National Health Interview Surveys (NHIS). Findings from the NHIS were similar to those of Manton, Corder, and Stallard (1997) with the NLTCS, in that there was a statistically significant decrease in overall disability among the elderly. However, this decrease was primarily due to a decrease in IADL disability—that is, disability in instrument activities of daily living such as household management tasks. While the decline in disability in the personal care activities of daily living (ADLs: e.g., bathing, toileting, dressing, and so on) was also statistically significant, the predicted decline in actual prevalence in this category was very small (approximately 2 percent). In the analyses based on the LSOA, no significant changes in disability rates over time emerged. Thus, Crimmins and colleagues (Crimmins 1998; Crimmins, Saito & Reynolds 1997) conclude that most of the improvement has been in the area of IADL disability, while for the most severe type of disability (i.e., personal care ADL tasks), the trend is not yet clear. Thus, even though there remains some controversy in the extent and type of disability decline identified, there is a basis for some optimism in the most recent data on aging and disability.

How do we explain the trend toward declines in disability rates? To a large extent, the answer can be found in the "coming of age," so to speak, of cohorts now entering the elderly population and the environments in which they live. That is, older people in the United States have grown up and are growing older in a society with better public health resources, improved nutrition, less infectious diseases, and more positive health habits in terms of smoking, diet, and exercise—factors that have a lifelong impact on the health of individuals as they reach old age (Crimmins, Saito & Reynolds 1997; Manton, Corder & Stallard 1997). Furthermore, educational attainment has been steadily rising among the elderly, and higher educational status is associated with lower rates of disability (Crimmins 1998). For example, whereas only 40 percent of the elderly aged eighty-five to eighty-nine had more than seven years of education in 1980, this proportion is expected to increase to between 85 and 90 percent by the year 2015 (Manton, Corder & Stallard 1997). Not only are individuals with higher education more likely to adopt healthy behaviors, they are also more likely to have had better medical care in early and midlife, and more easily comply with complex medical treatments, especially for chronic conditions with potentially disabling effects, such as diabetes and hypertension.

Nor can we overlook the advances in medical and surgical treatment which are now available to prevent the potentially disabling effects of age-related diseases and impairments. For example, cataract surgery is now commonplace in modern industrialized countries, practically eliminating this condition as an independent cause of disability in old age. Advances in orthopedic surgery, particularly hip and knee replacements, have played an important role in reducing functional mobility impairments that are common in older people. Improvements in treatments for conditions such as hypertension and diabetes have led to reductions in incidence and disabling effects of heart disease, kidney disease, diabetic retinopathy, and stroke (Blanchette & Valcour 1998). We will also soon have a generation of women entering the older cohort who have engaged in estrogen-replacement therapy with, as of yet, unknown effects on rates and disabling effects of osteoporosis and heart disease.

It is also important to note that the extent to which disability is experienced by individuals is also a function of their social and physical environment, and not solely biologically determined (LaPlante 1998). Current and future cohorts of older people have and will continue to benefit from a more accessible social environment, due largely to the advocacy effects of the disability movement and the provisions in the 1990 Americans with Disabilities Act. The importance of environmental modifications, such as access ramps for wheelchairs, more readable public signs, and the availability of hearing-enhancement devices in public places, should not be underestimated in terms of their effects in reducing functional disability and improving the quality of daily life among the elderly. There is also evidence that disability rates have been positively effected by the increased use of assistive devices and technologies (e.g., wheelchairs, hearing aids, optical magnifying devices) by older people (Manton, Corder & Stallard 1997) and that the use of assistive technology devices has grown substantially among the elderly over the past decade (LaPlante, Hendershot & Moss 1997).

Finally, challenging the stereotype of inevitable functional decline among older people with disabilities, recent data from several longitudinal studies (see, for example, Branch & Ku 1989; Manton 1988) clearly show that older people move in and out of a disabled status and that it is not unusual for older persons to report less disability in short- and long-term follow-up interviews than they did at baseline (Guralnik, Fried & Salive 1996). Thus, disability is neither inevitable nor intractable.

Trends in Aging and Disability—It's Not All Good News

Although the data support the general trend toward declines in rates of disability, several important caveats are in order. First and most obviously, even under the most optimistic assessment of declining disability rates, the size of the baby boom generation that will enter various stages of old age over the next several decades will result in significantly increasing numbers of older persons with some degree of disability. This dramatic increase in absolute numbers of older people nullifies any premature projections in terms of decreasing need for social and health care services among the older disabled population. It also further underscores the importance of public health and social policies which address the prevention of diseases and their disabling effects on multiple levels, including public health measures, medical/surgical interventions, assistive technology, and, as will be discussed in more detail in the following sections, appropriate integration of a rehabilitation philosophy and service network for older, as well as younger, disabled persons.

Most critically, not all members of the current cohort of older people, nor those now in the baby boom generation, will enter old age with the benefits of lifelong access to quality health care, high education, adequate income, and/or with a history of positive health practices (Alt 1998). Structural inequalities on a societal level will continue to put segments of the older population at greater risk of incurring and living with disability in later life. Specifically, gender, race/ethnicity, and socioeconomic status are each significant factors associated with increased risk of age-related disability.

Higher proportions of women continue to experience disability as compared to men. For example, data from the 1993 National Health Interview Survey indicate that the prevalence of IADL disability among women age seventy and older was 16.5 percent compared to 9.9 percent of men; for ADL disability it was 7.3 percent and 5.0 percent, respectively (Crimmins, Saito & Reynolds 1997). Further, Guralnik et al. (1995) note that women are particularly affected by disabling conditions. That is, although studies have shown that elderly men and women acquire disabilities at similar rates, more elderly women than men live with disabilities simply because they live longer than do men. Consistent relationships between low income status and severe disability for persons age sixty-five and older have also been documented (McNeil 1993). For example, Guralnik et al. (1993) found that loss of mobility was 1.5 times as common for those in the lowest income category as for those in the highest income group, even after adjustment for comorbid chronic health conditions. Disability rates for racial and ethnic minorities are also higher than those of white Americans, except for Asian and Pacific Islanders groups (U.S. Bureau of the Census 1992; U.S. Department of Education 1992). As Smart and Smart (1997) note, the disproportionate disability rates of minorities is further underscored by the fact that, given the relative youthfulness of minorities, one would expect fewer disabilities in this group but the opposite is the case. And it is important to remember that growth in the elderly population when the baby boomers reach old age will be most dramatic for minority populations. That is, while the number of whites over age sixty-five will double between 1990 and 2050, the number of African-Americans will triple and the number of Hispanics will increase fivefold (Morgan 1998). Further, educational attainment among African-Americans, Hispanics, and Native Americans is generally lower than the overall population and, given the relationship between education and disability, may account for some of the variance in ethnic differences in disability rates (Smart & Smart 1997). Thus, even optimistic scenarios based on declines in overall disability rates among the elderly must be tempered by the disproportionate representation of women, minorities, and low-income elders who are most at risk of incurring disabilities in old age.

Nor is there any evidence that the length of life spent in disability before death is decreasing (Crimmins 1998; LaPlante 1998). In 1980, Fries advanced the theory of the "compression of morbidity." This theory, which continues to engender great debate, postulated that there is a natural life span of approximately eighty-five years and that increasing longevity will be accompanied by increasing health and the delay of disease and disability, thus reducing the number of years during which disability is experienced (Fries 1980). Yet empirical evidence to date does not clearly support the hypothesis that "active life expectancy" (i.e., the average number of years an individual at any given year will remain in a disability-free state (Katz et al. 1983) is increasing. In fact, Guralnik, Fried, and Salive (1996) hypothesize that the "compression of morbidity" scenario in future cohorts is no more likely at this point than two alternative scenarios: first, that the postponement of disability onset will equal the increase in life expectancy so that the number of years spent in a disabled state will remain stable; or second, that disability-free life expectancy does increase, but to a lesser degree than does increases in life expectancy, resulting in an expansion of morbidity in the older population.

Aging with a Disability: An Additional Challenge to the Aging Network

Thus far, the discussion of future trends in aging and disability has focused on people who experience age-related disabilities. However, we will also be seeing an increase in a relatively new population that is coming to the attention of gerontological service providers and researchers; namely, persons who are *aging with a disability*. These persons include those with mental retardation and developmental disabilities as well as those with lifelong physical impairments such as polio, spinal cord injuries, and sensory impairments in vision and hearing. While it is has been recognized that people with lifelong disabilities have been living longer, most of the research attention in the gerontological literature has been given to *caregiving* issues in terms of the role of elderly parents as caregivers to adult disabled children, following the typical caregiving paradigm of caregiving stress and planning for future care.

However, while gerontological professionals are used to addressing age-related disability, the network does not necessarily understand how people with disabilities *age*, and the effect of the aging process when superimposed on the disability (Ansello & Rose 1989; Torres-Gil 1998). What, for example, are the psychological issues as well as the rehabilitation, social, and health care needs of a person who has been a lifelong wheelchair user and who is now experiencing age-related muscular and sensory changes? Or a person who has been functionally blind for most of his/her life and is now experiencing age-related hearing loss that reduces ability to rely on auditory cues for safe mobility? Understanding the differences in adaptation and coping processes between those aging with a disability and those experiencing an age-related disability is a relatively untapped area for future research and has been designated as a priority for research funding by the National Institute for Disability and Rehabilitation Research of the U.S. Department of Education. On a societal level, it is becoming apparent that the aging network is relatively unprepared in both training and resources, and is, in many respects, unwilling to provide services to this unique group of elders. Questions of how to modify and/or broaden services that meet the needs of this growing population represent still another challenge for the aging network as it confronts the changing nature of aging and disability in the new millennium (Torres-Gil 1998).

Changing Attitudes Toward Aging and Disability

Thus far, the changing face of aging and disability has been discussed in terms of disability rates and emerging subgroups. But there is also another important change that must be acknowledged—that is, a change in the *attitudes* of present and future cohorts of older people toward age-related disability. Although, as stated earlier in this chapter, there has been great progress in educating the professional and public communities that aging is not synonymous with disability, unfortunately many elders, their family members, and even the professionals who work with them too often accept disability as a "normal" part of the aging process. Nowhere is this more apparent than in the case of sensory impairments in vision and hearing due to age-related diseases. To illustrate, in a research demonstration project targeted at outreach to visually impaired elders in the community, refusals to accept referrals for vision assessment and rehabilitation services were met with comments such as, "If I needed help, my doctor would have told me," or "I'm old, what can I expect?" (Horowitz, Teresi & Cassels 1991).

However, it can be hypothesized that the same forces that are influencing disability rates (i.e., higher education, better lifelong access to health care, and more proactive behaviors regarding self-care) affect, and will continue to influence, the attitudes and behaviors of older adults when confronted with an age-related disability. We may expect that the current pattern of acceptance and/or toleration of functional decline in later life will give way in future cohorts to the expectation and active pursuit of interventions that will enhance functioning. In the future, we will be less likely to see older people passively accepting what their doctors tell them, primarily because they did not do so when they were younger. In short, the coming cohorts of older people will be demanding information about a range of health care issues, including choices in type of care options and, in particular, rehabilitation services that maximize functional abilities (Blanchette & Valcour 1998).

Research in Adaptation to Age-Related Disability: A New Approach

A major area of research in gerontology has been focused on the processes of adaptation to age-related disability and outcomes in terms of psychological well-being and general quality of life. Much of the current research in this area has been based on the "Stress and Coping" conceptual model, originally formulated by Lazarus and Folkman (1984). In this model, the processes of coping with and adapting to a stressor, such as the experience of disability, are heavily influenced by the individual's subjective appraisal of the stressor and the personal and social resources upon which she/he can draw. Appraisals, in turn, influence the type of coping strategies employed. Two broad types of coping strategies have been described, including problem-focused (manage/alter the problem) and emotion-focused coping (regulate one's emotional response) (Lazarus & Folkman 1984). Emotion-focused coping operates through cognitive acts such as avoidance, detachment, denial, or wishful thinking. While the objective situation remains the same, a more temperate emotional climate is created. While most stressors elicit both types of coping, problem-focused coping predominates when there has been an appraisal that the stressor can be modified, while emotion-focused coping is used when the stressor has been appraised as not amenable to change (Folkman & Lazarus 1980). Available data indicate that older people, when compared to younger adults, more often see stressful situations as out of their control and are more

likely to use strategies focused on emotion regulation rather than active behavioral change (Johnson & Barer 1993; Meeks et al. 1989).

But are we seeing a cohort effect? If, in fact, the older person appraises the
disability as amenable to amelioration, and not just a stressor to be tolerated,
will patterns of coping change to include more active employment of personal, social, and societal resources to deal with the stressor and, ultimately, more
positive adjustment among the disabled elderly? Again, these are important
areas for future research, with both practical and theoretical implications.

Attention to subjective appraisals of the disability also has important implications for how we design research to study adaptation to age-related disability. It is important to note that gerontological research has tended away
from a disease-specific approach when examining physical health impairments, in favor of a more global focus on functional status. Thus, studies of
disability, coping, and adaptation to disability have often drawn on community or clinical samples that are heterogeneous in terms of type of disability.
For the most part, this has been an appropriate approach, since it is typically
not the existence of a specific disease or impairment that gives us the critical
information for practice and program development, but the consequences of
the disease or impairment for the functional capacity of the individual. However, the importance of subjective appraisals of the stressor may lead us to re-
consider this approach for specific research questions.

Vision impairment, as one of the most common age-related chronic disabilities, will be used to illustrate this point. Recent research has highlighted
the profound effects that vision impairment can have on accomplishing the
most basic functional tasks of everyday life (see, for example, Branch, Horowitz & Carr 1989; Carabelese et al. 1993; Havlik 1986; Salive et al. 1994;
Thompson, Gibson & Jagger 1989). One of vision impairment's most unique
characteristics is the intense fear vision loss evokes in individuals. There are
strong social attitudes and pervasive myths that surround blindness in our
culture. In mythology as well as in religious and popular literature, blindness
has historically been associated with punishment for sin, with the abject beg-
gar, and/or with a total loss of autonomy (Monbeck 1975). These attitudes are
reflected in the current thinking of the general public. For example, one public opinion poll found that blindness ranks fourth, following only AIDS, cancer, and Alzheimer's disease, as the illness most feared by American adults of
all ages (National Society for the Prevention of Blindness, 1984–85). Elders
who become visually impaired in later life are rarely blind, but have often internalized this devaluating orientation, which in turn influences the subjective
meaning they ascribe to the vision disability. We may hypothesize, therefore,

that the functional implications of vision loss are perceived differently than those of other physical problems. For example, the older person who is experiencing problems in mobility due to problems with vision may have a totally different subjective reaction and experience of this limitation than would the older person who is experiencing the same objective level of functional difficulties due to arthritis. This subjective appraisal will inevitably have implications for long-term adaptation and well-being.

Thus, it is being suggested that it is time to swing the pendulum back somewhat in terms of thinking about the disease-disability relationship. Diseases underlying impairments can differ in several respects—for example, in terms of whether or not they are potentially life-threatening (e.g., cancer or heart disease), associated with pain (e.g., arthritis), or have an acute versus a gradual onset (e.g., stroke versus sensory impairments). In looking at the unique characteristics of specific impairments and the meanings ascribed to them by the older person, we may be able to better understand the diversity that has been identified in both functional and psychosocial adaptation to disability in later life.

Geriatric Rehabilitation:
The Forgotten Sector in the Long-Term Care Continuum

The foregoing discussion on disability trends and attitudes toward age-related disability implicitly suggests the critical role that geriatric rehabilitation should, and it is postulated, *will* play in the continuum of care for older people as we move into the 21st century. As alluded to earlier, the increased emphasis on rehabilitation for age-related disabilities will be driven by both individual forces, (i.e., changing attitudes toward the acceptance of disability and resulting consumer demand for such services), as well as societal forces (i.e., the increasing numbers of disabled elders and rising political concerns about the cost of long-term care services). Unfortunately, we do not at this time have a strong foundation on which to build and expand rehabilitation services as a critical component of the long-term care service system.

Rehabilitation, in general, has historically been the "stepchild" of the health care system in North America. Geriatric rehabilitation, in particular, has lacked priority in terms of both public policy and clinical practice. Furthermore, current rehabilitation interventions have been largely limited to the acute health care system and traditional health care therapies such as physical or occupational therapy, with much less attention paid to nonmedical aspects of rehabilitation that support independent living, such as assistive technology and environmental modifications (Sheets, Wray & Torres-Gil 1993). Although gerontologists talk about a continuum of care, professionals in the field have tended to maintain an "acute versus long-term care" mentality—that is, "If you can't cure them, take care of them." In this view, the response to age-related disabilities is supportive care, in home or institutional settings, substituting personal and home care attendants for assumed unalterable functional losses. The absence of discussions about rehabilitation in the current debate regarding the future of long-term care, as well as the virtual absence of aging advocacy organizations in enacting and implementing the 1990 Americans with Disabilities Act, is especially telling of the long road we need to travel to educate the gerontological community regarding the role geriatric rehabilitation can play in the prevention or minimization of disability.

Before proceeding, it is important to specify exactly what is meant by rehabilitation. In terms of health interventions, rehabilitation represents the tertiary level of care, which ideally works in conjunction and partnership with both primary and secondary prevention (Branch 1996). That is, primary prevention involves avoiding the event entirely (e.g., disease prevention through public health measures, lifelong positive health practices, and so on); secondary prevention involves recognizing and treating the event to minimize its impact (e.g., bypass surgery, cataract extraction, hip and knee replacements), while tertiary prevention involves intervening after the occurrence of the event to minimize its functional consequences (e.g., physical therapy for persons suffering a stroke, cognitive training for persons with Alzheimer's disease, exercise programs for persons with arthritis, prescription of low-vision optical devices and other rehabilitation training in skills of daily living for persons with visual impairments, as well as a range of possible environment modifications) (Branch 1996).

As Williams (1984:xiii) has noted, rehabilitation is "an approach, a philosophy and a point of view as much as it is a set of techniques." Consistent with Williams's conceptualization are the definitions of rehabilitation and geriatric rehabilitation offered by Torres-Gil and Wray (1993:832):

> Rehabilitation aims to improve, restore, or maintain functioning in order to optimize independence in persons with chronic conditions. The conditions may result in loss of function or ability to care for oneself at home, to carry out activities in the community, to work, or to fulfill social roles. Rehabilitation strategies include a mix of medical and nonmedical services.

Geriatric rehabilitation applies the principles of rehabilitation to the chronic disabling conditions of later life, taking into account the unique biologic, psychologic and social characteristics of the older person. These conditions may be single or multiple, and they may be the result of later-life effects of developmental or childhood disabilities or later-life accidents or diseases.

The development of a comprehensive rehabilitation system for older adults, encompassing both medical and nonmedical services, has been constrained by public attitudes and social programs that target rehabilitation services to younger persons with disabilities, with a focus on returning or preparing the individual for a "productive" role in society through employment. Unfortunately, there has been a historic schism between the aging and disability communities, although both service systems are based on a similar policy objective to promote independence. Disability programs tend to serve younger adults and place greatest emphasis on values of personal autonomy, consumer control of services, independence, and access to all aspects of society (Sheets, Wray & Torres-Gil 1993). Aging network services focus on supportive services, wherein independence for older adults is often narrowly defined in terms of maintaining "community" residence. Only recently have issues of autonomy and questions regarding the potential of social support services in creating "excess" social disability been raised. Reflecting societal biases, the disability community has historically been loathe to ally itself with the aging network, rejecting stereotypes of dependence and frailty often associated with aging. Concurrently, the aging network, with one of its goals being to counter the image of disability as an inevitability of aging, has failed to form linkages with the disability community. Thus, "ageism" and "disabilityism" have worked against the formation of what could be considered a natural alliance between the two services sectors.

The common ground that both networks cover in their goals of meeting the rehabilitation and social needs of disabled people of all ages is only recently being recognized. For example, on a systems level, interdepartmental committees comprised of representatives from federal agencies serving disabled and aging communities are being formed. There have also been attempts in professional organizations, such as the American Public Health Association, to foster collaborations between researchers in gerontology and disability studies.

While all of the above activities bode well for establishing linkages between disability and aging service networks, a word of caution is also in order. Lifelong experiences and cohort differences do distinguish the worlds of individuals who experience early- versus late-life onset of disability. Definitions of, expectations for, and routes to independence will have different meanings for a person who has been functionally unimpaired for seven, eight, or even nine decades prior to the experience of a disability. The model of consumer choice and consumer control of personal care service providers that prevails in the disability service network is not always directly transferrable to an aging population, where such preferences are not necessarily of top priority. Careful consideration of areas of commonalities and differences in social and health care needs, and how such needs translate into interventions, remains a priority for both clinical and empirical investigation.

Ironically, a major impetus for the development of a rehabilitation philosophy in aging social and health care services may come from the managed care delivery and financing systems which are currently proliferating in the United States. Driven by goals of reducing costs in the most expensive modes of care (i.e, inpatient hospital and institutional long-term care), managed care programs are beginning to promote the less expensive, preventive health services, including rehabilitation services for the prevention of disability (Silverstone 1998). For this trend to continue, one of the major challenges that gerontological researchers in disability and rehabilitation will face is the design of systematic evaluations of rehabilitation service interventions to provide empirical evidence of their value. But how does one define this value? It is proposed that research methodologies must not only carefully document inputs but comprehensively define outcomes. The latter should include short-term clinical outcomes, both short- and long-term functional and psychosocial outcomes, as well as recognizing the necessity to provide sufficient longitudinal follow-up to document outcomes relative to patterns of health care utilization and costs. To illustrate, in the case of vision rehabilitation, clinical outcomes could include whether the elder learned to utilize a low-vision optical or other adaptive aid for activities of daily living; for other physical disabilities such as stroke or hip fracture, clincial outcomes may be measured in terms of range of motion or ability to use mobility aids. It is argued, however, that these outcomes are important and necessary, but not sufficient indicators of successful rehabilitation. The ultimate goal of any rehaibilitation intervention is to maximize functional independence, foster psychosocial adaptation to the disability, and enhance general quality of life. These outcomes, which reflect improved functional and psychological health, may be linked in turn to stemming future declines and disabilities that would require more intensive acute or long-term care services. While it has been estimated that there are literally millions of disabled older people who could benefit from rehabilitation services (Hadley 1989), we have yet to amass the data to support this claim.

Beyond Caregiving:
The Family's Role in Geriatric Rehabilitation

Changing trends and attitudes toward age-related disability, as well as the anticipated future expansion of rehabilitative interventions for disabled older people, calls for a reconceptualization of the role of the family vis-à-vis older disabled relatives. This reconceptualization involves going beyond a "caregiving" perspective to a systems approach that views and involves the family as a partner in maintaining and maximizing the physical and emotional well-being of the older disabled relative.

Cumulative findings from three decades of gerontological research have consistently documented the importance of family members in providing emotional and instrumental support to older relatives (see, for example, Biegel & Blum 1990; Biegel, Sales & Schulz 1991; Brody 1985; Cantor & Little 1985; Dwyer & Coward 1991; George & Gwyther 1986; Horowitz 1985; Pruchno et al. 1990; Schulz, Visintainer & Williamson 1990; Stone, Cafferata & Sangl 1987). In fact, the growth in the body of knowledge in family caregiving, and the increasing sophistication in questions, methodologies, and measures, has been one of the great successes in gerontological research.

However, the vast majority of this research literature has focused on documenting and understanding the stresses and burdens experienced by family caregivers. In an early review of the caregiving research, this author wrote, "It is somewhat ironic that, when we discovered the family as caregiver, we seemed to forget about the older person as the recipient of care" (Horowitz 1985:226). Unfortunately, similar statements regarding the state of the caregiving literature are currently being made (see, for example, Newsom & Schulz 1998; Pruchno, Burant & Peters 1997). The elders' perceptions, reactions, and interactions with their relatives continue to receive much less attention. Some of this neglect is due to the fact that the caregiving literature has been dominated by research on caregiving to older people with Alzheimer's disease and related dementias. The situations of the physically disabled but mentally intact elderly have received much less attention. Thus, given the limited emphasis on this population, as well as the minor role rehabilitation has played in the system of care for elderly persons, it is not surprising that this substantial body of knowledge on caregiving support has virtually ignored the role families do, or may, play in the rehabilitation of their older relatives.

In contrast, we have seen an increasing awareness in the clinical rehabilitation literature of the importance of family involvement, attitudes, and support during the rehabilitation process as well as in the retention of short-term and long-term rehabilitation gains (Becker & Kaufman 1988; Kaplan 1990; Kelly & Lambert 1992; Osterweil 1990; Silverstone 1984; Weinberger 1980; Youngblood & Hines 1992). In fact, it has been noted that the initial decision to pursue rehabilitation services is often a function of the attitudes of family members (Granger 1984). Furthermore, the development of the initial rehabilitation plan for the individual is typically influenced by the professional's assessment of the willingness of the family to become a part of the process and to reinforce the gains made after rehabilitation is completed (Betts 1990).

Emerging research in rehabilitation, across disabilities, has begun to demonstrate the significant relationship between the availability and quality of social supports and positive rehabilitation outcomes. For example, among stroke patients, good family function predicted fewer days in the hospital, better adherence to the treatment plan, and better home care outcomes (Evans, Bishop & Haselkorn 1987; Evans et al. 1991). More complete physical recovery after a hip fracture has been found related to the presence of a spouse (Thomas & Stevens 1974), a greater number of close family supports (Cummings et al. 1988), greater feelings of attachment to the overall informal network (Roberto 1992), and family support resources available at discharge (Kaufman, Albright & Wagner 1987). Among diabetics, positive expectations of family members influence dietary compliance by the patients (Shenkel et al. 1985–86) and has been associated with better physical and psychological well-being (Mengee et al. 1990). For elders with age-related vision impairments, the quality of family support has been found associated with successful utilization of low-vision optical devices (Greig, West & Overbury 1986), and generally better psychosocial adaptation to the vision disability (Horowitz & Reinhardt 1992; Large 1982; Morrison 1982). Similarly, availability of social support, high family involvement, and better relationships with significant others have been found to predict greater compliance with treatment plans among arthritis patients (Oakes et al. 1970), better adjustment among hearing-impaired adults (Weinberger 1980), coping effectiveness among physically disabled wheelchair users (Mc-Nett 1987), and greater likelihood of survival among heart attack patients (Ruberman et al. 1984).

Based upon this growing body of evidence, there has been a recognition of the critical need to include the family as an active member of the rehabilitation team. Furthermore, there is growing awareness that the family has *unique* needs that must be addressed in addition to its role as "partner" and adjunct in the rehabilitation process for the older adult. As Brody (1986:88) notes, "Lack of attention to the experiences and needs of family members can sabotage the most meticulous sophisticated rehabilitation plan." Thus, there is an emerging consensus in the field for considering the entire family unit as the consumer of rehabilitation service (Brody 1986; Brummel-Smith 1988; Fulton & Katz 1986; Kemp 1986; Lawton, Brody & Saperstein 1990).

An important issue in working with families in the rehabilitation process is to address commonly observed overprotective attitudes and behaviors toward the disabled elder that can impede the rehabilitation process and limit the elder's autonomy (Axtell & Schoneberger 1990; Budde 1990; Plopper 1990; Stahl & Potts 1985; Silverstone 1984; Versluys 1980). Emerging evidence does suggest that caregiving can be both negatively perceived and have negative effects on the older care receiver. In a study of 276 spouse dyads (Newsom & Schulz 1998), 50 percent of caregivers provided help that the recipient did not report needing and 40 percent of care recipients reported some emotional distress in response to the help they received. Furthermore, helping distress predicted both concurrent depressive symptoms and depressive symptoms measured at the one-year follow-up. Similarly, S. C. Thompson et al. (1989) report that perceptions that families provided too much help was predictive of depression among stroke patients. Other earlier studies have also reported that a common care-recipient complaint is that the caregiver attempts to do too much for them, often inadvertently increasing the dependency of the older person (Fengler & Goodrich 1979; Noelker & Poulshock 1982). Interestingly, in a study of visually impaired elders and their family members, the latter were more likely to view themselves as overprotective than was this behavior perceived as such by the elder (Goodman et al. 1996). These findings support an earlier study (Horowitz, Silverstone & Reinhardt 1991) that found that family members did struggle, both behaviorally and emotionally, with balancing their concerns about the autonomy and independence of their older relative against their fears about the elder's health and safety. This was often a more pressing issue for the family member than it was for the older relative, who more typically placed greater value on the assistance received than on their fears about family members encroaching on their autonomy. Clearly, there are complex and often conflicting perceptions and reactions to receiving care among disabled elders that we have only begun to identify.

On the other hand, there are families who have belief systems that emphasize the continuing capabilities of older people, regardless of existing disabilities. While often a positive influence on the older relative, such beliefs can also reflect a denial of the seriousness of the disability and may lead to unrealistic expectations about the elder's capabilities (Plopper 1990; Silverstone 1984). Whether underestimating or overestimating the capabilities of the visually impaired elderly, Silverstone (1984:60) notes that "the well-intentioned efforts of the rehabilitation team can be subverted by well-meaning but confused family members who simply do not understand the rehabilitation process."

All of the above suggests the need to provide families with services in order to both facilitate the process of adaptation as well as meet the unique needs of the family. Assessments need to address not only what help the family can provide but also their attitudes and role expectations for themselves and their older relative (Brody 1986; Kelly & Lambert 1992; Silverstone 1984; Youngblood & Hines 1992). Providing accurate information about the elder's condition and the rehabilitation process through educational programs and psychosocial support services is critical if family members are to understand the concerns of the older relative, relieve their own anxiety, and learn how much support to give without doing too much (Brummel-Smith 1988; Der-McLeod & Hansen 1992; Kemp 1990; Smith & Messikomer 1988; Weinberger 1980).

The limited research to date offers beginning evidence that family interventions can influence both patient and family outcomes. For example, in the case of cardiac patients, Burgess et al. (1987) found that when families were provided information and support from the medical staff, the patient was significantly less stressed and less dependent during the rehabilitation process. Similarly, married persons who jointly attended classes in managing health regimens following a heart attack learned and retained material better than unmarried persons (Pommier 1992). Crews and Frey (1993) found that even when only limited informal services are provided for families of visually impaired adults, there was a significant reduction, at the completion of rehabilitation, in the proportion expressing concerns about their relative's safety and about their own role in assisting their relative.

In sum, the current state of the art in rehabilitation and aging provides ample evidence that families, for better or worse, are both influenced by and influential in the rehabilitation process and outcomes for older adults. But more extensive experience with family intervention models and careful evaluation of their results is critically needed as we move forward to include family members in the rehabilitation process. Underlying any such programmatic and/or evaluation effort must be a broader conceptualization of the family—one that goes beyond a unidirectional supportive relationship to one that focuses on a partnership with the elder in her/his recovery and/or compensation of functions comprised by age-related disabilities.

Depression and Disability: A Tangled Web

Any discussion of aging and disability must also address quality-of-life issues for the disabled elderly. Key among such issues is an awareness of the complex reciprocal relationship between psychiatric and physical morbidity in later life, especially in terms of the most common psychiatric condition in the elderly—depression.

Findings from the National Institutes of Health Consensus Development Panel on Depression in Late Life (NIH 1992) underscore that depressive illness is widespread among the elderly. Of the thirty-one million Americans age sixty-five and over, nearly five million suffer from serious and persistent symptoms of depression and one million suffer from a major depressive disorder. Rates for major depression are highest in nursing home settings, which are estimated to be between 15 and 25 percent, followed by primary care clinics (documented at between 6 and 9 percent), and dropping to about 3 percent for healthy elders living in the community. However, rates of significant depressive symptomatology without depressive disorder among community-dwelling elders are estimated to range from 15 to 20 percent.

These conference findings also stressed that depression is a serious illness in its own right and is not a normal consequence of aging. In fact, among healthy elders, rates are no higher than for younger cohorts, and many of the risk factors for depression among older and younger persons are similar. Higher rates of depression are documented among women, the unmarried (especially the widowed), those undergoing stress, and those without the support of a social network. If untreated, depression is associated with increased disability and increased risk of premature death. Unfortunately, depression among the elderly too often goes unidentified and untreated. As with physical disability in general, depression is too often accepted as a normal consequence of the losses in later life. The current cohort of older people tend not to seek mental health services and are more likely to attach a stigma to such a need. The lack of linkages in the United States between health care, mental health, and social service professionals and systems also presents many older people with a complex set of separate steps that must be negotiated in order to receive adequate treatment. In fact, it is estimated that only about 10 percent of older people in need of psychiatric treatment ever receive it.

A major conclusion of the NIH Consensus Development Panel was that physical comorbidity was the hallmark of depressive illness among the elderly (Lebowitz 1996). There is extensive evidence in the research literature documenting high levels of comorbidity between physical illness and depressive illness in later life (e.g., Berkman et al. 1986; Bruce et al. 1994; Gurland, Wilder & Berkman 1988; Parmelee, Katz & Lawton 1992; Turner & Noh 1988). But it is not simply that depression, medical illness, and disability coexist in elderly populations. There is a complex reciprocal interrelationship that is difficult to unravel and which is the focus of much of the research currently being conducted in the field of geriatric mental health. Emerging research indicates that physical disability is a major risk factor for the onset of depressive disorders among the elderly (e.g., Bruce & Hoff 1994; Kaplan et al. 1987; Kennedy, Klerman & Thomas 1990) *and* that depression is associated with increased risk for the onset of both illness and physical disability in later life (e.g., Bruce et al. 1994; Gurland, Wilder & Berkman 1988). Among disabled elders, across a variety of chronic conditions, depression is associated with greater levels of functional disability and poorer medical and rehabilitation outcomes (Katz 1996; Kemp 1990; Wells et al. 1989; Williams 1984). Thus, depression is a major source of excess disability in geriatric patients and can significantly affect the course and outcomes of medical, surgical, and rehabilitative treatments.

In fact, clinical literature consistently cites depression as a barrier to initial access and utilization of rehabilitation services, acting to negatively influence both medical referrals and patient motivation to engage in rehabilitation programs (e.g., Brody & Pawlson 1990; Dodds, Flannigan, & Ng 1993; Kemp, Brummel-Smith & Ramsdell 1990; Leinhaas & Hedstrom 1994; Lovett 1988; McDaniel 1976; Ringering & Amaral 1988; Williams 1984). Physicians are simply less likely to refer older patients to rehabilitation services who they label as depressed and thus deem unlikely to benefit from services. Unfortunately, these same patients are rarely referred to mental health practioners.

But there is emerging evidence that rehabilitation can also serve to ameliorate depression associated with disability among the elderly. In research conducted by the author and colleagues (Horowitz et al. 1994), use of low-vision services and a greater number of optical devices predicted declines in depressive symptomatology over a two-year period, after controlling for age, impairment severity, health status, and functional disability.

Such findings highlight the importance of rehabilitation services for the growing numbers of disabled elders. They also point to the importance of understanding the mechanisms by which rehabilitation may influence depression status. Given the well-documented relationship between functional disability and depression, a cogent argument, though still open to empirical investigation, can be made for hypothesizing that the primary pathway through which rehabilitation affects depression is by improvements in levels of functional ability. Yet the goal of rehabilitation is not only to maximize functional ability and stem functional decline but also to facilitate adaptation to the disability and instill a sense of empowerment and control (Warren & Lampert 1994). Thus, it is hypothesized that the pathways by which rehabilitation interventions influence depressive states also include the effects of rehabilitation on attitudes toward the disability, feelings of self-efficacy and mastery, and use of coping strategies, as well as on social support relationships. These are hypotheses that need to be tested in order to provide an empirical foundation for the design of future rehabilitation intervention strategies that can maximize mental health outcomes for the elderly with disabilities. The societal demands for increased accountability in health care services, as well as the projected consumer demand for effective interventions that will come from the coming cohorts of older adults, make this a research priority.

A Differential Approach to Aging and Disability

As stated at the beginning of this chapter, the goal of this essay has been to challenge the social work and gerontological professions to rethink current conceptual, empirical, and practice approaches to disabilities in later life. At the most basic level, this means that the assumption of "aging as disability," which for so long has implicitly dominated both public and professional responses to older adults, must be replaced by a differential approach to aging that explicitly recognizes the heterogeneity that exists among older adults in general and, specifically, among elders with disabilities.

Taking a differential approach to disabilities in later life forces one to move beyond simply defining older adults as the sum of their specific ADL task deficiencies which, in turn, defines the global need for supportive services from public and/or family resources. To do the latter implicitly embraces the "inevitable loss" model of aging, wherein the older person remains a passive recipient of care. In contrast, a differential approach explicitly acknowledges that not all the elderly are the same, that not all disabilities experienced by the elderly are comparable in their biopsychosocial consequences or in their trajectories, and, ultimately, that not all interventions are equally appropriate across the various cognitive, sensory, and physical disabilities experienced by older individuals. Most importantly, a differential approach recognizes that the elder is an active agent in the process of coping with a disability, including learning functional and psychosocial skills that help compensate for lost functions.

The natural question to be raised is why the gerontological community has, paradoxically, taken such a narrow and static view of disabilities in later life—virtually ignoring the rehabilitative potential and needs of older people with sensory, physical, and cognitive disabilities—even as issues of long-term care dominate practice and policy discussions? As argued throughout the chapter, both attitudinal and structural forces are at play.

Empowerment, however one chooses to define it, is a relatively new concept in gerontological practice and unevenly applied in practice. Rather, a "paternalistic" perspective has prevailed (a somewhat appropriate, if ironic, term given that the majority of the elderly with health and/or income needs are older women), which portrays the elderly as both needing and deserving of help. No where is this more obvious than when addressing the situations and needs of older persons with Alzheimer's disease. Given its devastating impact on both families and the health care system, Alzheimer's disease has appropriately been defined as a national crisis by very vocal and well-organized advocacy groups comprised of both family and professional constituents. While the broader range of disabilities experienced in later life (including depressive disorders as both a primary disability and a secondary condition associated with other physical and sensory disabilities) affect even larger numbers of elderly with equally devastating effects for the individual and the family, they are more likely to be seen as an "expected" part of the aging experience and have not received equivalent national attention. Whereas the early social welfare literature often referred to the elderly as the "hidden poor," it is not unreasonable to think of them as the "hidden disabled" as well.

Structurally, the social and medical service systems that respectively address the needs of older adults, adults with physical disabilities, and adults with psychiatric disabilities have developed independently over time. While a discussion of the specific histories of each system is beyond the scope of this chapter, for purposes of this discussion it is safe to say that competition, rather than cooperation and collaboration, continue to characterize relationships between these service systems. Each is competing for increasingly limited public resources, for public supporters, and for a prominent place on the national health and welfare agenda.

However, the message is not all bleak. A major theme of this chapter has been that attitudes toward disabilities in later life, as well as the interrelationships of the various service systems, are changing. Heralding these changes are shifting attitudes and expectations of the coming cohorts of older people, as well as increasing demands for effective use of health care resources. As discussed throughout the chapter, these changes are also giving rise to a new set of research questions and policy challenges. Research that provides a better understanding of the unique psychosocial and functional consequences of diverse age-related disabilities is critical to the identification and design of person/situation-relevant supportive and rehabilitative services. Investigations of family relationships in later life need to go beyond the current focus on caregiving stress. Rather, research is needed that turns greater attention to the perceptions and reactions of the disabled elder, and that explores the specific role of family attitudes, support, and involvement in enhancing and/or hindering the elder's ability to maximize functional independence. Disentangling the role of depressive illness as a predictor of excess disability and as a consequence of disability in later life also deserves high priority on our research agenda in aging and disability. Finally, rather than acting as if they are two ships passing in the night, it is imperative that gerontological and disability service networks recognize their common ground. On a structural level, we need to explore the types of organizational relationships and funding streams that can promote intersystem collaborations. Only when each system draws upon the unique knowledge of the other, pools resources, and consolidates their power where appropriate, will we be in the best position to meet our common goal of maximizing quality of life for persons with disabilities.

References

Alt, P. M. 1998. Future directions for public senior services: Meeting diverging needs. *Generations* 22: 29–33.

Ansello, E. F. and T. Rose. 1989. *Aging and lifelong disabilities: Partnership for the twenty-first Century.* The Wingspread Conference Report, University of Maryland Center for Aging. Palm Springs, Calif.: Elder Press.

Axtell, L. A. and M. B. Schoneberger. 1990. Physical therapy. In B. Kemp, K. Brummel-Smith, and J. W. Ramsdell (eds.), *Geriatric Rehabilitation*, 157–75.

Becker, G. and S. Kaufman. 1988. Old age, rehabilitation, and research: A review of the issues. *The Gerontologist* 28(4): 459–68.

Berkman, L. F., C. S. Berkman, S. Kasi, D. H. Freeman, L. Leo, A. M. Ostfeld, J. Cornonih, and J. A. Brody. 1986. Depressive symptoms in relation to physical health and functioning in the elderly. *American Journal of Epidemiology* 124: 372–88.

Betts, H. B. 1990. Rehabilitation and the elderly: A psychiatrist's view. In S. J. Brody and L. G. Pawlson (eds.), *Aging and rehabilitation II: The state of the practice,* 30–40.

Biegel, D. E. and A. Blum. 1990. *Aging and caregiving: Theory, research, and practice.* Newbury Park, Calif.: Sage.

Biegel, D. E., E. Sales, and R. Schulz (eds). 1991. *Family caregiving in chronic illness.* Newbury Park, Calif.: Sage.

Blanchette, P. L. and V. G. Valcour. 1998. Health and aging among baby boomers. *Generations* 22: 76–80

Branch, L. G. 1996. Research on disability: Where is it leading? *Journal of Gerontology: Social Sciences* 51B: S171–S172.

Branch, L. G., A. Horowitz, and C. Carr. 1989. The implications for everyday life of incident-reported visual decline among people over age 65 living in the community. *The Gerontologist* 29(3): 359–65.

Branch, L. G. and L. Ku. 1989. Transition probabilities for the elderly over a decade: Uses in long-term care financing. *Journal of Aging and Health* 1(3): 370–408.

Brody, E. M. 1985. Parent care as a normative family stress. *The Gerontologist* 25(1): 19–29.

———. 1986. Informal support systems in the rehabilitation of the disabled elderly. In S. J. Brody and G. E. Ruff (eds.), *Aging and rehabilitation: Advances in the state of the art,* 87–103.

Brody, S. J. and G. E. Ruff (eds.). 1986. *Aging and rehabilitation: Advances in the state of the art.* New York: Springer.

Brody, S. J. and L. G. Pawlson (eds.). 1990. *Aging and rehabilitation II: The state of the practice.* New York: Springer.

Bruce, M. L. and R. A. Hoff. 1994. Social and physical health rate factors for first onset major depressive disorder in a community sample. *Social Psychiatry and Psychiatry Epidemiology* 29: 165–71.

Bruce, M. L., T. E. Seeman, S. S. Merril, and D. G. Blazer. 1994. The impact of depressive symptomatology on physical disability: MacArthur studies on successful aging. *American Journal of Public Health* 84: 1796–99.

Brummel-Smith, K. 1988. Family science and geriatric rehabilitation. *Topics in Geriatric Rehabilitation* 4: 1–7.

Budde, J. 1990. Independent living rehabilitation: Concepts and practices. In S. J. Brody and L. G. Pawlson (eds.), *Aging and rehabilitation II: The state of the practice,* 57–73.

Burgess, A. W., D. J. Lerner, R. B. D'Agostino, P. S. Vokonas, C. R. Hartman, and P. Gaccione. 1997. A randomized control trial of cardiac rehabilitation. *Social Science and Medicine* 24(4): 3359–70.

Cantor, M. and V. Little. 1985. Aging and social care. In R. H. Binstock and E. Shanas (eds.), *Handbook of aging and the social sciences*, 745–72. 2d ed. New York: Van Nostrand Reinhold.

Carabelese, C., I. Appollonio, R. Rozzini, A. Bianchetti, G. B. Frisoni, L. Frattola, and M. Trabucchi. 1993. Sensory impairment and quality of life in a community elderly population. *Journal of the American Geriatrics Society* 41: 401–407.

Crews, J. E. and W. D. Frey. 1993. Family concerns and older people who are blind. *Journal of Visual Impairment and Blindness* 87(1): 6–11.

Crimmins, E. M. 1998. Is disability declining among the elderly? Trends and implications for the next millennium. Paper presented at the Annual Meeting of the American Society on Aging, San Francisco.

Crimmins, E. M., Y. Saito, and S. L. Reynolds. 1997. Further evidence on recent trends in the prevalence and incidence of disability among older Americans from two sources: The LSOA and the NHIS. *Journal of Gerontology: Social Sciences* 52B: S59–S71.

Cummings, S., S. Phillips, M. Wheat, D. Black, E. Goosby, D. Wiodarcyzk, P. Trafton, H. Jergensen, C. Winograd, and S. Hulley. 1988. Recovery of function after hip fracture: The role of social supports. *Journal of the American Geriatrics Society* 36: 801–806.

Der-McLeod, D. and J. C. Hansen. 1992. On Lok: The family continuum. *Generations* 17: 71–72.

Dodds, A. G., H. Flannigan, and L. Ng. 1993. The Nottingham Adjustment Scale: A validation study. *International Journal of Rehabilitation Research* 16: 177–84.

Dwyer, J. W. and R. T. Coward. 1991. A multivariate comparision of the involvement of adult sons versus daughters in the care of impaired parents. *Journal of Gerontology: Social Sciences* 46(5): S259–S269.

Evans, R. L., D. S. Bishop, A. L. Matlock, S. Stranahan, G. Smith, and E. Halar. 1987. Family interaction and treatment adherence after stroke. *Archives of Physical Medicine and Rehabilitation* 68: 513–17.

Evans, R. L., D. S. Bishop, and J. K. Haselkorn. 1991. Factors predicting satisfactory home care after stroke. *Archives of Physical Medicine and Rehabilitation* 72: 144–47.

Fengler, A. P. and N. Goodrich. 1979. Wives of elderly disabled men: The hidden patients. *The Gerontologist* 19(2): 175–83.

Folkman, S. and R. S. Lazarus. 1980. An analysis of coping in a middle-age community sample. *Journal of Health and Social Behavior* 21: 219–25.

Fries, J. F. 1980. Aging, natural death, and the compression of morbidity. *New England Journal of Medicine* 303(3): 130–35.

Fulton, J. P. and S. Katz. 1986. Characteristics of the disabled elderly and implications of rehabliliation. In S. J. Brody and G. E. Ruff (eds.), *Aging and rehabilitation: Advances in the state of the art*, 27–46.

George, L. and L. P. Gwyther. 1986. Caregiver well-being: A multidimensional examination of family caregivers of demented adults. *The Gerontologist* 26(3): 253–59.

Goodman, C. R., A. Horowitz, J. P. Reinhardt, and B. Bird. 1996. *Comparisons of older adult and family perceptions of vision impairment.* Poster presented at the Annual Scientific Meeting of the Gerontological Society of America, Washington, D.C.

Granger, C. 1984. The decision to rehabilitate. *Generations* 8: 9–10.

Greig, D. E., M. L. West, and O. Overbury. 1986. Successful use of low-vision aids: Visual and psychological factors. *Journal of Visual Impairment and Blindness* 80(10): 985–88.

Guralnik, J. M., A. Z. LaCroix, R. D. Abbott, L. F. Berkman, S. Satterfield et al. 1993. Maintaining mobility in late life I: Demographic characteristics and chronic conditions. *American Journal of Epidemiology* 137: 845–57.

Guralnik, J. M., L. P. Fried, E. M. Simonsick, J. Kasper, and M. Lafferty. 1995. *The Women's Health and Aging Study: Health and social characteristics of older women with disability.* Bethesda, Md.: NIA, NIH Publication no. 95–4009.

Guralnik, J. M., L. P. Fried, and M. E. Salive. 1996. Disability as a public health outcome in the aging population. *Annual Review of Public Health* 17: 25–46.

Gurland, B., D. E. Wilder, and C. Berkman. 1988. Depression and disability in the elderly: Reciprocal relations and changes with age. *International Journal of Geriatric Psychiatry* 3: 163–79.

Hadley, E. C. 1989. *Rehabilitation research programs of the National Institute on Aging. Report to the Panel on Physical Medicine and Rehabilitation Research.* Bethesda, Md.: National Institute of Health.

Havlik, R. J. 1986. *Aging in the eighties: Impaired senses for sound and light in persons age 65 years and over.* Hyattsville, Md.: National Center for Health Statistics, Advance Data Vital and Health Statistics of the NCHS, no. 125. DHHS pub. no. (PHS)86–1250. Public Health Service.

Horowitz, A. 1985. Family caregiving to the frail elderly. In M. P. Lawton and G. Maddox (eds.), *The annual review of gerontology and geriatrics,* 194–246. New York: Springer.

Horowitz, A., B. M. Silverstone, and J. P. Reinhardt. 1991. A conceptual and empirical exploration of personal autonomy issues within family caregiving relationships. *The Gerontologist* 31(1): 23–31.

Horowitz, A., J. E. Teresi, and L. A. Cassels. 1991. Development of a vision-screening questionnaire for older people. *Journal of Gerontological Social Work* 17(3–4): 37–56.

Horowitz, A. and J. P. Reinhardt. 1992. *Assessing adaptation to age-related vision loss.* New York: Lighthouse Research Institute.

Horowitz, A., J. P. Reinhardt, R. McInerney, and E. Balistreri. 1994. Psychosocial adaptation to age-related vision loss over time. Paper presented at the Annual Scientific Meeting of the Gerontological Society of America, Atlanta.

Johnson, C. L. and B. M. Barer. 1993. Coping and a sense of control among the oldest old: An exploratory analysis. *Journal of Aging Studies* 7(1): 67–80.

Kaplan, S. 1990. Social support, emotional distress, and vocational outcomes among persons with brain injuries. *Rehabilitation Counseling Bulletin* 34: 16–23.

Kaplan, G. A., R. E. Roberts, T. C. Camacho, and J. C. Coyne. 1987. Psychosocial predictors of depression: Prospective evidence from the Human Population Laboratory studies. *American Journal of Epidemiology* 125: 206–220.

Katz, I. R. 1996. On the inseparability of mental and physical health in aged persons. *American Journal of Geriatric Psychiatry* 4(1): 1–16.

Katz, S., L. B. Branch, M. H. Branson, J. A. Papsidero, J. C. Beck et al. 1983. Active life expectancy. *New England Journal of Medicine* 309(20): 1218–24.

Kaufman, R., L. Albright, and C. Wagner. 1987. Rehabilitation outcomes after hip fracture in persons 90 years old and older. *Archives of Physical and Medical Rehabilitation* 68: 369–71.

Kelly, S. D. M. and S. S. Lambert. 1992. Family support in rehabilitation: A review of research, 1980–1990. *Rehabilitation Counseling Bulletin* 36: 98–119.

Kemp, B. 1986. Psychosocial and mental health issues in rehabilitation of older persons. In S. J. Brody and G. E. Ruff (eds.), *Aging and rehabilitation: Advances in the state of the art,* 122–58.

———. 1990. The psychosocial context of geriatric rehabilitation. In B. Kemp, K. Brummel-Smith, and J. W. Ramsdell (eds.), *Geriatric Rehabilitation,* 41–57.

Kemp, B., K. Brummel-Smith, and J. W. Ramsdell (eds.). 1990. *Geriatric Rehablilitation.* Boston: College-Hill Press.

Kennedy, G. L., H. R. Klerman, and C. Thomas. 1990. The emergence of depressive symptoms in late life: The importance of declining health and increasing disability. *Journal of Community Health* 15: 93–104.

LaPlante, M. P. 1991. The demographics of disability. *Milbank Quarterly* 2(55): 55–77.

———. 1998. Recent trends in disability in the U.S. Paper presented at the Annual Meeting of the American Society on Aging, San Francisco.

LaPlante, M. P., G. E. Hendershot, and A. J. Moss. 1997. The prevalence of need for assistive technology devices and home accessibility features. *Technology and Aging* 6: 17–28.

Large, T. 1982. Effects of attitudes upon the blind: A reexamination. *Journal of Rehabilitation* 48: 33–34, 45.

Lawton, M. P., E. M. Brody, and A. R. Saperstein. 1990. Social behavior and environmental issues. In S. J. Brody and L. G. Pawlson (eds.), *Aging and rehabilitation II: The state of the pratice,* 139–49.

Lazarus, R. S. and S. Folkman. 1984. *Stress, appraisal, and coping.* New York: Springer.

Lebowitz, B. D. 1996. Diagnosis and treatment of depression in late life: An overview of the NIMH Consensus Statement. *American Journal of Geriatric Psychiatry* 4(4) (Supplement 1): S3–S4.

Leinhaas, M. and N. J. Hedstrom. 1994. Low vision: How to assess and treat its emotional impact. *Geriatrics* 49: 53–59.

AMY HOROWITZ

124 AMY HOROWITZ

Lovett, S. B. 1988. Adaptation to vision loss: A cognitive/behavioral perspective. *Journal of Vision Rehabilitation* 2(3): 29–35.

Manton, K. G. 1988. A longitudinal study of functional change and mortality in the United States. *Journal of Gerontology: Social Sciences* 43(5): S153–S161.

Manton, K. G., L. S. Corder, and E. Stallard. 1993. Estimates of change in chronic disability and impairment incidence and prevalence rates in the U.S. elderly population from 1982, 1984, and 1989 National Long-Term Care Survey. *Journal of Gerontology: Social Sciences* 48(4): S153–S166.

———. 1997. Chronic disability trends in elderly United States populations: 1982–1994. *Proceedings of the National Academy of Sciences (USA)* 94: 2593–98.

McDaniel, J. W. 1976. *Physical disability and human behavior.* 2d ed. New York: Pergamon.

McNeil, J. M. 1993. *Americans with disabilities: 1991–92.* Washington, D.C.: U.S. Department of Commerce, Bureau of the Census.

McNett, S.C. 1987. Social support, threat and coping responses and effectiveness in the functionally disabled. *Nursing Research* 36: 98–103.

Meeks, S., L. L. Cartensen, B. F. Tamsky, T. L. Wright, and D. Pellegrini. 1989. Age differences in coping: Does less mean worse? *International Journal of Aging and Human Development* 28: 127–40.

Mengee, M., R. Connis, M. Gordon, S. Herman, and T. Taylor. 1990. The relationship of family dynamics/social support to patient functioning in IDDM patients in intensive insulin therapy. *Diabetes Research and Clinical Practice* 9: 149–62.

Monbeck, M. E. 1975. *The meaning of blindness.* Bloomington and London: Indiana University Press.

Morgan, D. L. 1998. Facts and figures about the baby boom. *Generations* 22: 10–15.

Morrison, M. 1982. *The first steps: How to help people who are losing their sight.* Palo Alto, Calif.: Peninsula Center for the Blind.

National Society for the Prevention of Blindness. 1984. Survey '84: Attitudes towards blindness prevention. *Sight-Saving* 53: 14–17.

Newsom, J. T. and R. Schulz. 1998. Caregiving from the recipient's perspective: Negative reactions to being helped. *Health Psychology* 17: 172–81.

NIH Consensus Development Panel on Depression in Late Life. 1992. Diagnosis and treatment of depression in late life. *Journal of the American Medical Association* 268: 1018–24.

Noelker, L. S. and S. W. Poulshock. 1982. *The effects on families of caring for impaired elderly in residence.* Final report submitted to the Administration on Aging, Cleveland, Ohio: Margaret Blenkner Research Center for Family Studies/Benjamin Rose Institute.

Oakes, T. W., J. R. Ward, R. M. Grey et al. 1970. Family expectation and arthritis patient compliance to a hand-resting splint regimen. *Journal of Chronic Diseases* 22: 757–64.

Osterweil, D. 1990. Geriatric rehabilitation in the long-term care institutional setting. In B. Kemp, K. Brummel-Smith, and J. W. Ramsdell (eds.), *Geriatric Rehablilitation*, 347–56.

Parmelee, P. A., I. R. Katz, and M. P. Lawton. 1992. Incidence of depression in long-term care settings. *Journal of Gerontology: Medical Sciences* 46: M189–M196.

Plopper, M. 1990. Evaluation and treatment of depression. In B. Kemp, K. Brummel-Smith, and J. W. Ramsdell (eds.), *Geriatric rehabilitation*, 253–64.

Pommier, B. E. 1992. Factors affecting learning in a coronary artery disease rehabilitation class. *Rehabilitation Nursing* 17: 64–67.

Pruchno, R. A., C. J. Burant, and N. D. Peters. 1997. Understanding the well-being of care receivers. *The Gerontologist* 37(1): 102–109.

Pruchno, R. A., M. H. Kleban, J. E. Michaels, and N. P. Dempsey. 1990. Mental and physical health of caregiving spouses: Development of a causal model. *Journal of Gerontology: Psychological Sciences* 45(5): 192–99.

Ringering, L. and P. Amaral. 1988. The elderly low-vision client: Treatment issues. *Journal of Vision Rehabilitation* 2(3): 53–60.

Roberto, K. A. 1992. Elderly women with hip fractures: Functional and psychosocial correlates of recovery. *Journal of Women and Aging* 4(1): 3–20.

Ruberman, W., E. Weinblatt, J. Goldberg, and B. S. Chaudhary. 1984. Psychosocial influences on mortality after myocardial infarction. *New England Journal of Medicine* 311(9): 552–59.

Salive, M. E., J. Guralnik, R. J. Glynn, W. Christen, R. B. Wallace, and A. M. Ostfeld. 1994. Association of visual impairment with mobility and physical function. *Journal of the American Geriatrics Society* 42: 287–92.

Schulz, R., P. Visintainer, and G. M. Williamson. 1990. Psychiatric and physical morbidity effects of caregiving. *Journal of Gerontology: Psychological Sciences* 45(5): 181–91.

Sheets, D. J., L. A. Wray, and F. M. Torres-Gil. 1993. Geriatric rehabilitation: Linking aging, health, and disability policy. *Topics in Geriatric Rehabilitation* 9: 1–17.

Shenkel, R., J. Rogers, G. Perfeito, and R. Levin. 1985–86. Importance of "significant others" in predicting cooperation with diabetic regression. *Journal of Psychiatry in Medicine* 15(2): 149–55.

Silverstone, B. M. 1984. Social aspects of rehabilitation. In T. F. Williams (ed.), *Rehabilitation in the aging*, 59–79.

———. 1998. A grain of salt. Paper presented at the Annual Meeting of the American Society on Aging, San Francisco.

Smart, J. F. and D. W. Smart. 1997. The racial/ethnic demography of disability. *Journal of Rehabilitation* 63: 10–21.

Smith, V. J. and C. M. Messikomer. 1988. A role for the family in geriatric rehabilitation. *Topics in Geriatric Rehabilitation* 4: 8–15.

Stahl, S. and M. Potts. 1985. Social support and chronic disease: A propositional inventory. In W. Peterson and J. Quadagno (eds.), *Social bonds in later life: Aging and interdependence*, 305–323. Newbury Park, Calif.: Sage.

Stone, R., G. L. Cafferata, and J. Sangl. 1987. Caregivers of the frail elderly: A national profile. *The Gerontologist* 27(5): 616–26.

Thomas, T. and R. Stevens. 1974. Social effects of fracture of the femur. *British Medical Journal* 3: 456–58.

Thompson, J. R., J. M. Gibson, and C. Jagger. 1989. The association between impairment and mortality in elderly people. *Age and Ageing* 18: 83–88.

Thompson, S. C., A. Sobolew-Shubin, M. A. Graham, and A. S. Janigian. 1989. Psychosocial adjustment following a stroke. *Social Science and Medicine* 28(3): 239–47.

Torres-Gil, F. 1998. The future of aging and disability policy in the new millennium. Paper presented at the Annual Meeting of the American Society on Aging, San Francisco.

Torres-Gil, F. M. and L. A. Wray. 1993. Funding and policies affecting geriatric rehabilitation. *Clinics in Geriatric Medicine* 9: 831–40.

Turner, R. J. and S. Noh. 1988. Physical disability and depression. *Journal of Health and Social Behavior* 29: 23–37.

U.S. Bureau of the Census. 1992. *The Asian and Pacific Islander population in the United States: March 1991 and 1990*. Current Population Reports, P20–459. Washington, D.C.: GPO.

U.S. Department of Education, National Institute on Disability and Rehabilitation Research. 1992. *Disability statistics abstract no. 4*. Washington, D.C.: GPO.

Versluys, H. P. 1980. Physical rehabilitation and family dynamics. *Rehabilitation Literature* 41: 58–65.

Warren, M. and J. Lampert. 1994. Considerations in addressing the daily living needs in older persons with low vision. *Ophthalmology Clinics of North America* 7(2): 187–95.

Weinberger, M. 1980. Social and psychological consequences of legitimating a hearing impairment. *Social Science and Medicine* 14: 213–22.

Wells, K. B., A. Stewart, R. D. Hays, A. Burnan, W. Rogers, M. Daniels, S. Berry, S. Greenfield, and J. Ware. 1989. The functioning and well-being of depressed patients: Results for the Medical Outcomes Study. *Journal of the American Medical Association* 37: 1122–26.

Williams, T. F. 1984. *Rehabilitation in the aging*. New York: Raven Press.

Youngblood, N. M. and J. Hines. 1992. The influence of the family's perception of disability on rehabilitation outcomes. *Rehabilitation Nursing* 17: 323–26.

6

Aging and Caregiving in Ethnocultural Families

Diverse Situations but Common Issues

NANCY GUBERMAN AND PIERRE MAHEU

Social workers working with elderly persons and their families, in particular those needing assistance with the activities of daily living, are directly confronted with questions of values, meanings, norms, and attitudes concerning such themes as sickness, dependency, care, family dynamics, and gender relations. We are often acutely aware of these questions when it comes to working with persons of ethnic origins different from our own. Indeed, social work intervention models in a context of ethnocultural[1] difference between practitioners and "clients" are under increasing scrutiny for their applicability. The various immigrant groups that have settled in major metropolitan areas of Canada and the United States since the beginning of the twentieth century are now facing aging populations in proportions similar to those of the majority groups. As well, due principally to family reunification policies, many immigrants accepted in the 1980s and 1990s were sixty and over. Some of them arrived in a state of frailty, many have become so over the years. Given the immigration patterns of both countries over the past half century, it is probably best to assume that the elderly are culturally and ethnically diverse.

Despite their ever-increasing numbers, we know very little about the elderly of minority ethnocultural groups. However, what *is* clear is that we can no longer conceptualize the North American elderly population as being a mainly homogeneous group. Elderly persons of Western European extraction are no longer the norm. Indeed, given the rate of the diversification of the elderly population, we feel the time is overdue for researching and theorizing in this area in order to develop and transform existing paradigms and programs that are too often based on a perception of a homogeneous elderly population.

In this context, social workers—indeed all practitioners—are confronted with the challenge of how to open up their horizons and develop practice approaches that reflect sensitivity to ethnocultural differences. Training sessions now abound in the health and social service sectors to teach practitioners the knowledge and skills for understanding and appreciating differences. These efforts are to be lauded in making services more culturally adapted to the diversity of populations using them, but there are limitations to approaches that focus on the development of cultural competency (Devore & Schlesinger 1987; Ivey, Ivey & Simek-Morgan 1997; Jenkins 1988). Research on ethnicity and aging has not kept pace with these developments among practitioners. Until 1990, the majority of work available came mostly from the United States, was often limited to comparing blacks and Hispanophones to white Americans in large-scale surveys, and thus had limited applicability outside the States.

What literature does exist on ethnocultural groups, particularly with regard to social work practice with members of these groups, discusses ethnicity principally through the prism of understanding cultural difference—that is, how people from ethnocultural minorities differ from those of the majority group. It should be noted, on the one hand, that the prism of difference was an important angle to develop in the face of dominant assimilationist positions which suggested that immigrants and second- and third-generation citizens of other than European descent should simply adapt and become like "one of us" ("us," of course, generally meaning of white Western European descent). Invaluable work was thus undertaken on bringing to light ethno-specificities in the areas of aging, health, family practices, and service utilization to inform and transform practice (Bennett 1986; Cohen-Emérique 1993; Devore & Schlesinger 1987; Kadushin 1983). On the other hand, in our quest to show openness to diversity, to be sensitive to difference, is there not the danger of situating members of minority ethnocultural groups principally as *other*, rather than simply as *another*—that is, someone who, while different, has many things in common with "us"? It is this theme of differences and similarities and the place of ethnocultural groups in our understanding of some of the major issues facing gerontological social work practice which will provide the backbone of this chapter. While clearly refuting an assimilationist perspective, we would like to raise the question of the risks inherent in a position that emphasizes only differences, notably that of the ghettoization of health and social services to minority ethnocultural groups.

How can we understand ethnicity from a perspective that balances differences and similarities? To answer this question, we will refer to a body of research which we have carried out for more than ten years (Guberman & Maheu 1997; Guberman, Maheu & Maillé 1991, 1993). In the late 1980s and early 1990s, we coauthored several studies on family caregiving involving mostly respondents of the majority ethnocultural group. Of course, in Quebec we are refering to French-Canadians. Our research examined the nature of caregiving work, gender relations in caregiving, the formal and informal supports available to caregivers, caregivers' motives for assuming care, and the arrangements put into place by caregivers who combine caregiving and employment. Several key issues emerged from this research, including those around family availability and competency to assume caregiving to highly dependent elder relatives, women's specific place in caregiving, service accessibility, and the impacts of caregiving on women's employment and long-term financial situations.

The impetus for the research on which this chapter is based came from our interest in understanding practices and issues of family caregiving in minority ethnocultural groups to see if they were significantly different from the findings of our previous research, findings that generally were corroborated by most North American studies on the subject. This led us to study caregiving in Haitian and Italian families, as well as help-seeking behaviors and relations to formal and informal support systems among Chinese elderly.

Methods

Our first study of minority ethnocultural families was aimed at developing a better understanding of their caregiving experience. Given that we wanted to grasp, to the extent possible, the complexities and nuances of this experience, we opted to use qualitative methods to collect our data. To answer our questions we needed to have access to people's lived experiences, to the meanings and the representations they give to their reality. Qualitative methods seem to offer researchers more opportunity to understand the multiple facets that define participants' reality, to grasp its complexity and its movement in a dynamic fashion (Maxwell 1996; Patton 1990; Strauss & Corbin 1990).

Our main method of data collection was semistructured interviews with primary caregivers of frail elderly persons (Kvale 1996; Mason 1996). This type of interview allows participants the freedom to interpret the research question from their own perspective and to put emphasis on those themes or events which are of particular importance for them. As well, to a certain extent, our approach situates respondents as coinvestigators, as we ask them to share with us their analyses of the phenomenon being studied. We thus ask them not only to describe their experience but also to try and make sense of it.

Interviews were held in the homes of caregivers and lasted from one to two hours. We also organized focus groups both with home care practitioners working with ethnocultural minority families and with elderly persons themselves.

Sampling

Based on demographic data and statistics on the recent immigration patterns of persons sixty and older, and after verifying that the problem of care to frail elderly existed in these groups, we focused in on the Italian and Haitian communities. Besides responding to the aforementioned criteria, we were motivated in our choice of these groups by their contrasting characteristics in the following areas:

1. The length of time the groups have been established: Italians, having immigrated massively in the postwar period, represent the wave of European immigration of the 1950s, while Haitians in many ways reflect the immigrant groups of the 1980s and 1990s.

2. Integration problems: In terms of linguistic assimilation, older Italians are among the least-assimilated groups, with one third of Italian seniors speaking neither English nor French. Phenotypic visibility also plays a role in integration, and thus we chose Haitians as a visible minority.

3. Location: These two groups have largely settled in the same neighborhoods of the city, so they are served by the same CLSC (our local health and social service agencies, which are publically mandated to provide frontline services, including home care).

4. Degree of community organization: Italians, having been established for much longer, have a large network of associations and community groups offering services to their community. The social networks of Haitian groups are much more fragmented and limited.

Families were contacted in various ways. Several were referred by the local health and social service centers, others by local community groups. But most, particularly in the Haitian community, were recruited through word of mouth and introductions by a third party. In all we met with forty-nine caregivers from twenty-two Italian and twenty Haitian families. As we developed the sample, we tried to diversify the situations of the caregivers for characteristics such as their relation to the elderly person, age, education level, socioeconomic conditions, and employment as well as taking into account the length of residence of the elderly person in Canada. In this way we endeavored to seek out what Strauss (1987) calls the universe of possibilities.

When we were well into this study, we were invited by a downtown local health and social service center (CLSC) to collaborate on another project to study the problem-solving and help-seeking behaviors of Chinese elderly persons living in Montreal's Chinatown. Given the exploratory nature of the project and once again because we wished to grasp the complexity of the reality being studied, we opted for semistructured individual and group interviews with Chinese elders and focus groups with practitioners working with Chinese seniors. In all, we interviewed thirty-two Chinese seniors, including six couples, as to their personal pattern of help-seeking behavior. We also met with the nine-member board of administration of a Chinese seniors' organization to talk about the general problem-solving patterns of Chinese elders. Again, we tried to vary the sample so as to capture a diversity of situations in terms of age, marital status, gender, health status, socioeconomic conditions, level of education, type of housing, country of origin, languages spoken, religion, number of years in Canada, and the presence of family members.

The majority of the interviews were conducted by interviewers of the same ethnocultural and linguistic groups as the respondents (Italian, Creole, Mandarin, Cantonese, Toisan). They were transcribed and translated into French or English for analysis by the researchers.

Looking for Differences and Finding Similarities

Our departure point for both studies was to bring to light the differences in the three communities as to their caregiving practices and their relation to formal services. And, at the end of the research, we can affirm that there are indeed differences, based on varying values, norms, and experiences. But our major finding is that when you consider the overriding issues concerning family caregiving and service use, there are more similarities among all ethnocultural groups, including English and French-Canadians, than there are differences. Based on what we have seen in the three groups studied, we would advance the argument that when you look at care to frail elderly persons as a social issue, the analysis must go beyond cultures, individuals, families, and communities. Indeed, problems such as caregiver burden, the division of caregiving labor among family members, or service accessibility in a context of cutbacks and neofamilial ideology concerning the "proper" place for care, confront the majority of families faced with the needs of a frail or disabled elderly member.

As Blakemore and Boneham (1994) indicate, whether one emphasizes differences or similarities in assessing the needs of elders of minority groups depends on the level of generality at which such needs are defined. For example, elders of all groups may need help in food preparation. However, the specific foods to be prepared and their manner of preparation will differ from group to group and even within groups.

It is thus from a level of the general needs and conditions of elderly persons and their caregivers that this chapter will address some of the overriding issues facing elders, their families, and gerontological practitioners and attempt, on the basis of findings from our various studies, to demonstrate that elders and their families, no matter what their ethnocultural origin, are currently faced with many of the same problems and challenges. How these issues present themselves, how they are experienced, and the capacity of different sectors of the population to address the challenges and resolve the problems will depend on their social location in terms of class, race, ethnicity, and so on. At the end of the chapter we will draw out some of the implications of our position for future social work practice with elders of ethnocultural minorities and their families.

The areas of analysis which we will touch on are (1) the availability of families to care and the distribution of caregiving responsibilities among family members; (2) the nature of the caregiving responsibilities assumed by families; and (3) the question of access to formal support for frail elderly persons and their caregivers.

The Availability and Distribution of Caregiving Responsibilities

Studies in North America indicate that most people feel that the family should assume the major responsibility for providing help to its elderly members. In the three groups that we studied—Chinese, Italian, and Haitian—the stated value placed on the family as the main source of aid emerged even more explicitly than in our French-Canadian studies. As one Chinese senior explained: "Old people need to be looked after. Certainly this should be the responsibility of the children. We have a traditional saying, 'raise children to safeguard your old age,' because when you are old you cannot do anything and you expect your children to assist you." Or in the words of a Haitian caregiver: "The Haitian mentality considers that the family has to look after the mother or the grandmother. . . . In the Haitian mentality, even if you are married you live with your mother. You have to live with her, you have to take care of her." The importance of family values and family solidarity in the Italian community has been well documented (Carbone 1986; D'Abate & de Stephano 1986; Painchaud & Poulin 1983).

The cultural norm in all these groups is that elder care is family care, and there are normative pressures put on families by members of their community to reinforce appropriate behavior, as the following quotes from two caregivers of Italian origin illustrate.

> Children are obliged to care. Obliged precisely because, if not, they are subject to criticism . . . and this criticism is very, very important.

> For my mother it would be a dishonor to finish her days in a nursing home. It's as if in her head she would be insulting us, her children, because we weren't able to care for her and people would criticize us.

In short, the three ethnocultural groups of our studies share the same value regarding family care to elderly members that is dominant in North America, but probably adhere to it even more strongly. Likewise, elderly family members have very high expectations of being taken care of by their children. Of course, adherence to strong family values and dependency on family members must be situated in a context where, for many immigrants and people from minority groups, the family is the first line of defense both in maintaining their self-identitiy and in protecting them from the structural racism or ethnocentrism inherent in most dominant institutions and practices.

We, as researchers and practitioners, are very aware of ethnocultural groups' adherence to strong family values and norms. In fact, when we think about families from ethnocultural groups, what often comes to mind is a somewhat folkloric image of the large extended family where everybody chips in and helps out, where values and norms concerning filial piety and venerated elders dominate. It is important to ask elderly people and family caregivers to what extent our ideas about family solidarity represent reality. To what extent do these families meet the expectations of their elderly members?

Although our analysis is developed from a large body of research, both our own and that of others, we should point out that the nature of the samples used in ethnocultural studies might limit the degree to which one can generalize about family availability. In the work reported here it is important to remember that we did not interview comparable groups of Chinese, Italian, and Haitian respondents. In the case of the Italian and Haitian sample, we met with caregivers (that is, those members of the family assuming caregiving responsibilities). We did not meet with other family members or with families who had refused to assume care. The majority of Chinese elders we interviewed had moved out of their children's homes and were living on their own in Chinatown. We met with only a small number coresiding with their family. Nevertheless, we believe our findings are important for the reality which they do reveal.

The thirty-two Chinese elders with whom we met were very loquacious about the problems and limits that confront them when they turn to their families for help. Many of the interviews reveal an important gap between seniors' values and the aid available from their families, especially their children and grandchildren. In fact, the help received appears negligible when compared to their expressed expectations that all help should come from family.

> When I was ill, I was alone. My daughter had to go to work and could not take care of me. . . . Sometimes when I was in great pain, I wanted to phone emergency, but I didn't know how to call them. Even at the hospital, they will ask for your family members. But my daughter says: "I can't take care of you, I have to go to work to earn a living." She is a widow and the sole support for the family.

> I have two daughters here. The first one has two children and she doesn't have time for me. On the weekend she stops by for a short time and does my grocery shopping for me. The other daughter works and she also has a family. . . . My other children who live elsewhere phone me, but not regularly. Everybody is busy, they aren't available. My eldest daughter has a store, my sons have businesses. The grandchildren are in school. Everybody has to work. No one is available to visit me.

> When I'm feeling lonely I think that even though I have so many children it doesn't do me any good. They venerate me and are kind. But when I'm lonely I get angry that they aren't available for me.

Giving voice to the elders themselves revealed that the majority of Chinese seniors we interviewed were getting little or no direct help from family members. This situation can be explained by several factors. Many elders have moved far from their families and some have no family members still in Montreal. In some cases, the lack of linguistic and cultural competency on the part of other family members means that they cannot help elders to mobilize and mediate with mainstream resources. As well, some elders spoke to us of intergenerational and interpersonal conflicts with children and grandchildren which led to their moving to Chinatown. These, combined with changing values that come with immigration to North America, result in elders losing their venerated status and children loosening their attachment to traditional norms of filial piety. This has led to a situation where many elders cannot count on their families. Finally, the existence of a Chinatown that offers a small homogeneous neighborhood where seniors can function fairly autonomously changes the nature of their relationship to their children. We did not meet with a comparable sample of Italian and Haitian elders living on their own. We would postulate that there are a certain number who are not receiving help from their families. One Haitian respondent told us the story of her cousin who had been institutionalized because her daughter, a single working mother with two young children, refused to have her mother move in, and indeed rarely visited her. Undoubtedly, there are others. However, as stated, we met with family members offering care. This does not mean that the question of family availability for care was not an issue in Italian and Haitian families—many members were, in fact, not involved in caregiving activities. The question of availability has thus to be posed in terms of how caregiving responsibilites are shared among family members. On that level our findings corroborate the findings of other caregiver studies in North America (Cantor 1983; Sangl 1985). In the vast majority of the forty-two families studied, one family member or at most two assume primary caregiving responsibilities. The involvement of three or more family members is the exception, not the rule.

Women's Specific Responsibility for Care

Not surprisingly, women were the primary caregivers in the same proportion we find in all North American research, that is, from 70 to 80 percent (Cantor 1983; Johnson & Catalano 1983; Stone, Cafferata & Sangl 1987). Carla is of Italian origin. She is married, has adult children, six brothers and sisters, and cares for her ninety-year-old mother. She is very eloquent about her situation.

> I'm alone, I'm sixty-two and I'm sick. I have no more strength and I have pains everywhere. I can't do it anymore. I have no one to help me. I've

cared for my mother for twenty-five years. I'm alone to do all the work.
If one day I fall sick and am bedridden, who will look after her, who can
I call? That's the problem, that's my problem.

Carla's situation was, unfortunately, not atypical in our study. A home care
practitioner working with Italian families stated in a group interview:

> When you talk about attachment to the family, it's true that they're all
> there for marriages, baptisms, everybody. But when it's a question of sick-
> ness or death, what I've seen is that it's not everyone who's around. It's al-
> ways one person who cares for the elderly. Some families might share the
> work with the elder going two months to one home and two months to
> another. But what I see as today's tendency is that when you want the
> family or the collectivity to participate, this one can't, she works, that one
> has children or this or that. And you know what, no one wants to get in-
> volved. . . . As soon as someone is ill—oops! There's just one person to
> assume the care—the daughter, the daughter-in-law, or the son. The fam-
> ily is no longer around, it's completely disappeared.

Our findings thus lead us to the conclusion that, despite their explicit family value systems and cultural norms, in practice many ethnocultural families cannot provide the daily care required by their frail elderly members.
These Canadian findings corroborate similar results of U.S. studies which
question the assumption that minority families are more available to their
elderly members (Cantor & Little 1985; Mutran 1985; Sokolovsky 1985). As
Gratton and Wilson state, "Do not assume that a familialist culture among
minorities permits reduction in the provision of services" (1988:88). As well,
in the three groups studied, and in concordance with our findings concerning French-Canadian families, it is not the family unit that assumes the
care, but one or two family members, and these family members are most
likely to be women.

Women's role and place in the family are often seen as an element of cultural and ethno-specific values and practices which must be respected as such
when dealing with minority families. We would question this analysis, given
the universality of women's assignment to the domestic sphere and to caring
activities. This issue cannot be reduced to cultural values, but must be looked
at from the perspective of gender and class relations and the sexual division of
labor in all societies.

Issues of Family Availability and Sharing of Caregiving

Coming back to the question of family availability, how can we explain this disparity between values and practice in the three groups? Our studies point to a number of structural factors such as families' living conditions, children's lack of linguistic and cultural competency, intergenerational or family problems, and gender relations, as well as cultural factors such as changing values in the second and third generations, to explain this gap regarding the status of elderly persons and the duties and obligations of children.

Apart from the question of linguistic competency, structural factors invoked by respondents from the three groups point to the changing context and conditions of all families. Under the category of living conditions, we find geographical distance, lack of availability because of salaried work and other family obligations, or illness of potential carers—elements that are common to all ethnocultural groups. Intergenerational and family conflicts around family roles, inheritances, and divorce, which are also invoked, are certainly not specific to ethnocultural minorities. Nor are gender relations and the abdication of many men from caregiving responsibilities.

Thus, despite a more explicit attachment to family values, the elderly of the three ethnocultural groups and their caregivers are confronted with many of the same issues regarding the reality of family availability which our study of French-Canadian caregivers revealed, and which are undoubtedly common to the majority of families in North America:

- the myth of family solidarity
- the inequitable division of caregiving tasks among family members and between men and women
- living conditions that are irreconcilable with caregiving, including size of housing units, geographic distance and, notably, women's labor market participation

Indeed, families, including families of minority groups living in Canada or other Western countries, have undergone profound changes, including the transformation of traditional roles, integration of women with minor children into the workforce, changes in family structures, and so on. These structural changes, when associated with socioeconomic conditions such as poverty, small housing units, and increased life expectancy of seniors with chronic health conditions, place the ethnocultural elderly in the same position of vulnerability with regard to family support as elders of the majority groups. Likewise, women in the minority ethnocultural communities face the same gendered expectations as those of the majority in terms of caregiving work.

The Nature of Family Caregiving

The second area we would like to examine is that of the nature of the caregiving activities when the family—or should we say, a female family member—does assume care. On the one hand, we found that the health status and characteristics of the elderly being cared for in all our studies were similar. Many were over eighty years of age, and the majority were confronted with major physical and/or mental deterioration leading to such problems as confusion, memory loss, disorientation, loss of hearing and sight, paralysis, incontinence, reduced mobility, and respiratory difficulties.

On the other hand, with some minor differences, our studies show that caregiving to a frail elderly relative involved the same activities and responsibilities no matter what the ethnic origin of the family. Care for a frail elderly person, particularly in the case of severe dependency, is characterized by its complexity and a high degree of specialization. It involves a wide variety of tasks, competencies, and abilities which closely resemble those accomplished by paid professional workers in the health care system, work for which they have been trained for several years. Among other things, increasingly, family caregiving requires specialized medical knowledge; particular abilities and skills with regard to treating illness; knowledge of the health and welfare system; solid skills in management, coordination, and negotiation. Depending on the level of dependency of the frail elder, caregiving also requires a major investment in terms of time and energy and a high level of commitment.

Our studies have led us to subdivide the work of caregiving into three major categories: the tasks associated with hands-on care and assistance, the tasks associated with the mobilization and coordination of services and resources, and the tasks associated with the organization of care and the juggling of care demands with those of the other life spheres. Table 6.1 presents the organization of these categories.

As Glazer (1990) has pointed out: "[Women's] unpaid labor has changed from housekeeping and minor nursing to encompass the administration and monitoring of complex nursing-medical regimens once done only in acute care hospitals by physicians or registered nurses and specialists" (480)

Table 6.1   Tasks of Family Caregiving

1. Tasks associated with hands-on care and assistance

Nursing-medical care (administrating medication, controlling for effects)
Personal care (feeding, dressing, bathing, mobility)
Emotional and educational work (support, counsel, motivate, reassure, teach)
Support in organizing activities of daily life (housework, shopping, financial aid)
Surveillance/monitoring (supervision)

2. Tasks associated with the mobilization and coordination of services and resources

Identification and mobilization of services and resources
Mediation between the dependent person and services and resources
Management of services and resources and their integration within the context of the family
Coordination of the different services, resources, and actors (family members and outside help)

3. Tasks associated with the organization of care and the juggling of care demands with those of the other life spheres

Assuming the responsibility for the planning and accomplishment of all the caregiving work
Setting up of accommodations aimed at maintaining a balance between caregiving demands and those from professional, family, and personal life spheres

and "family caregivers 'practice' nursing and medicine, monitoring patients for everything from reactions to change in medication to medical crises requiring emergency readmission. Women use high-tech equipment to deliver treatments for acute and chronic conditions and to treat systemic infection and cancer. They supervise exercises and give mechanical relief to patients with breathing disorders, feed by tubes those unable to take food orally or digest normally, give intramuscular injections and more tricky intravenous injections, and monitor patients after antibiotic and chemotherapy treatments" (488). To these medical and nursing tasks, we would add all the work involved in helping the care-receiver accomplish personal care tasks (eating, dressing, bathing, washing, toileting), giving emotional and educational support (keeping company, listening, counseling, motivating, controlling behavior, crisis intervention), organizing activities of daily life (shopping, housework, banking, and so forth), and assuring continual preventive surveillance.

Beyond the Work: The Meaning of Care in Haitian Families

In terms of direct care activities, distinctive ethno-specific features emerged at the level of physical care and surveillance activities, in particular among Haitian caregivers. The attention they give to bathing and grooming goes beyond assuring simple personal hygiene, and these activities are accomplished even for persons who are in apparently good physical health. When elderly relatives are hospitalized or institutionalized, Haitian family caregivers tend to assure their toileting, bathing, and grooming. It is important to situate these activities within Haitian cultural codes that give specific meaning to such activities.

First, acts such as bathing and massages are part of rituals which are seen as having purifying, curative, and regenerating functions (when one is clean one is almost cured); they are thus seen as being physically and psychologically therapeutic. Second, physical care is also seen as being a form of communication expressing affection for the other person and a desire to please him or her. Haitians will administer massages and baths with special oils the way people from other cultures will bring chocolates or flowers. It's a way of saying "I care." Finally, when Haitian family members assume these activities in hospitals and institutions, it can also be a way of trying to help their elderly relatives overcome adaptation problems.

Surveillance tasks also seem to have particular meaning for Haitian families. Caregivers spoke to us using terms like prudence and thoughtfulness and even referred to a certain tendency to overprotect their elderly. These attitudes translate into forms of monitoring. Caregivers are extremely reluctant to leave elders alone no matter what their degree of autonomy. Elders must be constantly watched. In the case of hospitalization or institutionalization, caregivers assure constant control over the situation through regular visits and verifications. Haitians, our respondents told us, are socialized to respect their elders. One must be constantly preoccupied with the elder's welfare, to the point of being able to respond to his or her desires before they are even expressed.

To understand these actions, one must take into account the meaning of aging in the Haitian culture, the situation of increased dependency of Haitian elderly immigrants in a new context, and the lack of trust many Haitians have with regard to formal services. Aging in the Haitian culture is closely associated with a certain dependency and represents a state of vulnerability and fragility which requires constant attention and monitoring. In Haiti, we were told, elderly persons are never left alone. To do so is to neglect or abandon them. And given the state of health services in Haiti, a family member is never left alone in the hospital. Given the linguistic and cultural barriers of the majority of Haitian elders, this form of dependency reinforces the forestated attitude, that is, the need to assure constant presence. Finally, visits by Haitian family members to the hospital are not only aimed at monitoring the elders physical well-being, they also serve the purpose of assuring the quality of care. Between the lines, one can hear the fear of many caregivers that their elder will be neglected or even abused, a certain expectation that they will be confronted with racist attitudes. This inability to trust the system puts an additional burden on many minority caregivers who must be constantly present to prevent possible racist abuse. Thus, cultural sensitivity is important in understanding the meanings and significations behind certain behaviors and attitudes. However, this sensitivity must be situated within a context of a more general understanding of the common elements which compose caregiving work.

Mobilizing, Coordinating, and Juggling

In addition to these hands-on and emotional caregiving tasks, our research, in line with that of others (Archbold 1980; Horowitz 1985; Stephens & Christianson 1986), has led us to identify two other vital areas of labor that are less obvious in the evaluation of what family caregiving entails: *mobilization and coordination of services and resources* and *juggling to maintain a balance between caregiving demands and other aspects of life*. With regard to the first set of tasks, the fragmented pattern of the provision of services means that caregivers must often turn to a variety of institutions and professionals. One must choose between possible alternatives, combine a variety of resources, and adjust their services to the individual needs of the care-receiver, which must be previously assessed by the caregiver. The caregiver must try to set up a somewhat standardized routine and offer, herself, those services which are not available elsewhere. Caregivers must also monitor and coordinate the work of the various professional and home care personnel passing through the home, assure the quality and continuation of service, intervene if there are problems, defend the elderly person's right to service when necessary, and so forth. These tasks of mobilizing and coordinating are extremely demanding and time-consuming, although rarely considered in agency evaluations of caregiver burden. When they are performed by professionals, they are clearly recognized as elements of case management work. When similar work is done by families, it is hidden in the vague concept of informal care.

For all the groups we studied—Haitian, Italian, and Chinese—the area of mobilization with regard to public institutions and community services takes on particular importance given the linguistic and cultural barriers facing elderly persons who speak neither French nor English, have almost no knowledge of existing services, and even less knowledge of how to access them. The role of linguistic and cultural interpreter is thus very central for most caregivers. As well, these problems are compounded by the fact that caregivers have to grapple with an array of institutional practices that exclude them because they are based on the perceived realities of only one cultural group, the dominant one.

The third series of tasks are those associated with the work of *juggling* to maintain a balance between the often conflictual demands of the different aspects of one's life: caregiving, salaried employment, family life, and personal and social activities. The feminist literature on caregiving has documented this reality for most women. What we wish to highlight is the added complexity of factoring into the work-family balancing act, caregiving to a dependent adult. Contrary to hospitals, residences, or treatment centers, homes have not been specifically designed and organized on the basis of the needs of a person requiring assistance with the activities of daily living. They are not arranged accordingly and do not have appropriate equipment. Also, family members, including the primary caregiver, do not necessarily have the knowledge, skills, or the training to meet the specialized needs of severly ill or handicapped members. Finally, contrary to institutional care, family caregiving takes place in the context of daily family life. It comes as an addition to all the other demands of family living: salaried employment, family relationships, social activities. The demands of caregiving often conflict with those from other spheres of life. Everything must be readjusted, rearranged, to accommodate caregiving.

As a result of these conditions and given the often difficult, complex, and monopolizing tasks that must be assumed, caregivers of Haitian and Italian origin spoke to us of the same burden, the same feelings of overwork, physical and mental exhaustion, powerlessness, worry, and frustration as caregivers of the majority groups (George & Gwyther 1986: Guberman, Maheu & Maillé 1991; Hooyman & Gonyea 1995; Neal et al. 1993). Caregiving has the same negative impact on their personal, social, and family life—reduced time for oneself, one's mate, other family members and friends, often resulting in the social isolation so well documented among other caregivers. Caregiving also affects labor force participation in the same negative way.

Thus, regarding the nature of the responsibilities assumed by family caregivers, we would advance that the main issues are the same for all social groups:

- the lack of social recognition that caregiving is real work and that too often it involves labor which goes far beyond the responsibilities that one can normally expect from families

- the invisibility of much of the caregiving work and the trivialization of its complexity and the skills required for assuming it because it takes place within the context of the family and the home

- the risks for caregivers to their physical and mental health, to their labor force participation and, in the long term, to their financial security caused by the weight of responsibilities assumed and the conditions under which they are assured

Despite the specific meanings that different people give to the caregiving work they accomplish, the objective (and often the subjective) burdens are similar. Taking care of a frail or severely ill elderly family member is real labor, and because of its monopolizing, invasive nature, this labor can have serious short- and long-term consequences for the caregiver no matter what her ethnocultural origin.

Use of Formal Support

There is a fairly high degree of consensus in the literature regarding the fact that elders from minority ethnocultural groups have unequal access to formal services owing to linguistic barriers and their lack of knowledge of existing services (Bibeau 1987; Harel, McKinney & Williams 1987; Lebel 1986; Maclean & Bonar 1987). As well, we tend to consider that many of these groups have beliefs and attitudes which lead them to prefer other modes for resolving their problems, mainly turning to family and community members (Carbone 1986; McCallum & Shadbolt 1989).

In the case of the Chinese community, the literature suggests (Helley 1987; Zhang 1990) that this group is so culturally distant from the mainstream culture that its members have particular difficulty in accessing most aspects of North American dominant culture. This cultural distance prevents them from fully benefiting from the services to which they have a right. We began our study with Chinese elders with this idea in mind. At the end of our project, we were confronted with the reality that the Chinese elderly living in Chinatown were the most open to using public and community services of any of the groups we had studied, including French-Canadians, as long as they had linguistic access through interpreters or Chinese-speaking personnel.

Once they had accepted the reality that their families could not or would not provide the help they needed, our Chinese elderly respondents were fairly pragmatic. Despite their value system and their beliefs, these seniors showed a high degree of openness to alternative sources of aid, even non-Chinese ones. Our interviews revealed that public medical and home care services, community groups, family doctors, friends, and neighbors were used almost interchangeably as a substitute for family care, and that the choice of turning to one or the other is made on the basis of fairly pragmatic factors. These factors include knowledge of the resource, availability, accessibility and linguistic competency, geographic proximity, the seriousness of the problem, the perceived efficiency of the service, and the cost of the service. The affective quality of the relationship is also very important. It should not be forgotten that the majority of Chinese seniors we interviewed had moved out of their children's homes to live alone in Chinatown.

Italian and Haitian caregivers and their descriptions of the attitudes and behaviors of the seniors they cared for, as well as what the Haitian and Italian elderly persons who participated in our focus groups revealed, more closely fit the portrait described earlier of groups that have little access to public and community services. Specific factors in the history of the Chinese elders have led to their experiencing a somewhat different reality to that of Haitian and Italian elders. As noted earlier, these Chinese elders live in a specific community where they can have a fair degree of autonomy because culturally and linguistically adapted services and businesses are available. Chinatown offers a high level of what has been called "institutional completeness" (Breton 1964); that is, a well-developed network of institutions, offering services in parallel to mainstream institutions, are available. For instance, there are Chinese Golden Age groups, church-run medical clinics, community social service groups, as well as a Chinese geriatric hospital. Even the public health and social services, including the local health and social service clinic (CLSC) and the local hospital have Chinese-speaking staff and a history of serving Chinese clientele. Given the diversity of the downtown population, there is a higher tolerance of differences than is found in some of the CLSCs and hospitals in less heterogeneous areas, such as those where Haitian and Italian families live. Indeed, although somewhat concentrated in the northeast areas of the island of Montreal, there are no agencies that specifically serve the Haitian community, although there is an Italian hospital. This may explain some of the differences in the relationship each group has with services. Haitian and Italian caregivers that we interviewed rarely solicited formal services; they used them when referred. The use of outside help is an act born of necessity, something one must resign onself to, especially for Italian families. Thus, at the level of these groups' relation to formal services, a certain number of specificities linked to values, norms, attitudes, and past experience must be considered.

Major illness is a regular occurrence among elderly persons and thus, despite deep reservations, Haitian and Italian caregivers turn to hospitals for serious situations or when the level of care required goes beyond their competencies. From the hospital, many families are referred to the home care services of the CLSC. When they do accept services, these are mainly nursing and home-help services. The Italian families we interviewed also sent their elderly relatives to an Italian day center. We found that psychosocial services were seldom used and nursing home placement was seen as an ultimate and much-dreaded recourse to be used only when families could no longer provide the care required (although there is a waiting list for the sole Italian long-term hospital). However, home care use remains problematic and meets with much resistance from caregivers and elderly persons alike. Factors that explain the help-seeking patterns can be divided into two categories—cultural factors and structural factors.

The cultural factors are associated with modes of problem-solving. They refer to what anthropologists call the cultural representation of needs, and include values, perceptions, attitudes, past experience, linguistic and cultural compentency, and knowledge of available services. These factors determine the definition of the problem, the solutions one should use, and which problems are in the private or public domain.

Cultural Factors in Explaining Help-seeking Patterns

As previously mentioned, for the Italian and Haitian caregivers we met with, the use of public and community health and social services does not seem to be part of their problem-solving patterns. In this section we examine factors that might help us understand this behavior, including values, perceptions, past experience, linguistic and cultural abilities, and knowledge of services and how to access them.

Haitians come from a society where mutual help and reciprocity in the exchange of services are fundamental values because of the socioeconomic situation that makes these values essential for survival. Not surprisingly, the same cultural universe is reproduced upon immigration to a new country. When looking for assistance, Haitians place high value on turning to people they know and trust and with whom they can establish an affective bond.

That is why their social network and church brethren are highly valued as help providers.

One of the determinant factors in the help-seeking patterns of Italian caregivers is the tremendous importance placed on the family. Problems are seen as personal and private, to be resolved within the immediate family, thus the importance put on blood ties. Going outside the family is perceived as a transgression of traditional values.

The use of community services is tainted with mistrust and suspicion. Our respondents explained that, for Italians, the use of outside help from strangers is associated with shame and an admission of the family's inability to solve its own problems. Outside help is seen as an intrusion into the private domain. Italian seniors and caregivers have difficulty talking about their personal and family life with strangers and particularly in divulging their financial situation. As well, Italians spoke to us of their system of exchange of services, where to receive something from someone puts one in a situation of debt. One is obliged to give in return. It is unacceptable to be indebted to someone, including professionals.

For the Haitian respondents, mistrust and fear of anything related to government is very prevalent, and this mistrust exists even in relation to their own community. These feelings stem from their long experience of dictatorship and oppression in their country of origin, the existence of political factions in community groups and fear of reprisals, and the fear of how information given to a public organization will be used.

For both groups, values, perceptions, and past experiences with institutionalization lead them to equate placement with abandonment, abdication of one's duty, and a step toward an elder's death. These values and perceptions can be so strong, particularly for first-generation caregivers, that going outside the family for assistance is extremely guilt-inducing and can create numerous family problems. As well, there is a high refusal rate among the frail elderly when community services are suggested by the caregiver.

The first generation, those being cared for, have little experience with our health and social service structure. When they left their home countries, such services were not generally available and are not part of their reality. Often what contacts they have had with public services, such as immigration, have been negative.

Many people we interviewed were afraid of not being understood and thus not being adequately helped. It appears that beyond linguistic ability, cultural ability is also important. This refers to the ability or capacity to understand the cultural meaning of words, to interpret the other's message correctly, to accurately decode verbal and nonverbal messages and to grasp the sense of the words in their sociocultural context.

There is widespread lack of knowledge of services among ethnocultural minorities. A 1987 study of the Italian community in Montreal showed that 70 percent of respondents had never used a public service and that they didn't know of their existence. In our study, a number of caregivers didn't use home care services because they didn't know how to access them and explain their situation properly so as to fit admission criteria, and also because they didn't know how to use the help offered.

Structural Factors in Explaining Help-seeking Behavior

Structural factors, including those associated with the support networks themselves, as well as socioeconomic/political context and conditions, must also be considered. We have already dealt with the limits of the family network. In terms of community resources, when Italian and Haitian caregivers or Chinese elderly turn to these services, they are confronted with the same problems facing many families: that of insufficient human and material resources, as well as the difficulty of accessing appropriate services, all likely to be compounded by language barriers and lack of cultural sensitivity on the part of practitioners. Finally, factors related to the socioeconomic context include the immigration experience, the transformation of the family, sexual division of labor, generational differences, and social class and educational attainment levels. Cultural and structural factors cannot be disassociated. They are in constant interaction in the decision to use one or the other forms of help.

Once again, our various studies lead us to conclude that if there are many specific traits that influence use of formal and informal support among the three minority groups studied, there are equally many problems with regard to service use which confront frail elderly people and their caregivers in all ethnocultural groups—in particular, the lack of services or the adequacy of services with regard to families' needs as well as the incredible bureaucratic complexity of the service system. Moreover, cultural factors such as lack of knowledge of services or cultural barriers exist for many families of the majority groups, especially for poor families or those with little formal education. We are sure that the average Anglo- or Franco-Canadian is just as confused by professional jargon, administrative red tape, and the myriad professionals he or she has to deal with as any recent immigrant.

While we in no way want to downplay the necessity of understanding and dealing with cultural differences in values, attitudes, and behaviors that clearly hinder people in demanding services they have a right to, in the present context of cutbacks and downsizing, the problem resides less with the minority communities that do not access services than it does with the lack of services, along with a concerted effort by policymakers to transfer more and more caregiving responsibilities to the family. In terms of support to family caregivers, we would advance that this is a major issue confronting us all.

Implications for Practice with Ethnocultural Elders and Their Families

The above analysis leads us to conclude that, despite the very real and important specificities identified for each of the three groups, which must be seriously considered if we want to develop services to meet the needs of the changing profile of elderly persons in major metropolitan areas, the most serious issues to be addressed affect *all* frail elderly persons and their families. These are the issues associated with family reciprocity and solidarity, the gendered division of labor, current family conditions resulting from recent societal transformations, insufficient and inadequate community resources in conjunction with policies based on the assumption of family care.

These common issues force us to look beyond ethnocultural differences and to reflect on how to integrate ethnocultural groups into our understanding of caregiving dynamics and the resulting consequences for the people involved. As we have seen, across ethnocultural groups women assume most of the caregiving work, and they do so with little support from other family members or community agencies. It is they who have to juggle their caregiving responsibilities with the demands of their family life, their personal and social activities, and, in the case of many caregivers, their employment. This laborious act of juggling is stressfully intensive and demanding and makes almost irreconcilable demands on the caregiver's time and presence. Further, it is usually the women with the least resources who are most affected by having to juggle these nearly impossible schedules. In one study (Brody 1985), 28 percent of the nonemployed women had left the labor force to care for a disabled mother. Another American study, based on a national representative sample reports 11.6 percent of caregiver daughters who quit their jobs to assume care, while 28 percent of caregivers who remained in the workforce reduced their working hours (Stone, Cafferata & Sangl 1987). Brody and her collaborators (Brody et al. 1987) identify women with lower family incomes who hold jobs of lower status as those most likely to leave the workforce to assume caring work. Unfortunately, these are too often the women who can least afford the drop in income, both in the short term and in the long term, due to the impact on their pensions. Women of minority ethnocultural groups too often find themselves in less skilled, low-paying jobs, owing to the underlying racism that structures much of the labor market. The consequences of caregiving on workplace participation can thus not be reduced to elements of cultural difference; they must be seen also as the result of race and ethnic relations which lead to the oppression of minority groups.

In the same way, barriers to accessing appropriate health and social services are not solely a question of ethnocultural difference. We have already mentioned the cultural barriers that many Anglo- or Franco-Canadians meet when trying to access social and health services. Massé (1995), for example, documents the important cultural distance that exists between poor people in Canada and representatives of the socio-medical professions. But somehow questions of meanings and values, of problem-solving patterns, are examined almost exclusively through the eyes of cultural diversity when we are dealing with ethnocultural minorities. Our work suggests that it is important for practitioners and researchers to pay close attention to these questions in all their practices. Sensitivity to cultural distance is just as important when dealing with the various subgroups of the majority ethnocultural groups as it is for minority groups.

Based on the analysis that emerges from our findings, it appears important to us that researchers and practitioners develop an approach that stresses not only the differences but also the common elements between minority ethnocultural groups and the majority population. This approach, while taking into account cultural differences, recontextualizes them within their social, political, and economic environment. Too often researchers and practitioners have a tendency to overemphasize cultural factors to the detriment of considering other social and economic barriers facing old people and their families. A more structural model for understanding ethnicity, while incorporating elements of culture such as ethnic identification, history, values, beliefs, and language as important determinants of behavior and ways of thinking, would also highlight the importance of economic, social, political, and ideological factors as conditions that impede access to services and shape the attitudes and policies of the host society. We propose that the emphasis be placed on how the dialectical relations between ethnicity and these factors work themselves out in the specifics of our practice and service structures.

In short, our results invite health and social service practitioners and agencies to develop cultural competence, but this competence is far more than a tool kit of knowledge and skills to be called upon when the person you are working with is categorized as culturally different. Such an approach to cultural competency could lead to what Kaufert (1990) calls the "boxification" of culture, where culture is reduced to a giant matrix, a checklist of values, beliefs, and attitudes which one need only consult to understand how to deal with a person of a specific culture when confronted with a specific problem. Rather, the competency proposed here rests on an analysis which, while taking into account cultural differences, situates them within the socioeconomic context of the groups in question and within the larger picture of dominant social relations. As McCall, Tremblay, and Le Goff (1997) point out, the more practitioners get to know their clients, the more they look for explanations to their problems in the complex universe of relations and conditions which underlie their situation, and the more the explicative value of cultural differences disappears from their analysis: "We are less differentiated by our cultures of origin than we are united by the conditions in which we live: housing conditions, income inequality, health problems, aging, isolation, conjugal violence, family breakdown, despair in the face of layoffs" (McCall, Tremblay & Le Goff 1997:102; our translation).

It would appear to us that if we do not adopt a more structural approach, we run the risk of reducing problems confronting caregivers of minority ethnocultural groups to ethno-specific problems and of excluding these groups when considering fundamental issues and problems facing all old people and those who care for them. This could lead to "ethnicizing," to the point of ghettoizing, the social and health services offered to these groups, leading to what Massé (1995) calls a form of self-management of exclusion.

Note

1. Terminology with regard to ethnicity is the object of numerous debates within North American society. There are multiple definitions of concepts such as ethnicity, race, and nation which refer to various theoretical models. In this text, we have chosen to employ the term *ethnocultural groups* in contrast to the dominant Canadian government concept of cultural communities, to indicate that the differences between the various groups cannot be reduced to a question of culture but also include a number of characteristics which are often motives for discrimination, such as color and phenotypical traits. We define ethnocultural group as a group of individuals who have the following common characteristics: (1) language; (2) links

to a given territory, be it real or imaginary; (3) a culture of origin or one that has been reconstructed; (4) a certain awareness of belonging to what can be called "ethnicity" (Jacob 1994).

References

Archbold, P. G. 1980. Impact of parentcaring on middle-aged offspring. *Journal of Gerontological Nursing* 6(2): 78–85.

Bennett, J. M. 1986. Modes of cross-cultural training: Conceptualizing cross-cultural training as education. *International Journal of Intercultural Relations* 10(2): 117–34.

Bibeau, G. 1987. A la fois d'ici et d'ailleurs: Les communautes culturelles du Québec dans leurs rapports aux services sociaux et aux services de santé, avec la collaboration de J.-M. Vidal, J.-P. Dupuis et D. Bélanger, Québec. *Commission d'enquete sur les services de santé et les services sociaux* (Synthèse critique no 2). [From here and from elsewhere: The cultural communities of Quebec in their relations to the social and health services. *Inquiry Commission on Health and Social Services* (Critical synthesis no. 2.]

Blakemore, K. and M. Boneham. 1994. *Age, race, and ethnicity: A comparative approach.* Buckingham, U.K.: Open University Press.

Breton, R. 1964. Institutional completeness of ethnic communities and the personal relations of immigrants. *American Journal of Sociology* 70(2): 193–205.

Brody, E. M. 1985. Parent care as normative family stress. *The Gerontologist* 25(1): 19–29.

Brody, E. M., M. H. Kleben, P. T. Johnsen, C. Hoffman, and C. B. Schoonover. 1987. Work status and parent care: A comparison of four groups of women. *The Gerontologist* 27(2): 201–208.

Cantor, M. H. 1983. Strain among caregivers: A study of experience in the United States. *The Gerontologist* 23(6): 597–603.

Cantor, M. and V. Little. 1985. Aging and social care. In R. H. Binstock and E. Shanas (eds.), *Handbook of aging and the social sciences*, 745–81. 2d ed. New York: Van Nostrand Reinhold.

Carbone, A. 1986. A personal perspective on the Italian family system with treatment and intervention applications. *Intervention* 74: 56–60.

Cohen-Emérique, M. 1993. L'approche interculturelle dans le processus d'aide. *Santé mentale au Québec* 18(1): 71–92.

D'Abate, D. and J. de Stephano. 1986. Ethnicity and culture: Implications for the mental health professional. *Intervention* 74: 34–40.

Devore, W. and E. Schlesinger. 1987. *Ethnic-sensitive social work practice.* Columbus, Ohio: Merrill.

Gelfand, D. E. and C. M. Barresi (eds.). 1987. *Ethnic dimensions of aging.* Adulthood and Aging, no. 18. New York: Springer.

George, L. and L. P. Gwyther. 1986. Caregiver well-being: A multidimensional examination of family caregivers of demented adults. *The Gerontologist* 26(3):253–59.

Glazer, N. 1990. The home as workshop: Women as amateur nurses and medical care providers. *Gender and Society* 4(4): 479–99.

Gratton, B. and V. Wilson. 1988. Family-support systems and the minority elderly: A cautionary analysis. *Journal of Gerontological Social Work* 13(1–2): 81–93.

Guberman, N. and P. Maheu. 1997. *Les soins aux personnes âgées dans les familles italiennes et haïtiennes* [Caregiving to the elderly in Italian and Haitian families]. Montréal: Les Éditions du Remue-Ménage.

Guberman, N., P. Maheu, and C. Maillé. 1991. *Et si l'amour ne suffisait pas . . . : Femmes, familles, et adultes dépendants* [What if love is not enough . . . : Women, families, and dependent adults]. Montréal: Les Éditions du Remue-Ménage.

———. 1993. *Travail et soins aux proches dépendants* [Employment and care to dependent kin]. Montréal: Les Éditions du Remue-Ménage.

Harel, Z., E. McKinney, and M. Williams. 1987. Aging, ethnicity, and services: Empirical and theoretical perspectives. In D. E. Gelfand and C. M. Barresi (eds.), *Ethnic dimensions of aging*, 196–210.

Helley, D. 1987. *Les chinois à Montréal: 1877–1951.* Québec: Institut québécois de recherche sur la culture (IQRC).

Hooyman, Nancy R. and Judith Gonyea. 1995. *Feminist perspectives on family care: Policies for gender justice.* Thousand Oaks, Calif.: Sage.

Horowitz, A. 1985. Sons and daughters as caregivers to older parents: Differences in role performance and consequences. *The Gerontologist* 25(6): 612–17.

Ivey, A. E., M. B. Ivey, and L. Simek-Morgan. 1997. *Counselling and psychotherapy: A multicultural perspective.* Boston: Allyn and Bacon.

Jacob, A. 1994. *Politique de la gestion de la diversité a l'UQAM.* Montreal: Université du Québec à Montréal.

Jenkins, S. 1988. *Ethnic associations and the welfare state.* New York: Columbia University School of Social Work.

Johnson, C. L. and D. J. Catalano. 1983. A longitudinal study of family supports to frail elderly. *The Gerontologist* 23(6): 612–18.

Kaufert, P. A. 1990. The "box-ification" of culture: The role of the social scientist. *Santé—Culture—Health* 7(2–3): 139–48.

Lebel, B. 1986. Les relations entre les membres des communautés culturelles et les services sociaux et de santé [The relations between members of cultural communities and health and social services]. *Canadian Ethnic Studies/Études ethniques au Canada* 18(2): 79–89.

Kadushin, A. 1983. Cross-cultural interviewing: The social work interview. New York: Columbia University Press.

Kvale, S. 1996. *InterViews: An introduction to qualitative research interviewing.* Thousand Oaks, Calif.: Sage.

Maclean, M. J. and R. Bonar. 1987. Cooperative practice to overcome socially constructed hardship for ethnic elderly people. In D. E. Gelfand and C. M. Barresie (eds.), *Ethnic dimensions of aging*, 211–23.

Mason, J. 1996. *Qualitative researching.* Thousand Oaks, Calif.: Sage.

Massé, Raymond. 1995. *Culture et santé publique* [Culture and public health]. Montréal: Gaëtan Morin Éditeur.

Maxwell, J. A. 1996. *Qualitative research design: An interactive approach.* Thousand Oaks, Calif.: Sage.

McCall, C., L. Tremblay, and F. Le Goff. 1997. *Proximité et distance,* Montréal: Éditions Saint-Martin.

McCallum, J. and B. Shadbolt. 1989. Ethnicity and stress among older Australians. *Journal of Gerontology* 44(3): 589–96.

Mutran, E. 1985. Intergenerational family support among blacks and whites: Response to culture or to socioeconomic differences. *Journal of Gerontology* 40(3): 382–89.

Neal, M. B., N. J. Chapman, B. Ingersoll-Dayton, and A. C. Emlen. 1993. *Balancing work and caregiving for children, adults, and elders.* Newbury Park, Calif.: Sage.

Painchaud, C. and R. Poulin. 1983. Italianité, conflit linguistique et structure de pouvoir dans la communauté italo-québécoise. *Sociologie et Sociétes* 15(2): 89–104.

Patton, M. Q. 1990. *Qualitative evaluation and research methods.* 2d ed. Newbury Park, Calif.: Sage.

Sangl, J. 1985. The family-support system of the elderly. In R. J. Vogel and H. C. Palmer (eds.), *Long-term care: Perspectives from research and demonstration.* Rockville, Mass.: Aspen.

Sokolovsky, J. 1985. Ethnicity, culture, and aging: Do differences really make a difference? *Journal of Applied Gerontology* 4: 6–17.

Stephens, S. A. and J. B. Christianson. 1986. *Informal care of the elderly.* Toronto: Lexington Books.

Stone, R., G. L. Cafferata, and J. Sangl. 1987. Caregivers of the frail elderly: A national profile. *The Gerontologist* 27(5): 616–26.

Strauss, A. L. 1987. *Qualitative analysis for social scientists.* Cambridge: Cambridge University Press.

Strauss, A. and J. Corbin. 1990. *Basics of qualitative research: Grounded theory procedures and techniques.* Newbury Park, Calif.: Sage.

Zhang, J. D. 1990. Pour l'amélioration de l'accessibilité des services de santé et des services sociaux à la population âgée chinoise de Montreal [For improved accessibility to health and social services for Montreal's elderly Chinese population]. Essay submitted to l'École de service social de l'Université Laval, Québec.

7

Feminist Lessons from the Gray Market in Personal Care for the Elderly

So What If You Have to Spend Your Own Money?

SHARON M. KEIGHER

The question is, when you have the freedom to make choices, what do you do?
What are the choices that you make?
—Warren Beatty, movie star (quoted in Hirschberg 1998:22)

As the "mixed economy of welfare" has proliferated and market principles have permeated policies governing provision of in-home services to the elderly (Doty, Stone & Jackson 1997; Evers & Leichsenring 1994; Keigher 1997; Stone & Keigher 1994), a profound restructuring is occurring in regard to who benefits from social programs. Home care is one of many benefits now provided to middle-class, disabled, and frail elderly Americans with public revenues that were previously restricted to the destitute. On its face, this seems like a move toward universal entitlement, surely a positive development. Unfortunately, this "middle-classification" of government services is coming at the cost of abandoning an ever-larger array of critical safety-net provisions for those who are poor and experience gender and race inequities (Estes and Close 1997; Estes, Swan & Assoc. 1993; Gilbert 1995).

Certainly in the United States, as federal and state governments increase support for the middle class and start to underwrite some of the caring functions of the domestic domain (Ungerson 1997), it is learning to do so in an increasingly controllable, cost-effective, targeted, efficient, and local fashion. As Neysmith notes in chapter 1, today's neoliberal policy responses seek efficiencies through market forces in providing whole ranges of public goods. Personal care is idealized, and that which is decentralized and relegated to the

family and other informal caregivers is widely portrayed as being optimal for
and desired by people in need of care. Best of all, such care is "costless"—well,
at least to government. The data presented in this chapter indicate that this
facile presumption has profound implications for all women, but especially
for low-income women.

Part of this transformation is the appearance of "consumer-directed care,"
"self-managed care" and "care choice," philosophies regarding the social care
of frail and disabled people. These are currently ascending the public policy
agenda in North America and Europe in response to political and economic
forces (Evers 1998; Keigher 1997; Keigher 1999). Despite its patina of accep-
tability and improvement, the rhetorical ideal of "consumer hegemony" hides
a public policy of cost-cutting, devolution, and abandonment of the poor.
Consumerist ideology in state initiatives and private-local-state partnership
innovations effectively obscure the fundamental forces reshaping modern provisions of in-home care. Such tinkering with "benefits" helps enforce the
maintenance of responsibility for care with the very women whose needs for
government assistance are greatest, whose alternative employment (and earnings) options are least, and whose families have always been the ones asked to
bear a disproportionate share of the real cost, namely, ultimate responsibility
for providing care when there are no other options.

The "consumerist," cash, or direct-payment philosophy as a model of care
has profound implications for women now, as well as for normative expectations regarding women's roles in care arrangements in the future. By showing
in this chapter how individuals and families *use* personal care when given discretion, or choices, to "buy" what they need, larger aspects of the political
economy that shape gender oppression are illuminated. Illustrations in the
chapter are based on cases drawn from a qualitative cross-sectional study of private and publicly funded care, delivered through a consumer-directed model
that provides home care through independently employed personal care workers. Conducted in one midsized Midwestern American city, this research highlights some of the differential interests of poor and upper-middle-class women
needing and providing care. In doing so, some of the race, social class, and gender equity issues embedded in and easily obscured by use of independent, consumer-directed workers are identified.

In setting the stage for this feminist policy analysis, it is helpful to lay out
some basic principles. One useful framework for considering community care
of the elderly in the past has explicated the extent to which given policies support principles of "gender justice." This model was developed by Suzanne England (Osterbusch), Sharon Keigher, Baila Miller, and Nathan Linsk in 1987, in

assessing the fairness and impacts of policies proposing to compensate family members for providing care (Osterbusch [England] et al. 1987; Linsk et al. 1992). Using a feminist critical analytic lens to examine state policies, we identified several "dimensions of choice" (Gilbert & Specht 1986) on which government and private provisions for home care can be evaluated. These dimensions are outlined in table 7.1.

First, examining basic assumptions in the operative policy model, we asked whether home and community-based care is a means-tested benefit to be rationed or one available universally, such as exists in some public utility, education, or health systems. In the means-tested rationed model, a minimal level of care is provided. This "safety net" or residual approach has meant that elders (not their caregivers) qualify for benefits according to need as defined by lack of income and resources. Costs are "saved" by excluding as many persons as possible and limiting benefits to the minimum needed for survival outside a nursing home.

Underlying this model is the fear (unsubstantiated by research) that informal caregivers, including family members, would gladly cease or reduce their own efforts to provide care, letting the government take over or substitute for family care. This assumption of "substitution effects" is the reason Medicaid restricts access to its benefits. It assumes that new or extended benefits would "just substitute" government money for the home care presently provided by relatives and friends (Rich 1985), or for care that could (and should!) otherwise be covered by private insurance, employers, or individuals. A recent example of this is the 1997 Childrens' Health Insurance Program that is mandated to exclude children whose parents "could" otherwise insure them through their employers, even if the cost for doing so is excessive (Mann & Guyer 1997).

Furthermore, there is the concern that even programs designed to help only those who would otherwise have to be admitted to nursing homes may attract large numbers of applicants from "out of the woodwork," unless deterrents are established. Several congressional actions restricting Medicaid have aimed to prevent states from making home care an entitlement program. For example, ceilings were imposed on Medicaid waiver programs so that per capita costs would not exceed the program's anticipated level of nursing home expense had the waiver not been granted.

By supporting home-based care only as a lower-cost substitute for institutional care, Medicaid waiver polices have forced state programs to limit payment for home support to those who are so ill as to be eligible for nursing home care. Thus, a key concept is that the target for benefits must meet the "but for" criterion, as in "this person would be in a nursing home 'but for' the

Table 7.1 Comparison of Assumptions of Present Community Care Policies with Policies That Maximize Gender Justice

Policy Dimensions	*Present Policies*	*Policies to Maximize Gender Justice*
	Community care is welfare (e.g., a safety net). It must be rationed and means-tested.	Community must be a social utility, like public education. It should be available according to a broadened definition of need.
	Only minimum benefits should be given.	Equal access should be provided through income support, availability of goods and services, and, when appropriate, compensated family care.
	Government-supported care should be the "last resort."	Public provision should be the foundation for care.
Locus of responsibility	Care of the elderly is a family responsibility.	Care of dependent individuals is a responsibility shared by family and government.
	Government's only responsibility is to fill the gap.	Most families provide as much care as they can.
	Families should exhaust their own resources before turning to the government for help.	Many families need government help to carry on.
	Government-assisted care should not substitute for unpaid family care.	Government help is an add-on rather than a substitute for family care.
Values	Women are the primary caregivers in the family.	Women are not obliged to be the primary caregivers in the family.
	Women are responsibile for the direct care of dependent members of the family, even if they have to give up other roles.	Men and women family members should be equally free to choose between caregiving and other roles.
	It is more important for men to realize their full economic potential than it is for women	Women are entitled to realize their full economic potential.
	Family care is a "private good."	Family care is a "social good."

Table 7.1 *(continued)*

	The State's primary responsibility to the family is to assure freedom from State intrusion.	In addition to freedom *from* intrusion, the State should assure the freedom *to* provide care by making the necessary resources available.
	Families, not society, benefit from family care.	Families contribute to society by providing care.
	Most family care is not compensable.	Family care is compensable.
Targets of benefits	The impaired individual at highest risk is the sole target.	Those too ill or disabled to be helped effectively by the health care system alone and those who care for them are the targets.
	Those without available family qualify for government help.	Those with family qualify for government help.
Objectives	Avoid or delay institutionalization as a way to curtail costs to the government.	Provide support for family care and protection to family carers.
	Encourage families to provide care.	Integrate family care into a continuum of services and programs.
	Maintain the "balance" between family and government care, that is, let families "pay the first dollar."	Provide cash transfers to elders and/or their carers.
Cost-benefit concerns	Benefits are measured by savings to taxpayers first and the welfare of caregivers last.	Benefits are measured by family and community welfare.
	Benefits or incentives to caregivers would bring caregivers "out of the woodwork" and drive up costs.	There is no evidence of the "woodwork" effect; initial increase in cost may be due to pent-up demand, but costs will probably level off.
	Family-provided care saves government money because it does not cost anything.	Family stress from unsupported caregiving burden can result in costs to the community.
	The costs borne by families are not accounted for, even if they become public costs in the future.	Women presently bear an inequitable share of the social and economic costs of caregiving.

services provided by the community care program" (Doty 1985). The "but for" approach effectively discounts the unpaid caregiving of family and friends from the total amount of benefits to be paid. Thus, an elderly person without friends and family will receive a higher benefit than an equally disabled person who has family members apparantly available to provide care. However, family care is not calculated as a direct contribution (or a real cost) to the program, nor are family caregivers accorded any recognition or compensation. Under such policies, even respite and caregiver training are hard to justify.

The values implicit in home care provisions covered by Medicaid are those of familism and traditionalism, which assume that women's "proper" role is that of primary caregiver. Ironically, families are assumed to be self-supporting as well, with a full-time breadwinner present. Quite simply, home care is framed as a private good instead of a societal or community responsibility; "freedom" from state "intervention" is more important than assurance of access to care for all who need it. Benefits are not targeted to the impaired individual but rather to the family unit or household (in which the vast majority of disabled elders live), whose members are assumed to be available, able, and willing to provide care. Only elders without family, or who live alone, qualify for maximum levels of whatever care is available, followed by those whose primary caregiver "needs to be" employed full time outside the home. Retired family members and spouses, especially wives, who provide vital care and assistance are taken for granted.

The objectives of policy are basically to curtail institutional (nursing home) utilization, and its consequent costs for government, by enforcing on individual applicants the expectation that they give care themselves and liquidate their assets by purchasing care or private long-term care insurance, to their maximum ability before requesting government help—a residualism deriving from the Elizabethan Poor Law. Even though the costs borne by family or informal caregivers effectively free up public money, making it available for other taxpayers, the welfare of caregivers is not considered. Rather, family and other cheaper labor sources are viewed as resources to be "used up" before public resources are released. Indeed, any benefits to or recognition of caregivers are assumed to simply drive up costs, and so are ill-advised.

Independent Home Care in Milwaukee's Gray Market

Research on the gray market in elder care in Milwaukee demonstrates how families and elderly individuals obtain private, self-employed caregivers to substitute for and/or supplement the efforts of family caregivers, in assisting elders to remain in their own homes. The research also examines the workers who provide such services and how relationships within the triads of worker, elderly client, and client's family are structured. A major interest guiding the research is to document how care is negotiated between these three parties.

To understand the dilemmas arising from systemic reliance on "consumer direction" of care as public policy, this project gathered data on two samples of service users: middle- to upper-income families who purchase services privately with their own money, and low-income families (users of the Community Options Program—COP) who essentially receive a government subsidy or authorization to "buy" such services. Data were collected through interviews with eighteen cases in the self-pay (or private pay) group and twenty-one cases in the subsidized group—that is, those receiving services from the Milwaukee County Department on Aging's COP program. In nearly all cases contact was made with workers before contacting clients and family members. Workers in the self-pay group were sought through contacts with a variety of community agencies, nursing homes, personal contacts, and newspaper ads. In the subsidized group, workers were sought through contacts made at COP worker-training classes. Workers were interviewed twice, with four to six months in-between interviews, while clients and relatives were interviewed only once. Workers were paid $15 for the first interview, and $25 for the second. The following analysis describes and compares some of our findings on these two samples.

Powerlessness and Disadvantage Among the Subsidized Clients and Black Workers

Among the thirty-nine cases studied (eighteen self-pay, twenty-one subsidized), a total of forty-one workers were interviewed. Among the self-pay cases, the worker was hired by the family in 61 percent of the cases, whereas in the subsidized set, the worker was hired by family members in only 35 percent of cases; in over half the subsidized cases, the county case manager facilitated hiring the worker. Family members were much more available to the self-pay clients, who were either married or had children living nearby and available who strongly influenced the decision to hire help. Further, and importantly, we saw very few cases where a severely cognitively impaired elder was living alone. In a few unusual cases in the subsidized sample, COP workers had actually taken legal steps to become guardians for their clients, largely because there were no nearby family members or close friends.

The social support available to clients in the two samples appears to be qualitatively different. It is well documented that elders without social support rarely remain in the community long if they become unable to at least express gratitude to persons caring for them. Isolation is a key reason for nursing home admission, especially as public case managers realize they are the only agents taking responsibility for this person (Cantor 1991). But elders who have social support—spouses especially, but any relatives or friends who help out—have better life chances in general (Antonucci 1985). Low-income subsidized clients who do not have spouses or other close relatives are at an obvious disadvantage; their personal care workers are often thrust into roles much like that of family and become vital to these elders' remaining in the community.

The Two Samples Studied

The cases studied and the respondents interviewed in the private pay and the subsidy program samples are shown in table 7.2. A total of thirty-nine cases of home care were studied, including a total of forty elderly disabled clients (one case includes both husband and wife) and forty-one personal care workers. The thirty-nine cases include eighteen in the private pay sample and twenty-one in the subsidy program sample. Since not all the clients could be interviewed (for reasons explained below), actual interviews were conducted with thirty elders (twelve were in the private pay sample and eighteen in the subsidy sample). Some demographic data are available on all the elders, including those who were not interviewed. Six elders (five private pay, one subsidy) had more than one worker in the study, but in no case did we interview more than two workers per client. Not all elders had a relative available who could be interviewed, particularly those in the subsidy program sample. A total of twenty family members were interviewed, including twelve with elderly relatives in the private pay sample, and only eight with relatives in the subsidy sample. A similar number of personal care workers were interviewed in both samples (twenty private pay and twenty-one in the subsidy set). One worker in each set had two clients in the study, and one private pay worker had three clients.

Finally, the data gathered can only represent the points of view of all three parties in these relationships when it is complete on all three respondents. As noted in table 7.2, interviews with all three parties—elder, family member, and worker—are complete for seventeen of our thirty-nine cases. Interviews with client and worker are complete for twelve, and interviews only with per-

sonal care workers are complete for nine. Personal care workers were interviewed twice, however, and they report information on the changes in elder
clients' status and situations over time.

The needs of the elderly clients served in the two samples of elders are
generally similar, but their demographic characteristics are different on some
key dimensions. Only 6 percent of the private pay clients are African-American (one of eighteen), whereas 45 percent of the subsidy program clients sampled are African-American. The remainder are European-American as there
are no Hispanic elders in either sample. (Milwaukee County's population over
age sixty is more than 90 percent European-American, about 8 percent
African-American). The private pay clients are somewhat older (mean age of
83.3) than the subsidized clients (mean age of 78.5), and include a higher proportion of males (33 percent) than the subsidized sample (27 percent).

While a slightly higher proportion of the private pay sample is widowed (58
percent compared with 48 percent of the subsidy program clients), the private
pay clients are much more likely to be currently married (42 percent) and living with their spouses; only 10 percent (two) of the subsidized clients are living
with spouses. Indeed, fully 42 percent of the subsidy clients were unmarried
(five had never married, three were separated, and one was divorced), as were
none of the private pay clients. With their lower likelihood of being married, 29
percent of the subsidy sample have *no* grown children who they might rely upon
for help, whereas all the elders in the private pay sample have grown children.

Table 7.2   Cases Studied and Interviews Conducted

	Private Pay Cases	Subsidized Cases	Total
Cases studied	18	21	39
Interviews conducted with			
Triads—Client, family, worker	10	7	17
Dyads—Client, worker	2	10	12
Dyads—Family, worker	0	1	1
PCW only	6	3	9
	(total 18)	(total 21)	(total 39)
Numbers of individuals interviewed			
Clients	12	18	30
Clients not interviewed	6	4	10
Family members	12	8	20
PCWs	20	21	41

The elders in the private pay sample are also more likely to be living in secure affordable housing. As can be seen in table 7.3 (under "Living arrange-
ment"), half of the private pay sample own their homes, as do only 19 percent
of the subsidy sample. On the other hand, only 8 percent (one) of the private
pay clients live in subsidized senior housing, compared to 29 percent (six) of
those in the subsidy sample. In addition, another 29 percent of the subsidy
sample elders live in homes or apartments belonging to others, either their
children or nonkin, all of which reflects their limited financial resources.

While similar proportions of elders in both samples live alone in their
own homes, condos, or apartments (42 and 43 percent), the patterns of coresidence of those living with others also differentiate the two samples. Of those
living with others, in the private pay sample 17 percent (two elderly widows)
live with one of their children, as do 29 percent of the clients in the subsidized
sample (five with a daughter, one with a son). Another 19 percent of the subsidy sample (four clients) are living with nonrelatives, in all cases their personal care worker. The greater rates of coresidence with nonspousal kin
among the clients in the subsidy program reflect a common pattern within
low-income ethnic and immigrant communities, one typically the product of
economic necessity (Hoch & Slayton 1989; Stack 1974).

Finally, the OARS scores from the client assessments done during the interviews were collected to identify any particularly unique needs in either
sample. Comparing these scores, displayed in table 7.3, indicates that the total scores are not remarkably different (total scores 18.00 versus 17.40), although the private pay clients are slightly "needier" on three of the rating
scale's five dimensions. As expected, the subsidy clients' economic needs are
greater (3.35) than those of the private pay sample (1.96), and since many of
the private pay clients had Alzheimer's disease, they have higher ratings for
mental health needs (4.50 versus 3.40). The only other dimension on which
the subsidy sample has a higher rating is physical health, which may reflect
the medical necessity criteria of the Medicaid program, which funds the subsidy program.

Comparison of the actual care needed by the elderly clients as assessed by
workers and family members in the interviews reveals that a greater proportion
of the subsidy program elders are utilizing a higher level of care intensity. Only
10 percent were receiving care mainly for companionship, housekeeping, monitoring, and caregiver respite, whereas 28 percent of the private pay care was for
this purpose. Fully 90 percent of the subsidy clients required total care, compared with 72 percent of the private pay clients. Within this latter category a
higher proportion of the subsidy clients needed total personal care requiring

heavy lifting and physical strength from the care provider; thirty-three required such heavy care, as did only 17 percent of the private pay clients.

Since in the subsidy program clients may hire any family member except a spouse to be the paid carer, the involvement of the seven daughters (among the eight relatives interviewed) in the subsidized sample is informative. Why did they choose *not* to be the paid provider when they had this choice? It

Table 7.3 Comparison of Private Pay and Subsidized Clients

	Private Pay Clients		Subsidized Clients	
	Number	*Percent*	*Number*	*Percent*
Living arrangement[a]				
Own their house	6	50	4	19
Rented home or apartment	5	42	5	24
Subsidized apartment	1	8	6	29
Living in others' home	0	0	6	29
Alone	5	42	9	43
With others	7	58	12	57
With son/daughter	2	17	6	29
With spouse only, and others	5	42	2	10
With PCW	0	0	4	19
Care needed[b]				
Companionship mainly (Monitoring, social interaction, meal prep, outings, relief and support of regular caregivers)	5	28	2	10
Light total care (Companionship plus total care; no heavy lifting)	10	56	12	57
Heavy total care (All ADLs, IADLs, companionship, dispensing meds, catheter care, exercise, sometimes housework)	3	17	7	33
Mean OARS scores[c]				
Social support		2.42		1.93
Economic resources		1.96		3.35
Mental health		4.50		3.40
Physical health		4.04		4.15
ADL		5.08		4.58
Total OARS score		18.00		17.40

[a] Sample sizes reported include 12 private pay, 21 subsidized clients.
[b] Sample sizes reported include 18 private pay, 21 subsidized clients.
[c] Sample sizes reported include 12 private pay, 20 subsidized clients.

turned out that one daughter was serving as a paid care provider (along with a nonrelative PCW who worked thirty-five hours per week) at the time of our first interview, while three of the daughters had been paid caregivers in the past. Currently, each had hired other women, depending on their own occupational prospects and, in one case, the needs of the PCW who was a young family friend. By our second interview, a second had become the PCW (described below). The daughters, all in their fifties, expressed concern about needing to keep their regular jobs because they themselves needed health insurance and pension credits. The workers they hired were typically younger than the daughters. Most had lower occupational prospects, less education, and less work experience than the daughters.

Social Support and Supportive Living Situations

Private pay clients. Aside from the seven clients living with their spouses, the five private pay clients living alone vary widely in the amount of care they purchase. Paid round-the-clock care is provided to only one, Mrs. Anderson, but for seven others twenty-four-hour care is provided between family members and paid workers. However, the three elders living with a spouse or daughter purchased as little as two to three hours of care per week.

Mrs. Anderson's daughter handles writing paychecks to nine different PCWs over the course of a week, including workers who stay over with Mrs. Anderson every night. A private case management agency recruits and schedules the workers. Living in literally two apartments (which her recently deceased husband had converted into one) in an expensive religiously affiliated congregate care facility, Mrs. Anderson has dementia-like symptoms, osteoporosis, and a previous hip fracture; she needs constant availability of care, catheter maintenance, help maintaining a range of motion, and help with all ADL tasks. Having had both a maid and a cook in their previous home, Mrs. Anderson is comfortable having household help and is a generous employer. For instance, she pays vacation time for her three longest-term employees, including the former family cook.

In contrast are a few families who only sporadically hired PCWs for respite, to relieve a spouse or daughter. Typical of low-income families using private pay independent care is Mrs. Wilson, age eighty-nine, whose daughter, a recently retired sixty-one-year-old schoolteacher, cares for her full time. Even though her need for respite was great, Mrs. Wilson's daughter hired very little help, trying to stretch her mother's savings. Admitting she is glad her mother is finally in the late stages of Alzheimer's disease, the daughter now feels she can safely leave her mother for up to three hours, securely fastened to the bed, without worry she will get up and hurt herself.

Subsidized clients.   As might be surmised from table 7.3, subsidized clients were more often living in less stable situations, less likely to be living with a spouse or in their own homes, more likely to be in rented or subsidized apartments, and with others. Indeed, they are quite different from the private pay group, of whom no one resided with others except with a spouse or adult child.

The four subsidized clients who were living with their paid workers are especially interesting. These cases include, for example, a sixty-eight-year-old African-American woman seriously disabled from a gunshot wound some eighteen years before, who resides with her worker (age thirty-nine) and her worker's husband. The worker has been known to this client since childhood and began providing a home for her after a couple of other arrangements did not work out; the worker's daughter (who lives in the upstairs flat) also helps out sometimes. COP provides this worker's only earnings. COP pays her about $600 per month for up to twenty-one hours of work per week, providing for the client all cooking, laundry, cleaning, and shopping chores as well as putting her to bed, giving her a bath, and so on. In the past both client and worker have abused alcohol.

A second coresiding client is a seventy-seven-year-old African-American male veteran diabetic who has shared his subsidized one-bedroom apartment with his fifty-year-old worker for ten years. Having been good friends with the worker's mother, he originally asked her to move into his apartment and care for him so he would not have to go to a nursing home. At the time of our interview, the "case" was being served temporarily by the regular worker's twenty-two-year-old daughter, who "needs the work" to get off welfare. She often brings her three young children to the client's home with her. The regular worker, who keeps this tiny apartment sparkling clean, sleeps on a convertible sofa in "her space," the living room, while the client, who regularly goes to day care at the Veterans hospital, spends the rest of his time sitting up or in a hospital bed in his bedroom.

Another client is a sixty-year-old developmentally disabled European-American woman living, along with another developmentally disabled client, in an Adult Foster Home operated by her worker. This worker, a fifty-five-year-old recently widowed African-American woman, is probably the only black worker in this study who is "better off" socioeconomically than her white client. Finally, an eighty-four-year-old European-American woman with multiple health problems (dementia, pressure sores, arthritis, cardiac problems) following a stroke is living in the home of her "ex-daughter-in-law," age forty-four, and her several teenage children who all pitch in caring for "Gramma," to whom only the youngest son is actually related. These naturally occurring shared-housing arrangements typify residential patterns in low-income neighborhoods (Hoch & Slayton 1989; Stack 1974). Such living arrangements were more common among African-American clients but were unusual among European-Americans.

The needs of elders receiving subsidized independent care are more diverse and their situations certainly more fragile than those of elders and their families purchasing independent care themselves. As was shown above, more subsidized clients needed total care. Although they are younger, the subsidized group has more medical diagnoses and more conditions with long-term functional impairments (i.e., paralysis, immobility, amputations, developmental disabilities, and cardiac disabilities plus dementias). The PCW is vitally important because she knows this client, and because the whole long-term service system, such as it is, hinges on her. In this study, private pay clients' impairments were more acute and the length of time involving needed care was was less certain. In two cases clients were waiting for eligibility for the subsidy program, and in one case a family was only paying privately for worker hours beyond those covered by the subsidy program. Clearly, the family remains the backbone of care that exists when family members are nearby, available, and willing to take this responsibility.

Differences Between the Private Pay and the Subsidized Workers

Comparing the experiences of all forty clients in both client samples by race reveals that all black clients (n = 13) were served by black workers, all but one were in the subsidized sample, and their workers in most cases lived close by. Of the thirty-nine total cases sampled, however, white clients (n = 28) were served by black workers in fifteen cases.

The workers in the subsidy program are younger on average than the workers paid privately (mean age of forty-six compared with fifty-six), including four workers in their twenties, whereas no private pay workers were younger than thirty-eight (see table 7.4). This suggests that it may take time and experience to "break into" independent care work in the private pay market, and that doing so requires maturity, experience, and "connections." "Access" to the county subsidy program is entirely different in that most workers were asked to participate by someone who already knew them. Most had not had formal health care experience previously.

Table 7.4 Comparison of the Private Pay and Subsidized PCWs

	Private Pay PCWs (n = 20)	Subsidized PCWs (n = 21)
Mean age	56 years	46 years
20–29	0	4
30–39	2	3
40–49	3	6
50–59	7	4
60–64	4	2
65–69	1	0
70–75	2	2
Number of blacks	10	15
Marital status		
Married	6	4
Widowed	6	4
Single, never married	1	6
Separated	1	2
Divorced	6	5
Education		
Less than high school	5	8
High school graduate	10	4
Some college	1	7
Assoc. or prof. degree	4	2
Training for personal care work		
None	3	0
Hospital/nursing home program	4	1
CNA program only	3	2
LPN/RN	3	0
Personal care training by local nonprofits	7	2
Required DOA PCW training	—	21
Transportation available		
Have a car	13	12
No car	4	7
Get rides occasionally	3	2
Rely on public buses	7	9
Source of health insurance		
Own private insurance coverage	13	9
Public only or none	6	12

Thus, almost three out of four of the subsidized workers and half the private pay workers were African-American in this strongly working-class residentially segregated city. Not only were subsidy program workers younger on average and more likely to be unmarried, but 38 percent had not completed high school (however, 42 percent had completed some college or an associate's degree, and one had a bachelor's degree).

Few seem to have had much training in health care, however, compared to the private pay workers, although all had had at least the forty-hour course in personal care provided by the Department of Aging. (At the time of the interviews, all COP program workers were required to take this training.)

As a group, both the private pay and subsidized workers had very significant health problems of their own, plus a lack of access in all cases to health insurance, as shown in table 7.4. The latter is a very serious problem. Although twenty-two have health insurance, ten have it through their spouses' employment, three through other full-time employment, and six purchased it privately. But eighteen had no health insurance or only public coverage through such programs as Medicaid/Healthy Start, which are rapidly being curtailed. This health care insecurity was the biggest concern raised by all independent care workers and the main deterrent to women's relying full time on such employment.

Interestingly, poor clients in the subsidized program were more likely than private pay clients to have known their workers before they "hired" them; many had known each other for many years, some since the workers were children. Nine of the twenty-one subsidized workers had known the client before, whereas no workers in the private pay sample had known their clients previous to being hired. In finding workers privately, clients and families had had to take on many new tasks and develop skills through experience: devising ways to ask friends for direct help, advice, and assistance in locating workers; learning to advertise; turning to churches and agencies for referrals; screening potiential workers; and learning to relate to a stranger in their home. Of the subsidized cases, a high proportion of clients had had long-term relationships with their PCWs. These workers lived much closer to their clients and in neighborhoods comprised largely of low-income people. Such neighborhoods offer distinctly more availability of potential home care workers.

This may reflect one of the problems created by sprawling American metropolitan areas, where communities are segregated by income as well as race, so that people with resources to hire help simply do not have regular social opportunities to meet working-class women who do home care work. The social distance, which many fear is increasing, is manifest in the multiple dilemmas regarding communication, reliability, transportation, and child care which challenge both workers and the families and elders depending on their care.

Accommodations Made Among the Three Stakeholders in Care

How do political and economic structures shape care in the gray market where people buy and direct care themselves? These forces can be seen vividly in the day-to-day strains felt by private pay workers and their clients, and the kinds of pressures and expectations with which both parties regularly contend. England and Ganzer (1994) have called this the "micropolitics of care." Their analyses of narrative dialogue in film portrayals of caregiving with older people have demonstrated how social constructions position different participants. Berenice Fisher and Joan Tronto's (1990) and Tim Diamond's (1992) work has similarly focused on these relational dimensions to identify the convergences of race, class, and income along with gender in the commodification of caregiving.

Our research used tape-recorded and transcribed interviews with the three "stakeholders" in private pay care—the elder, her relative (typically, a daughter or spouse if one is available), and the PCW. Two PCW interviews, conducted six months apart, permitted us to capture a substantial amount of contextual detail about each case, including changes that occurred over this period of time in the client, the worker, and/or the situation. Analysis focuses on the different positions from which the three view their situation, identifying details suggestive of points of view, strength of feelings, similarities and differences in interpretations of events, and attitudes regarding the other person or both parties. Potent emotionally laden issues such as power, control and influence, mutuality of purpose, reciprocity, and comfort/discomfort cue the analyst to key factors related to status and strain. The following vignettes, summaries of situations that were described to us, illustrate a few of these areas of strain. While quoting directly from some statements made by respondents, we use pseudonyms and have altered a few identifying features. However, the stories remain "true" to the sentiment of the message shared with us.

Independent home care workers' experiences vividly illustrate political (power) and economic (value) forces, beginning with the very experience of being hired and hiring. An experience common to all workers and employers are the negotiations required between them to agree upon the conditions under which work will be done, and the amount and basis for compensation.

Few interviewees dwelt on this process except to acknowledge that negotiation was often stressful for both parties.

The strain derives from the larger reality that employer (either client or family) and worker are, typically, being squeezed to fit available resources. One worker, Doris Miller, detailed for us the many prescriptions she had developed for effectively negotiating independent jobs with prospective employers, suggesting, we believe, that some of her past employers have either undervalued her skills or attempted to exploit her goodwill.

Negotiating the Job: Workers' Needs to Set Limits

Doris Miller, fifty-seven years old, became a Licensed Practical Nurse in 1958 and has done private duty work for over twenty-five years. Highly professional and confident in her capacities, she emphasizes the importance of negotiating one's salary with potential employers before anything else, setting a limit (a daily or hourly rate of pay) below which a PCW absolutely will not negotiate. Doing this, of course, requires knowledge of local market rates and conditions—information most workers and employers have no way of knowing. She recommends the PCW also insist on clarification regarding the dates one will be paid, scheduling and hours of work, flexibility and availability, time off, vacations, and employers' responsibilities for providing necessary supplies. A worker must be very clear about limitations (one's unwillingness to do housework, for example, or heavy lifting). Clarity regarding job expectations is critically important, Doris says, "from the very beginning."

Doris knows from experience that the best-laid plans when one is hired seldom work out, and it is in this process of change that workers get taken advantage of. One of the many dilemmas workers can get into is with older couples, because the spouse usually needs care as well as the client. "So you find that you sometimes are taking care of two clients and being paid for one." Workers are having to remind the second person to eat and take their medication. But "you don't usually know that [the spouse needs help too] until you are in the home working . . . and at that point, you've already negotiated the job."

Similar rising expectations occur as a client's condition declines, requiring more and more daily care simply to maintain the status quo. When something has to give, it is typically the worker, at least until either a crisis occurs or the worker "puts a foot down" or quits. This dilemma is illustrated in the case below, which was described somewhat differently by the worker and the employer. Families often try many alternatives before spending money to hire more help. In this case the employer and the worker struggled, with Mr. Johnson (the client's husband) relinquishing his domestic privacy only bit by bit, and the worker, as graciously as she could, using her limited leverage to extricate herself from a situation she felt had become too much for her to handle.

Ed and Edith Johnson and Fay Coury: Renegotiating More Care

Fay Coury began working for Mr. and Mrs. Johnson two and a half years ago, caring for ninety-year-old Edith Johnson, who has had Alzheimer's for over four years. Fay was the first person Ed Johnson ever hired to do the housework that Edith had done entirely by herself for more than forty years.

An experienced fifty-seven-year-old African-American nursing assistant, Fay has done care work all her life, most of it private duty. She was referred to the Johnsons by the Interfaith registry. Fay had grown up with eight siblings (all of whom are nurses or doctors) and feels she is able to get along "with just about anyone." Ed says she and Edith really had come to enjoy each other.

While doing some cleaning, dusting, and sweeping, Fay says, "the main thing is Edith, 'cause I'm a companion for her. After I get there in the morning, I'll give her a bath, put her clean clothes on, comb her hair, take and brush her teeth." Then Fay fixes breakfast and sits and has coffee with both Edith and Ed. "And if she's having company, we fix her up real pretty."

At first Fay just worked a couple of hours a day, making $7 an hour, but after a year "it had worked up to three or four hours," and Fay felt that Ed and Edith needed even more help. Ninety-one-year-old Ed had had coronary bypass surgery; low blood pressure and dizziness prevented him from standing or lifting. He could no longer cook or help around the house. Feeling they needed round-the-clock help, Fay urged him to hire more help and finally talked this over with the trainer at Interfaith, who agreed.

Ed subsequently announced he had found a "live in" through a friend. Relieved, Fay immediately took another job in a different northern suburb. The live-in, a recent Russian immigrant who spoke little English, and her daughter, had trouble communicating and getting Edith up in the mornings. Becoming impatient, the live-in was unable to establish a relaxed relationship with her. After about a month the Johnsons' middle-aged son returned from an extended trip to find that Edith was suffering skin problems from her increasing incontinence and not being bathed properly. Upset with his father, he insisted that they "get somebody in here with Mom, and you too, Dad."

Fay states simply, "The live-in didn't pan out."

Ed started calling Interfaith every day and finally asked Fay if she would come back. Acknowledging there was more to do now, he offered to pay $9 an hour if she would stay at least six hours a day and prepare their supper too. Fay decided to keep her other client on Wednesdays, and then resumed working for the Johnsons four days a week. She now makes $9.25 per hour.

Tension remains between Fay and Ed, but Fay would never say it this way. She giggles somewhat nervously, admitting, "He wants me there at 8:30; I get there at 9." Never having owned a car, Fay rides a bus for over forty-five minutes from her home to a bus stop several blocks from the Johnsons' home. Ed used to pick her up there, but he no longer drives because of his heart condition. Now Fay walks, slowly and with difficulty because of her arthritic knees. She feels she is working all the hours she can handle, given her knees and her responsibilities at home to her own children and grandchildren.

Part of Fay's reticence, and Doris's as well (as described above), is the subtlety of the expectations and the enormity of the responsibility put upon them by their employers. As experienced independent workers, both are gracious and nonconfrontational in handling their job, but not always effective at rebalancing the fairness quotient. Our study identified workers who have accommodated clients and families in some extraordinary ways, and rarely, if one looks closely enough, without cost to themselves. One, for example, comes to a client's home at 6:00 A.M. in order to allow a middle-aged daughter to get off to work without tending to her mother's care; this worker gets the client up, bathed, and dressed by 9:00 A.M. when she takes her to the day care center where she also works until 4:00 P.M. After work she usually takes her client home, staying another couple of hours, sometimes starting dinner before the daughter returns home. Another worker actually moved from the northwest side to the south side of the city to be closer to her client. Many PCWs work split shifts and are "on call" all hours of the day and night. In being so accessible they take a calculated risk that the case will continue, that such an investment of time and effort in this relationship will "pan out."

In all cases we found workers strongly oriented toward being accountable to their client, or the client's family members, even when these were grown children living great distances away. Elders living alone presented special concerns and responsibilities to workers, especially elders who had no relatives locally to oversee their affairs or to call upon for decisions. Of the five elders living alone in the private pay sample (table 7.2), two lived in congregate housing and so had some services available (Mrs. Anderson and Mr. Stein had meals and cleaning provided by their facilities), and Mr. DeBoer was entirely competent. However, Mrs. Walker and Mr. Pollack were confused and forgetful enough that the concommitant sense of responsibility borne by their workers was quite great. However, Mr. Pollack, a retired professor, has a housekeeper with him from 9:00 A.M. to 7:00 P.M. daily, whereas Mrs. Walker, a retired bookeeper who was widowed at an early age without any savings or life insurance, lives in subsidized housing. Her children employ, for about one hour a day, a skilled RN (a mother herself with several children) who lives nearby and who "looks in on Mrs. Walker," bringing meals, checking medications, and keeping in touch with neighbors and family. As Mrs. Walker's dementia increases, they hope she will qualify for the COP program and thus be able to have more hours of care. Short of living with others, there is no other realistic way to assure her safety over time.

These data suggest that being a reliable independent worker requires a considerable amount of altruistic behavior. However, this low-waged work, as commodified interpersonal arrangements, makes workers vulnerable. Despite such working conditions, independent PCWs displayed disarming comfort with being freelance workers. Indeed, for most this independence was the main attraction of home care work. They frequently contrasted independent care work with nursing home or home care agency work, indicating their preference for the former because the one-on-one relationship of freelancing allowed them to do better work by not having to "go through a supervisor," and being free to do exactly what the patient wanted done. Other important needs of these women that were met by independent home care work included the ability to set one's own schedule, the feeling of competence, the ambiguity of the work and its limits, satisfaction, and convenience.

With this independent status comes a strong sense of personal investment in the work and reliance on their own personal standards for giving good care. Workers elaborated at length regarding the importance of measuring up to their own standards, having continuity in the work, having the same patients over time and thus being able to observe changes, being able to "detect a physical change or change in personality" and respond to these individual needs. They are able to establish routines that become familiar and comforting to clients. They can "tell what they [the clients] don't like, and what they like." Clients and relatives value this continuity as well and, when a good match appears to have been made, worker and employer quickly establish a kind of mutual dependency.

This relationship becomes cemented through small acts of compassion and reciprocity as workers come to understand the total vulnerability of the elder in their care, want to know more about this person, and strive to treat her "like I would like to be treated myself." Workers come to identify strongly with their clients; as one explains, "I hope that there are people around that will give me the care that I've given." Many workers have deeply held religious values, or feel gratitude for the good things that have happened in their own lives. Many spoke of feeling they have a special gift or of having "the touch" to work with the elderly.

This compassion, affection, and identification with clients is revealed in the respectful ways some describe, minimize, or actually hide their clients' less attractive qualities. Claudia, for example, struggles with her client's ill-tempered, verbally abusive husband—another element of care over which she has little control—using her detailed knowledge of him to explain his difficult behavior.

Peacekeeping

Claudia's client, Mrs. Wise, is severely forgetful and easily confused. Her client's husband's frustration with her frequently explodes in verbal assaults aimed at whomever is there. Claudia says it helps that Mr. Wise reminds her of her father. Besides carefully remembering obscure details of his childhood, she is sympathetic to his potentially embarrassing health problems (a colostomy and occasional urinary incontinence), which she feels keep him from socializing. Maintaining a distant, casual relationship with him, preserving his independence, she patiently and unobtrusively scrubs down the malodorous bathroom after he changes his colostomy bag with his own arthritic hands and clouded eyes. While "providing personal care only to the wife," her attention to maintaining the husband's reign and dignity preserves stability in the apartment.

Workers described elaborate strategies for cueing, making suggestions, and cajoling confused persons, especially in regard to bathing, in order to obtain cooperation and avoid ever being confrontational. Whether they did personal care or mainly companion work, most saw their role as preserving client dignity, with basic tasks related to maintaining personal cleanliness, attractiveness, and the individual's familiar appearance. Rose notes that "the patient feels more independent when they are at home giving *you* the orders," rather than in a facility where the worker would be "taking orders" from a nurse. Workers demonstrated many interpersonal skills in facilitating that control through their attention to a wide range of details meaningful to the client, and in individualizing and personalizing care. That clients and families feel the impact of their skill is illustrated in the extent to which they describe activity in terms of "we did it together." Or as Mary Walker, a client in the early stages of Alzheimer's disease declares, "Oh, yes. She helps me a lot. She helps me even when I don't wanta be helped . . . She's good in that way. She can talk you into things."

Maintaining and facilitating client, as well as family, control is a part of this, and it seems that in many ways the most skilled workers, as with mothers, are those who are most nurturing, self-effacing, and willing to share credit for their accomplishments with others. Such work, "of course," provides little recognition or compensation. The potential dilemmas here are illustrated in the very different way key events are sometimes related by workers as opposed to family members.

Empowering Families, Disempowering Self

One of the three workers with Mrs. Smith, who has advanced Alzheimer's disease, explained how Mrs. Smith's bowel and swallowing difficulties require constant adaptation of diet to give her sufficient nutrition and fiber. Disturbed that the client's husband had previously fed her TV dinners, she devised a regular routine of blending quantities of cooked well-seasoned meat and vegetables, and freezing it in meal-sized plastic pouches that can be easily thawed and reheated.

The client's husband, delighted with how well and conveniently the blended packets worked, described this creative process a bit differently, entirely through the perspective of his own responsibilities. "We [myself and the workers] do a very good job," he explained. "I think we've got a good solution [a soft diet]. She gets a well-balanced meal. I talked to a dietician to make sure . . . We make sure she gets enough liquid because I don't want a urinary tract problem."

Both are correct interpretations of what was done. Mr. Smith believes these ideas to be largely his own because of the years of heavy responsibility which he carried alone. The workers feel great compassion for him, respectful of how he carried on ("for a man"), yet worried that he can't let go and let them do even more for him.

In such circumstances, efforts to promote client empowerment are costly to workers, as well as family caregivers, who literally have to absorb pressure, tension, and unmet needs without any institutional support that recognizes or compensates the real value of the work. One of our student interviewers was reminded of Eleanor Roosevelt's having said, "You just do the things that you thought you never could do."

Similar dilemmas and ultimatums face families who become dissatisfied with a worker after arrangements have been in place for some time. Typically, the contract continues unless broken by some crisis or event that disrupts and releases the feelings of obligation that tie both parties on a day-to-day basis. Knowing that threats to quit are potent and upsetting to a family, one worker, Athena, expressed how upset she gets with younger workers who sometimes talk casually of quitting a job. "You *never* threaten like that," she declared emphatically, "you never talk loose about quittin'." In home care, such "threats" have an urgency like yelling fire in a crowded theater, with the potential to destroy fragile good will built up over time, and this reflects badly on other independent workers like Athena.

Workers whose only employment and income is from their independent work, as is Athena's, were especially vulnerable because even if they made a living wage (which only a couple did), they had no health insurance or other fringe benefits. For this reason, some maintained other regular employment in nursing homes, hospices, day care centers or other home health agencies that typically provide at least some health insurance (usually with the worker paying part or all of the premium), retirement contributions, workers' compensation, and unemployment insurance.

Elder care is work dictated by many factors that neither workers, families, nor clients can control, factors leading to a high turnover rate among workers, and that often leads to sudden unemployment. My colleagues and I were struck by the huge, unpredictable array of changes in workers' careers that occurred over the four to six months between the first and second interviews. In the private pay sample, four of the twenty workers had ceased doing independent home care work by the second interview, two because of their own health problems (both had started dialysis), a third because of an alcohol relapse, and a fourth because she took a full-time job working with children. Among the sixteen who continued, nearly all saw a change in caseload and the health of their clients. For example, Mrs. Smith (described above) was hospitalized for what turned out to be a hip fracture, and Mr. Smith eventually hired his daughter, a nurse, to stay full time, thus terminating all three of their PCWs. Several other private pay PCWs also had clients die or become hospitalized.

Among the subsidy program PCWs, workers' own reasons for not working were more temporary or due to their own health problems. Two had had babies and had taken time off (without pay, of course), but another two had had cancer relapses, including one worker we never reinterviewed because she was dying. Several lost their clients, of whom at least two died, but one young mother obtained a "better job" on a night shift at a nursing home. Each story is complicated by changes in the lives of clients or the worker, crises in the lives of other workers (who shared client responsibilities), or changing circumstances within the workers' and the clients' families. All of these micro-level tensions were experienced against a backdrop of welfare reforms at this time in Wisconsin that were pushing some women into independent care work while pushing others out of it.

Despite the satisfactions of closer and more long-term relationships with clients, for many workers independent care work simply does not provide vital security: there is no health insurance, pension, or even Social Security coverage for most, not to mention paid vacation, or sick days. And the urgency of some workers' (as well as their family's) own health problems tends to push a high percentage of women into very stressful but isolating alternatives. Which is to say, even the fondest relationships can be struck down by the precarious conditions of the work. Indeed, precarious conditions sometimes predominate for all three stakeholders, as everyone's focus becomes quite short term: paying the next bill, moving, getting a bus to work, "just" getting the phone back on.

This discussion has so far minimized the public policy advantages of the subsidy program examined here, a government-supported direct-payment program that does not discriminate between relative and nonrelative caregiver. There is no doubt that the model offers a flexibility to all participants that does not exist in the traditional agency home care model where PCWs are agency employees. The following case captures vividly the strengths and weaknesses of direct payment for independent care, illustrating the distinct "interests" of both the caregiver daughter, Molly, and the personal care worker, Angeline.

The Witt Family: Low-Income Women with Real Choices

Molly Witt, age 48, has never been married. She "fell into being the family caregiver" when her father became ill in 1982; she was just 33. After his death a year later, Molly's mother, Dorothy, needed help, and in the ensuing year, her mother, then 65, was hospitalized seven times for heart bypass, cataract, and bowel surgeries. Molly continued living with her mother and older sister, and the three of them eventually moved into their present apartment.

Fourteen years later, Dorothy, age 79, has had a series of ministrokes, and Molly had become the full-time family care manager as well as breadwinner, monitoring all her mother's medications, preparing meals, and keeping her clean, plus looking after her sister who, while similarly devoted to caring for their mother, is developmentally disabled. Molly knows she can handle it, but is resentful that, as the second youngest of the family, her four siblings provide little if any help.

Molly worked full time as a grocery checker for four years, earning $6.20 per hour, until her mother started needing more help. The family began paying a care worker privately before they got the present worker, Angeline. Shortly after that Molly cut back her employment to part-time. They began receiving the COP payment in July 1996, after Dorothy had been disabled with Parkinson's and Alzhiemer's for over a year.

Because Dorothy has "her good days and bad days," which are very taxing emotionally and physically, Molly feels very responsible for her mother's care. "It can be very monotonous and you do resent it once in awhile. Human beings do. But that's the time you have to really, really remember, and think, if I've ever been through a test in my life, this is it . . ."

Responding to her mother's need to go to the toilet several times a night, Molly rarely gets a full night's sleep. She is always tired. "When I'm done with my job, I come home and have another. There is like no in-between time." Very grateful to have had Angeline for the last year, Molly believes the relationship between her mother and Angeline is remarkable. "Angeline is a gem, she is a real gem. My mom connected with her right off the bat. She was just, it was like you either do or you don't kinda thing, and we were fortunate. I trust that woman completely. She's just become a member of our family. She's been a better support for me and has done more for us here in this household than my family has. That woman is a rock for me."

What Molly values most is Angeline's intuition. "She's a real treasure. . . . Every health care worker should be as conscientious as Angeline is about her job. She is a very clean person; she does things you don't even have to ask her to do. She just automatically does em."

Ten months before our first interview Angeline had taken over this job from her cousin, shortly after which Dorothy became eligible for COP. Age 49, separated from an abusive husband, with five grown children and 15 grandchildren, Angeline had completed a two-week home care training course with Interfaith just before taking the job. Despite years of factory and hotel housekeeping employment, and lifelong experience caring for her own family, Angeline has no formal health care experience. Like many African-American women her age she has hypertension, diabetes, and no health insurance. She also has a painful wound in her leg where her husband stabbed her three years ago. She relies on a local public clinic for her medical care.

From the beginning COP paid Angeline $9 per hour for 27 hours per week and Molly paid for up to 12 hours more, depending on her own work schedule. Angeline could have taken on more clients, but she became quite fond of Mrs. Witt and her daughters. Shortly after being hired, she moved from Milwaukee's inner city to their Southside neighborhood so she could walk to work and be on call. She shares a two-bedroom apartment with her youngest daughter who works full time at a nearby university. Angeline's schedule was unpredictable from week to week, dependent upon Molly's work schedule at the grocery store.

Within a year, COP had increased Mrs. Witt's care level to 40 hours per week, giving Molly, who felt constantly exhausted, a real choice between working and staying with her mother full time. Her decision was settled in spring 1997 when the grocery store closed and she lost her job. Rather than seek another, she decided to accept COP's $1,500 per month, becoming her mother's full-time caregiver.

This was temporarily disasterous for Angeline who was just as abruptly displaced. But she soon began working for an elderly couple back on the Northside, despite having fled that neighborhood before—her first husband had been murdered in a park there, and she had been abused and attacked there by her third husband—and even though the new job, again several miles from her home, requires another hour-long bus ride. A resilient, resourceful networker who loves her new professional identity as a caregiver, Angeline volunteered at Interfaith, and quickly landed several more clients.

The respectful relationship between Molly and Angeline remains important to them. Angeline continues to be "on call" for Molly who now pays her out of her own COP reimbursement. Angeline hopes someday to become an LPN [licensed practical nurse]. Her children call her the "Speed Racer," because she is always in a hurry, but Angeline says that care work has given great meaning to her life. "I'm—you know how squirrels do? They store up nuts and stuff for the winter? Well, I want to do all I can while I'm able to do this, you know."

Lingering Concerns About a Consumerist Model
for Home Care

The experiences of clients, their families, and workers already engaged in "consumer-controlled" care arrangments are very instructive. Having known the worker before payment for care began and having control of the payment is a very much more personal experience for a client than having a bath "from XYZ Home Health Corporation," or finding a worker through telephone contacts. The key question should be, how well do direct-payment arrangements serve all sectors of communities in need, including the providers of care?

My colleagues and I have concluded that the model needs to carry a "consumer beware" tag. The model can be precarious to one's health even "when you have the freedom to make choices." What you do and what choices you make depend on the options available. Some of the concerns raised in our interviews with workers, clients, and families include the following:

The difficult client. What happens to the "difficult client" for whom no one wants to work? All elders are not equally sweet and compliant personalities, and relatives' and workers' descriptions of challenging client behaviors clearly reveal who is the least desirable to work for. What happens when such a "client" cannot or does not conform to expectations that they share responsibility for care? Not all seem able to comply with emerging self-help norms. Does a consumerist model actually violate a client's *right* to have care? Given that a right to have care is not assured under current U.S. policies, it certainly can. In other words, relying on a consumerist model does not guarantee that care will be provided: certainly not to the poor, and possibly not even to those with the means to purchase care themselves. Yet the private pay model requires that *someone* assume responsibility. The question is, where does responsibility lie and how will obligations be enforced?

The workers' real needs. Many home care workers come from difficult or troubled backgrounds themselves, living in circumstances that make it difficult for them to obtain and keep employment. Many of the workers we interviewed had health problems of their own, about a third had reading difficulties, and another third lacked reliable means of transportation. Many younger women also needed work that could accommodate their child care arrangements, and workers of all ages had family responsibilities of their own. Still, there is much demand for independent home care on a part-time basis, and many workers feel independent work accommodates them best. This raises important questions about how traditional home health agency or institutional care work should be reorganized. In addition, most workers said they liked independent care work very much. Despite going through difficult periods emotionally and financially when a client dies, most valued and felt closer relationships with their private-pay clients than they had when working for home health agencies. Yet the relatively high turnover rate among both clients and workers forces even committed independent workers to take a businesslike approach toward constantly cultivating possible new clients, and for families to plan how to obtain backup workers.

Both parties' experience of power and dependency.   A central issue is how power and control, dependency and autonomy, are managed in these three-way relationships. Does choosing the worker really give the client power? In many respects private pay clients have more freedom in that their "care" is whatever they feel they need or want on a given day. There is no question that the private pay client, or her family, command the situation, but does the subsidized client have similar control? Relationships were very fluid, but generally more hierarchichal. Several family caregivers also admitted to being uncomfortable with the vagueness in such relationships, unfamiliar with how to contract for personal care services, and uncertain whether to treat the worker as a friend or an employee. This was especially difficult for daughter and spouse caregivers in the private pay sample who admitted liking their worker, having enjoyed discussing personal issues with her, and having felt they knew her "like a friend."

The importance of ambiguity when parties have different perceptions.   Close examination of the narrative data reveals a great deal of ambiguity in the terms and definitions used to describe independent home care work and the relationships that exist within it. There appears to be a lot of vagueness about what gets done, how much time it takes, and about the various specifics of the work that are of most interest to managers and analysts. In private pay arrangements, both client and worker have a great deal of discretion about how to use their time together; no one worries much about delineating time frames for tasks to be completed. In fact, the importance of this "vague" relational work is that it is essential to the coproduction of care. The work requires a great deal of cooperation and respect from both parties. And, basically, each party has its own very different definition of what they are doing together.

Such casualness does not fit well into the measured-work units required by publicly funded programs, however, sometimes causing great difficulties to all parties. For instance, workers who had several clients, especially in the subsidized sample, felt prohibited from using time "to just sit around and talk." One worker told of carefully scheduling her COP clients for the end of the day; indeed, clients would ask her to do so. Despite having one of the heaviest schedules, often seeing six to ten clients a day, she did schedule these clients late so she could take an hour of her own time and "shoot the breeze" with them. She had been with them for ten years and knew how eagerly they awaited her arrival.

Whose money is this, anyway?   Many workers and clients could not name the source from which their payment came; only a few knew that they were paid by the County Department of Aging. Such confusion regarding accountability never existed among private pay workers, other than that some did not know if the relative or the elderly client had more control of the payment. One of the dilemmas of the mixed economy of care is the "funder-provider split" (whether this be through contracting out of services, or giving cash or vouchers to clients to purchase such care themselves), so that the public forgets that these are, in fact, government benefits. Indeed, a major problem with the new "mixed welfare economy" is that it is difficult for citizens to know their rights or the sources of their benefits. They may attempt to hold government accountable, or not, depending on their understanding, but ultimately what occurs is an erosion of confidence in public-sector programs, fueling the destruction of social provisions.

The foregoing analysis has sought to identify several problems with a consumer-directed approach to paying for and controlling home care. A consumerist perspective assumes that markets exist that will determine the best price and provide the best service. The very existence of markets, price sensitivity based on supply and demand, highlights women's vulnerability as buyers and sellers. It makes a difference if citizens are expected to "spend their own money" on basic care, quite simply because women have less money. Markets in independent home care, the gray market today, are characterized by easy entry and thus concerns about quality, arising from a lack of public price information, exist.

   Alternatives to market arrangements are possible: personal care work could be performed equally by men and women, full-time workers could be assured adequate wages along with health insurance and pension coverage, and all citizens could be guaranteed a basic level of personal care services when agreed-upon levels of impairment exist. Finally, these two direct-payment models of home care delivery demonstrate that care can be provided in ways that honor comfort and familiarity without looking and feeling uniform, standardized, and impersonal. Whether such individualized care will be made available for all who need it in the future is another question. Such social care provisions would require a funding base well beyond the capacity of most local communities. A federal response, such as social insurance, is needed to assure basic equality of provision for all.

References

Antonucci, T. Social supports and social relationships. In R. H. Binstock and L. K. George (eds), *Handbook of Aging and the Social Sciences*, 205—26. 3d ed. San Diego: Academic Press.

Cantor, M. 1991. Family and community: Changing roles in an aging society, *The Gerontologist* 31(4): 337–46.

Diamond, T. 1992. *Making gray gold: Narratives of nursing home care*. Chicago: University of Chicago Press.

Doty, P. 1985. *Family care of the elderly: The role of public policy*. Washington, D.C.: Office of Legislation and Policy, Health Care Financing Administration.

Doty, P., R. Stone, and B. Jackson. 1997. Beyond alternatives to institutionalization: "Negotiated choices." *Home Care Research Initiative*, Robert Wood Johnson Foundation (Author).

England, S. and C. Ganzer. 1994. The micropolitics of eldercare in momento mori: Diary of a good neighbor and a taste for death. *International Journal of Health Services* 24(2): 355–69.

Estes, C., J. Swan, and Associates. 1993. *The long-term care crisis: Elders trapped in the no-care zone*. Newbury Park, Calif.: Sage.

Estes, C. and L. Close. 1997. Public policy and long-term care. In P. Lee and C. Estes (eds.), *The Nation's Health*, 177–91. 5th edn. Boston: Jones and Bartlett.

Evers, A. 1998. The new long-term care insurance program in Germany. *Journal of Aging and Social Policy* 10(1): 77—98.

Evers, A. and K. Leichsenring. 1994. Paying for informal care: An issue of growing importance. *Ageing International* 21(1): 29–40.

Fisher, B. and J. Tronto. 1990. Toward a feminist theory of caring. In E. K. Abel and M. K. Neson (eds.), *Circles of care: Work and identity in women's lives*, 35–62. Albany: State University of New York Press.

Gilbert, N. 1995. *Welfare justice: Restoring social equality*. New Haven: Yale University Press.

Gilbert, N. and H. Specht. 1986. *Dimensions of social welfare policy*. 2d edn. Englewood Cliffs, N.J.: Prentice-Hall.

Hirschberg, L. 1998. Warren Beatty is trying to say something. *New York Times Magazine* (May 10), 20–25, 38–40, 53, 62.

Hoch, C. and R. A. Slayton. 1989. *New homelessness and old: Community and the skid row hotel*. Philadelphia: Temple University Press.

Keigher, S. 1997. Austria's new attendance allowance: Prototype for a consumer choice model of care for the frail and disabled. *International Journal of Health Services* 27(4): 753–65.

Keigher, S. 1999. The limits of consumer-directed care. *Canadian Journal of Aging* (June).

Keigher, S. and C. Luz. 1997. *Common stakes in home care of the elderly: A pilot study of Milwaukee's gray market in independent care*. Milwaukee: The Helen Bader Foundation and the University of Wisconsin–Milwaukee, School of Social Welfare. November.

Linsk, N. L., S. M. Keigher, L. Simon-Rusinowitz, and S. England. 1992. *Wages for Caring: Compensating Family Care of the Elderly*. Westport, Conn.: Praeger.

Mann, C. and J. Guyer. 1997. *Overview of the new child health block grant* (August 6). Washington, D.C.: Center for Budget and Policy Priorities.

Morris, R., F. Caro, and J. Hansan. 1998. Testing an improved personal service system for home care: Another option for life at home with a disability. Authors.

Osterbusch [England], S., S. M. Keigher, B. Miller, and N. Linsk. 1987. Community care and gender justice. *International Journal of Health Services* 17(2): 217–32.

Rich, S. 1985. The home care debate. *Washington Post National Weekly Edition* (June 10), 85.

Stack, C. 1974. *All our kin: Strategies for survival in the black community*. New York: Harper and Row.

Stone, R. and S. Keigher. 1994. Toward an equitable, universal caregiver policy: The potential of financial supports for family caregivers. *Journal of Aging and Social Policy* 6(1–2): 57–75.

Ungerson, C. 1997. Social politics and the commodification of care. *Social Politics* 4(3): 362–81.

8

Being in Health

Versions of the Discursive Body

ANNE OPIE

Examining my qualitative research study on social work practice with care-givers and people with a dementia enables me to revisit two critical issues raised by that research. One is the competing representations of the caregiver pro-duced by different players in the long-term care drama: the funders and those organizations that define service content and priorities; social workers who as-sess and respond to care needs; and family caregivers, who must adapt and fill in the gaps so that a generic formal service can meet the particular needs of a frail spouse or parent. I explore how each constituency has a different, and not always complementary, representation of the aging body that is the supposed object of care. These representations offer different constructions of needs and service provision. The second issue explores complications embedded within the concept of "empowerment." The complications of having cast the study in a "collaborative" quasi-"empowerment" framework rapidly became apparent once the fieldwork got under way. Rather than refocusing on these particular dissonances (see Opie 1995), this chapter discusses the implications of "em-powerment" in knowledge, practice, and research methods.

The first section ("The Work of Discourse") begins with a discussion of a key theoretical term—*discourse*. It then moves into a brief account of the methodology of the research reported on here and contextualizes the study within changing economic and social discourses in New Zealand and inter-nationally, followed by an account of the three discourses (those of the orga-nization, the social workers, and caregivers) constructing the caregiving body. The second section ("Discourses of Empowerment") takes up the ques-tion of "empowerment."

The Work of Discourse

My use of *discourse* is informed by the work of the French philosopher, Michel Foucault (see, for example, Burchell, Gordon & Miller 1991; Foucault 1977, 1978; Gordon 1980; Kritzman 1988; Martin, Gutman & Hutton 1988). "Discourse" refers to the social allocation of truth values to certain types of knowledge and behaviors and to the socially validated outcomes of this process. It highlights the interrelation of knowledge, power, and the ability to define truth in order for the state to maintain particular forms of social relations and to produce desired forms of subjectivity. Discourse is intimately linked with power. As a consequence of the power held by some groups within a society, certain modes of knowledge and behavior (or "micropractices") are privileged. The intersection of what Foucault refers to as "power/knowledge" results in the allocation of truth to particular discourses; their truth status assists in their validity being continuously confirmed and reproduced. What is a *social* construction is seen as "natural." Being taken for granted, a particular mode of construction of the social world goes substantially unnoticed and its truth value largely unquestioned. Any discourse then *includes* some modes of understanding the world; equally it *excludes* others. The process is not, however, entirely deterministic. There is always more than one discourse circulating at any given time. Changes in dominant discourses, and the emergence of alternative ones, are made possible because no discourse is monolithic; all occupy contradictory positions, enabling over time the appropriation or modification of a previously dominant discursive position.

Inevitably, discourses offer partial representations of the social world. These representations are structured by the positioning of those who both speak and are spoken by those discourses. By this I mean that an individual speaks from within a discourse and, as a consequence of articulating that discourse, is spoken by it. What one sees and knows is affected by one's social, gendered, ethnic, and economic location within a society and by the interpretative strategies available as a consequence of that positioning. No event or fact is transparent. All are mediated by language, and the entry of language into the construction of that event or fact immediately locates the speaker within a set of discursive strategies. No representation, however "objectively" cast, can claim neutrality; all are informed by discourse. It is impossible to operate beyond discourse, but there are choices about the discursive strategies in which one locates oneself, although these choices may be significantly more constrained for some.

Part of Foucault's thesis attends to the role of discourse in the regulatory processes of the state and the ways that these write or produce certain types of "bodies" through the operation of micropractices and disciplinary systems (Castel 1991; Grosz 1994; Martin, Gutman & Hutton 1988: see esp. ch. 8). As the analysis I develop below indicates, there is more than one way of writing/producing the caregiving body. Furthermore, each mode defines the appropriate shape and structure of services and of resource allocation because discursive constructions have material or real social consequences. A critical issue for social work practice is understanding what each caregiving discourse encompasses and from where it is spoken—that is, the power it is able to command and the knowledge on which it is constructed. Let me put this differently. The "business" of human services organizations is in part to meet the "needs" of the service users for whom those organizations are responsible—and how needs are defined is a business in which the state, professionals, and other groups have a significant interest! As Fraser (1989) has indicated in her complex discussion of needs interpretations, the mere act of defining needs is a highly political action, although the politics of needs interpretation are often occulted. As I demonstrate in the following pages, in my research I found that there was a persistent tension between providers' rhetoric of the needs of caregivers, the caring elderly "body" produced by that rhetoric and the ensuing representation of the necessary service provision, and the social work discourse, particularly that of the more sophisticated workers.[1]

It is important to emphasize that in writing of a discursive "body" I am referring to how that complex intersection of belief, ideology, and behavioral practices structures the physical body—in other words, to how actual bodies and actions of individuals are so shaped by social conventions and the micropractices which discourse reproduce that particular physical and intellectual actions which could be performed by them are not regarded possible while other ways of being in the world are. To focus on the discursive body is to attend to these processes of inscription or production. Rather than focusing on the supreme power of the state, the central concern in many discussions of power that make up traditional political economy analyses, Foucaultian/feminist analyses address "the body as the site of power, that is, as the locus of domination through which docility is accomplished" (Diamond & Quinby 1988:x). By offering a more complex account of the caregiving situation, the sophisticated social work discourse produced a more complex, more differentiated "body" than that produced by the providers. This discourse addressed issues of difference and changing needs. It worked against the grain of ageist discourses, articulating "need" in terms of assistance with

everyday tasks (household and/or personal) *as well as* in terms of responding
to the psychosocial needs of older people.

The practice necessary to respond to the social workers' discursive construct of the caregiving body had few points of connection with the organizations' discursive constructs. For example, part of effective social work
practice related to the imparting of information about services. Social workers spoke of the giving of information as a process which had an emotional
context. Caregivers' anxiety, fear, guilt, exhaustion, not knowing what questions to ask, and degree of trust—all these affected what could be heard and
what could be immediately absorbed. This situation was further compounded when service users had a dementia but were still in a position to be
involved in decisions about their lives. Defining the giving of information as
a process, as more than a factual exchange (the organizational discourse),
points to the "need" for a more indeterminately structured service where
workers attend to the emotional and social issues generated by the provision
of information. This may mean, for instance, that the work to be undertak-
en is more effectively done through a home visit rather than by phone and
that, as one caregiver noted in talking about his initial reluctance to contact
a worker, some persistence by the worker may be called for in developing
a relationship.

Methodologically, attending to the discourses that structure the texts
which guide researchers' analyses calls for a radical departure from detailed attention to the construction of data trails—the involvement of others in assessing the efficacy of coding and the collapsing of codes one into the other—
which appears to be the stuff of some writing about qualitative research
methods (see, for example, Beck 1993).[2] Although some of this may be part of
data analysis routines, this writing gives the impression that following such a
set of prescribed procedures is sufficient to produce valid research outcomes.
The effect of this routinized gaze, itself a mode of discursive practice, is to re-
site qualitative research in an "objective" mode, that mode of research still accorded primary significance within Western scholarship.

Practices such as these obscure the critical interaction between texts that
constitute the data and the interpretative processes brought to those texts by
readers/writers, who are themselves intertextual fields.[3] In undertaking an
analysis informed by postmodern theory, researchers' attention is not only on
content and immersion in coding processes. It is also on the production of a
close reading of the texts and their location within the social—that is, how
these texts generated by individual actors are not about those actors alone but
instead how these actors are located within different discursive positions and

social processes. Rather than writing of the separation of the micro and macro, this approach emphasizes how each is embedded in the other.

In undertaking an analysis, I may code (as part of the very beginning of the formal phases of analysis, under a heading that may or may not change)[4] a piece of text as being about an aspect of social work practice experienced by a caregiver. This of course is not the end of the process. Reading the range of texts coded under this heading, and reading those against texts coded elsewhere, generates further questions. I will be asking how these texts work, how they interrogate others, what micropractices they describe, what "shape" of body they produce, and what are the implications of that production? The developing responses I propose to these questions are then placed against the accumulating evidence: how does this affirm or deconstruct the analytic possibilities I am proposing to myself? How do the implications of this data intersect with or raise questions about other studies in the field and relate to my knowledge of professional practice? How do I respond to internal contradictions, marginalized comments, the richness of detail of one text, and the relative paucity of another? The significance of a small phrase is not merely because of its particular content (although that is part of it), but how that phrase opens up a fuller reading of the social.

The Context for the Research

Undertaking a study of social work support to people with a dementia and their caregivers (Opie 1995) was a consequence of a previous research project (Opie 1992). Although social work support is often noted in the international literature as critical to caregivers, those who participated in the 1992 study spoke of its substantial absence; some also commented on its perfunctoriness. Social workers were "too busy." The study was, then, a response to this caregiver-identified absence. An initial question ("Where were the social workers and what did they do?") developed rapidly into more complex questions about where social work practice was positioned within discourses of aging and how practice was in part further affected by the (then) emerging (and persisting) managerialist discourses generated by New Right economic theory.

I undertook fieldwork at four sites in 1992. One site was in a major urban area, the other three were in provincial cities of varying sizes. One dimension of the research design was its emphasis on the need for triangulation in order to develop a representation of practice informed by multiple data sets. I therefore observed thirty-eight meetings (primarily social work and multidisciplinary team meetings) which social workers attended as part of their everyday

work. I observed and audiotaped thirty interviews conducted by social workers (interviews with caregivers, interviews with people with a dementia, family meetings to discuss care plans, and assessment interviews), and I reviewed
sixty-one social work files (Opie 1993). I also conducted audiotaped interviews
with twenty-two social workers, four managers, and fifty-three health professionals with whom the social workers worked closely (e.g., nurses, occupational therapists, home care workers, geriatricians) as well as the fifty-three
caregivers (whose texts I discuss later).

I defined the study as "collaborative," in part to emphasize researchers' dependence on participants' active involvement and representations of the phenomena which constitute the subject of the study, thereby challenging models of research which accord primacy and power to the researcher. I also
conceptualized the study in terms of "empowerment." Knowing from my
own practice experience how difficult it is to find time to think through the
ground and implications of practice, I hoped that workers would find the opportunity to discuss their practice professionally empowering, particularly in
light of the challenges that changing health discourses pose for social workers.
Despite some ambivalence about social work as a profession, I hoped further
that a research project that located practice within a complex contextual field
would also assist in empowering the profession by underscoring the breadth
and intricacy of its work; and that it would empower caregivers in demon-
strating the significance of and the need for quality, nuanced services. While
interviews with caregivers were to focus on the caregivers' evaluation of social
work services rather than individuals' particular circumstances, I thought it
likely that some would discuss the situations that led to social work interventions. I hoped that this process would be itself therapeutic, would be empowering, albeit on a different plane. Finally, I hoped that my research would
contribute to critical discourses surrounding health practices and "needs" interpretations but was highly dubious about the extent to which it would benefit participants in the immediate future.

The research took place at a time of major social, economic, and discursive changes in New Zealand which had begun in 1984. While similar changes
have occurred elsewhere (Hadley and Clough 1996; Taylor 1990), what has
been peculiar about the New Zealand "experiment" (Kelsey 1995) has been the
speed, intensity, and extensiveness with which the restructuring occurred (and
continues to occur) despite significant and long-term opposition from the
public. These changes have been paralleled by major changes in public discourse. Particularly significant has been the reformulation of the discourse of
the beneficence of state intervention and of collective social responsibility into

one that defines such intervention as encouraging dependency and irresponsibility.[5] As a major social and capital-intensive institution, the health sector was the object of constant restructuring in efforts to control expenditures and improve efficiency and accountability, with the most radical "reform" being effected in 1993 (Upton 1991).[6]

The Organizational Production of Work and Its Effects

When I carried out the fieldwork, contracting for services was not yet in place. Social work practice was, nonetheless, becoming much more highly regulated than previously and the degree of indeterminacy in professional practice was restricted in two ways. One was through organizational protocols such as those that gave service priority to the needs of inpatients rather than to those informal caregivers and their relatives with a dementia who were in the community. This occurred despite aged care policy stressing the importance of community care, and of the provision of support to family caregivers (Shipley & Upton 1992).[7] The other way was occasioned by changing organizational pressures and demands for accountability which restructured social work practices. In two of the research sites, the sheer quantity of the work because of frozen positions, high referral levels, and the need to achieve high outputs[8] meant that home visits were being replaced by telephone calls and regular follow-up work was cut back. Management expected social workers to build a good rapport with caregivers in the course of a single brief contact, at which point their needs would be determined and met and the case would be closed. As a consequence, responsibility was placed on the caregiver to recontact the worker when faced with a crisis, contrary to past practice where the worker offered an option to maintain the association. Most social workers considered that the assumptions informing such policies sat poorly with what they understood to be the complex and demanding nature of caregiving, where caregivers often found it difficult to request assistance.

Different organizational and professional accounts about practice are far more than just competing accounts about what constitutes good practice. Each discursively constructs, through its representations of what work is needed, and through its micropractices of engagement with service users, competing accounts of adequate professional practices, caring bodies, and, correspondingly, caregivers' needs. The political (and hence organizational) discourses, grounded in one knowledge domain about the effects of big government and the importance of self-help (or help given by family and community), prioritizes the model of minimalist intervention, to be terminated the moment the crisis is passed. Placed within other discursive contexts of economic scarcity and what are defined as "budget blowouts" requiring targeted services, these produce the "need" for highly economically efficient organizations with well-defined areas of professional work from which outputs can be properly measured to ensure government finances are properly targeted.

The object of service, the body that these discourses generate, is a self-reliant one, requiring brief interventions only at points of crisis—a rational, competent, active, decision-making body with ties to family and/or community, from whence support will be offered. It follows, then, that such a body will need only intermittent contact with service providers, that the information required to make competent decisions about needs and how to meet them will be easily digested, and that services are those where inputs and outputs can be measured and targeted at those who "need" them most. Targeting therefore introduces the requirement for well-defined, "objective" criteria for including and excluding possible subjects. "Need" is defined in terms of supposedly objective predetermined criteria—it stands alone, divorced from its complex contextual and political underpinnings.

The Social Work Discourse of the Caring Body

Recent accounts of social work practice with older people (e.g., Biggs 1989; Froggart 1990; Fry 1992; Hughes 1995; Marino 1991), and care issues for people with a dementia (Kitwood 1989, 1990, 1997; Lyman 1993) emphasize the complex emotional (not just practical or instrumental) work to be undertaken with older people and the corresponding high levels of skills and knowledge required for effective professional work. Defining social work in this manner introduces potentially more fluid concepts of assessment and evaluation *with* the person about the physical and psychosocial domains of their lives. It does not exclude prioritizing, but does not operate in relation to abstract, often simplistic, categories of "need" which form the backbone of most decisions of "targeting."

In reviewing social workers' relationship to these discourses, and the caring body that they produce, it can be said that most endorsed this more complex articulation of practice, but there were considerable variations in the knowledge and skills possessed by workers, as well as variations in their positioning in ageist discourses. Out of the twenty-two workers involved in the study, five women demonstrated sophisticated work practices. These few workers brought an unromanticized commitment and a high level of social work skills to their practice. They were particularly concerned about the increasingly reductivist work they were producing in the changing organizational environments. In contrast, my observations of other workers' practices suggested that they addressed only practical or instrumental needs, whatever their convictions about the significance of psychosocial components of work with older people.

The sophisticated work practices exhibited by the five women in the study sought to include complex interrelated issues in needs determination. Their assessment of the degree of support needed from family reflected an appreciation of possible practical and emotional constraints in accessing that support, and the difficult decisions required (for example, in deciding about placement in residential care). Whereas the political and organizational discourses represented the needy body in regulatory and administrative terms as part of its targeting mechanisms, the more sophisticated social work discourse produced a "thick" description of the differing psychosocial "needs" and the importance of focusing on the different bodies of caregiver and care recipient, affirming both their joint and separate needs and the complexity (ethically and practically) in responding to some of those needs. Smale and Tuson (1993) have described two main models of assessment. One model is the "questioning" model, wherein "the professional is assumed to be the expert in identifying need" (7) and where "the questions reflect the worker's agenda, and not other people's. Enshrined in the questions asked will be implicit or explicit criteria or perceptions of the problems that [the client has] and a view of the resources available" (9). An alternative model is the "exchange" model, which Smale and Tuson define as more empowering of service users because "the professional concentrates on an exchange of information between themselves" and the user (9), resulting in positive interactions between workers and users rather than question/answer behaviors. This model enables the sharing of perceptions of "the situation, its problems, availability of resources and the need for more" (11). The social work discourse was located in the latter model, thus highlighting the production of work within the context of a relationship.

Inscribing the Caring Body: The Caregivers' Representations

It is now time to bring on the caregivers. What did they have to say about the social work services they received? Where did they discursively locate themselves?

I interviewed fifty-three caregivers, selected by the social workers in response to preestablished criteria. While all the caregivers' texts informed my knowledge of the issues, I carried out a detailed analysis on twenty-five interviews, representative of the whole group in terms of gender, kin relationship, and the evaluations offered of the social work service they had received.

Given the gendered nature of caregiving, it is not surprising that I interviewed predominantly women, many of whom were older spouses. To define responses to the social work interventions in terms of gender is, however, difficult. Two women (a middle-aged nonresident daughter and an older spouse) were the most critical of that service. A husband whose female social worker had left and been replaced by a male worker was markedly less enthusiastic about his contact with the latter, citing the absence of the emotional support provided by the previous worker, who also had had a good rapport with his wife—something the male worker did not.[9] One son, who had only sought limited contact with the social worker and had kept the discussion focused on practical issues, described the service he received as having been quite inadequate in terms of the support he wanted. Some of the other male carers emphasized the value of affective, not just instrumental, support, despite one or two who felt initially suspicious in talking about the emotional aspects of the work—something a few women commented on as well. There tended to be a qualitatively more affirmatory but not gender-specific difference in caregiver response from caregivers who had had contact with the more sophisticated social workers. Overall, however, the caregivers' texts highlighted the significance and value of the relational dimension of their contact with social workers, including those where work had focused on service provision and information-giving. The social worker was someone with whom the caregiver could talk, plan, and in many instances "fall back on"[10].

There were, however, some criticisms. Only three caregivers (two referencing the same young, inexperienced, and unsophisticated worker) provided a sustained negative critique of the service they had received. Some, while being substantially positive, offered points of qualification, such as the worker's tendency to rely on phoning rather than on face-to-face contact, and the statement by one person who thought his worker should have been much more knowledgeable about services—but then complicated this assertion by saying that, given his general emotional state at the time, he may have not taken in much that was said.

One line of argument would define these criticisms as being relatively minor. An alternative perspective—the one I adopt here—seeks to contrast the organizational discourses with those of the social workers and the caregivers. Let me return to the issue of providing information. There was a high level of congruence between the social worker arguing for the need to "drip-feed" information over time as the caregiver is able to accept that information, and caregivers' texts. Both sets of texts speak of a stressed body, where the emotional dynamics of the situation are such that not all the complex information outlined at one interview is heard or retained. This writing of the body as emotionally structured, as being situationally audibly "impaired," stands against organizational writing pointing up rationality and the "audibility" of information. Each account is embedded in micropractices endorsed or challenged by organizational definitions of that practice.

I want now to a address a more complicated and contradictory position advanced by some of the caregivers. If the overwhelming majority of their texts highlighted *presence* and *understanding* as a key dimension of their contact with social workers, about half spoke as well of workers' failures to ask about, or to take up, emotional issues which the caregiver was confronting, or to respond to their grieving processes, and of how workers terminated contact at a critical moment, such as following the older person's death or the admission of the older person to institutional care.[11] Less skilled workers either did not respond to the situation or tended to reassure the person of the normality of grieving rather than encouraging caregivers to actually talk about their feelings. One woman concluded that her worker had assumed she had it all under control, whereas she had "grasped it intellectually" but not emotionally. Another spoke of the two months she had spent coming to a decision to put her husband in care. Her recollection was that the worker focused on what was the "best decision" for him, and her deteriorating ability to cope. The approaches adopted by both workers emphasized logicality and rationality in the decision-making process and were doubtless intended to be reassuring—equally both inscribe or write caregiving in ways which suppress its emotional component. As the second of these women noted, there was no discussion of what this decision meant for her in relation to loss and subsequent refocusing of her life. She commented,

> Logically I knew I could no longer *cope*. I knew that logically I couldn't but in my heart I didn't want to really face it so um I had this sort of caring sensation of . . . I wanted him *at home* but then I knew that if I brought him *home I really wouldn't* be able to cope and so I was, you know, was going through a *terrible* guilt thing . . . *shocking* guilt thing because I, because I didn't have him at home.

Such a text writes the body (if I may be allowed to mix metaphors) as being "at sea," as being "adrift." There was no process that allowed her to talk through some of these feelings.

Not all carers wanted to become involved in more counseling-oriented discussions focusing on issues of grief and loss. However, those who did wish to
talk things through more fully, but were faced with the unavailability or inability of the social worker to do so, rationalized this absence by positioning
their needs in relation to a discourse of "scarcity," which created an interesting
dynamic. To criticize the worker was difficult when he/she had been a "life-
line." Instead carers drew from the discourse of scarce resources and rationed
themselves, thereby protecting the worker from too many demands. They
only made contact when, for example, they were "desperate," but further
comments indicated the relativity of this concept. One woman who may have
been abusive toward her mother said, "I felt as if I were taking up valuable
time and I didn't want to be a nuisance." Others placed their "needs" against
the needs of unknown others and concluded they were not as needy; wishing
not to become burdensome, they therefore refrained from making contact or
did not raise the issues that were concerning them. This process did not produce a body with no emotional needs, but a body whose needs could become
so overwhelming that they could alienate their one source of help.

The bodies constructed by these lay texts were complexly textured and
multiply-sited bodies (for example, in relation to age, gender, relationship,
multiplicity of demands) with different degrees of "neediness" across the psychosocial plane. They were informed substantially by uncertainty and confusion, loss, emotionality, exhaustion. They received different degrees of support. As such, these bodies bore little relationship to the homogenized frail
aging body constructed within political and administrative discourses.

The bodies produced within the caregivers' texts did have significant connections to those constructed within social work discourses, and it was these
more complex bodies that the more sophisticated workers sought to articulate,
despite their organizationally restricted practice. In this instance, there was a
high degree of congruence between the lay and what Fraser (1989) calls "expert"
discourses. Both foregrounded complexity and variability: variability in the
complexity of situation and circumstance of both carer and care recipient and
the variety of responses necessary to attend to these; in the presence, availability, and supportiveness of those charged constructs "family" and "community";
and variability in positioning within the emotional nexus of caring (Opie 1994).
They emphasized the degree to which decisions cannot be defined as informed
only by rationality, contradicting the valorizing of rationality and self-interest of
the discourses of the New Right. Both defined effective social work practice
with caregivers (and people with a dementia) as being nuanced, as being responsive to the particularity of situation, as being reflexive, as responding where

necessary to the emotional dynamics embedded in the caregiving situation, of attending to the dyad of caregiver and care recipient, not just to the identified "consumer." Both highlighted the heterogeneity of caregivers.

There is, however, a further point that needs to be made. All discourses operate around exclusion, not just inclusion. While the social work discourse in particular and caregiver discourse to a significantly lesser degree emphasized the needs of the latter in the context of the stress and distress generated by the desire, duty, and obligation to care, in defining services necessary to respond to caring responsibilities the needs of the person with a dementia were relegated to the margins. The care recipient entered the social work discourse largely as a "burden," as one whose personhood is in the process of becoming lost—in effect, "becoming a 'nonperson.' " Reclaiming this marginalized body involves disrupting the range of mainstream professional discourses constructing this body (Gilmour 1997; Kitwood 1997), attending to issues of psychic discomfort generated by the aging body (Biggs 1989), and rewriting the positioning of the caregiver and person with a dementia in order to attend to their joint *and* to their competing needs.

A second point of exclusion is that while the distant political and administrative discourses exclude the more complex articulation of caring bodies, through highlighting the economic savings of attending to minimalist versions of caring and aging dementing bodies, the social work discourse, developed through a daily encounter with those bodies, excludes a detailed discussion of resources and resource allocation. The binary between the economic and the social remained.

Discourses of Empowerment

The question of whose voices are heard in the construction of needs takes a further interesting twist when placed within the context of empowerment, a significant concept in the discourses of collaboration, particularly in action research methodologies, and within government health and welfare policies that emphasize "consumer" empowerment in the development of services and choice. It is to this issue that I now turn.

If I adopt the definition of "empowerment" as focused on the allocation of power and authority (*Oxford Dictionary of Current English*), then this emphasizes the extent to which empowerment is deeply embedded in relations of power and foregrounds those Foucauldian questions about who speaks and why now? from what position? and what is heard of that speaking? The objective of empowerment is to make available those lay or marginalized voices/positions that are typically written out, rendered invisible by the dominant discourses (McLean 1995; Opie 1998; Smale & Tuson 1993; Young 1994). Achieving this objective—the introduction of alternative knowledge, voices, and discourses with the concomitant intention to dislodge or disrupt the dominant discourses—involves highly complex processes. Achieving change involves more than shifting personal ideologies or belief systems, attitudes, or behaviors. It involves achieving institutional shifts across these domains. That such shifts are possible is demonstrated, for instance, by the Maori renaissance in New Zealand. But there is also a point where success and redistribution of power may engender further (and possibly more strident) resistance and disruption. Such points of resistance, and the resistance to the resistance, leads to the articulation of further discursive positions informed by revisited and recast representations of "reality" held by dominant, not just marginal, groups. It is, however, important not to be overly sanguine about rapid discursive shifts and changes in the distribution of power.

Empowerment and Research Practice

In the 1980s feminist social science researchers, only too aware of the colonizing tendencies of much social science research, wrote the concept "collaboration" into research design (see Reinharz 1992 for a discussion of some of this literature). Collaborative projects would actively involve participants in all aspects of the research process, ensuring that the results were "owned" by the participants. An objective of such research is to privilege participants' voices, affirm their knowledge as necessary to more fully informed appreciation of issues, and (possibly) shift the balance of political power in their direction. In the 1990s the concept of "collaboration," as papers presented at the 1997 American conference Reclaiming Voices emphasized, appears to have shifted more to "empowerment" as a research objective in much qualitative research (see, for example, Fine 1997). Its current discursive positioning has become complicated—discourses of resource distribution (here accessing principles of social equity and justice) and affirming individual dignity are intertwined with those of dependency avoidance, self-help, and the retreat of the state.

Since the argument about empowerment and discursivity I want to develop works against that developed by Yvonna Lincoln, I wish to quote from her writing. In writing of the "authenticity criteria" (Lincoln 1990:71), which Lincoln asserts assist in the evaluation of the validity of qualitative research, she outlines a model of empowerment and action research which includes a discussion of the "states of being" for respondents, participants, and stake-holders. These relate to

(a) levels of understanding and sophistication and to (b) the enhanced ability of participants and stakeholders to take action during and after an inquiry and to negotiate on behalf of themselves and their own interests in the political arena. Those "states of being" criteria included *ontological authenticity*, or the heightened awareness of one's own constructions and assumptions, manifest and unspoken; *educative criteria*, or the increased awareness and appreciation (though not necessarily acceptance of) the constructions of other stakeholders; *catalytic authenticity*, a criterion that is judged by the prompt action generated by inquiry efforts; and *tactical authenticity*, the ability to take action, to engage the political arena on be-half of oneself or one's referent stakeholder or participant group.

(Lincoln and Guba 1986, quoted in Lincoln 1990:72)

She writes of how "the written report should demonstrate the passion, the commitment, and the involvement of the inquirer with his or her copartici-pants in the inquiry" (73), and of "action criteria" which relate to the taking of action as a consequence of the research study (74).

Taking the "community" of caregivers as an exemplary construct, I want to engage with the problematic of this particular discursive construct of re-search methodology (noting the hierarchical structure embedded within the verb—those who are to be empowered as subordinate to those dispensing empowerment).

A decision to locate a research project within a "community" immediate-ly raises definitional problems: Who is "the community" and what assump-tions are being made about its relational immediacy and cohesiveness?[12] Who is excluded by that definition? What are the researchers' agendas? Part of the objective of involvement is to ensure that "the community" owns the project, ownership facilitating researchers' entrée, community participation, and (in some cases) willingness to use the results. There may well be also a clear ed-ucative and employment component, as ongoing activity in the project is like-ly to require "community" involvement in meetings and the development of literacy as well as political skills. Further, such research is likely to be time-in-tensive for both researchers and "the community." These factors highlight the resources necessary to satisfactorily meet the methodological demands. Yet, as Peterson and Lupton (1996) have pointed out, socially marginal communities which may be most likely to attract empowering projects are those where members' resources to be so involved are likely to be extremely limited.

How then to identify my "community" of caregivers? While I was able to meet twice with the social workers to discuss the study prior to its commencing, similar forms of consultation (with their attendant difficulties and limitations) were not possible with the caregivers. Consultation with the local Alzheimer's society would not have helped. The society could not have spoken for all those whom I finally did interview as the majority were not members. They could not be distinguished in relation to a particular geographical location, and even thinking of them as a group was problematical because of the weighting it gave to a single shared characteristic—the responsibility of caring, or having cared for someone with a dementia. Other factors such as kinship, gender, age, socioeconomic status, ethnicity, family support, and so on emphasized their heterogeneity, not their homogeneity.

The model of empowering research points to political action by participants and to their increased political sophistication. It writes an active body, able to engage with the political implications of the research and its findings. Yet many of the caregivers whom I was seeking to "empower" were elderly, a number were exhausted and not in good health, and what energy they had was generally absorbed by a very demanding and time-consuming role. The support groups that some attended focused on survival strategies. Was it my role to "educate" them about their political responsibilities, to insert my agenda into their lives? What does that say about positioning and power? Moreover, a question that has somewhat belatedly occurred to me as I write this is, "which political role?" The interpretation of the politics of care which informs my writing is that complex rather than simplistic models of "needs" should inform service provision, that longer-term goals about gender equity and social justice should direct attention to structural issues, and that assumptions about the availability of a "supportive community" require constant challenge. The problem with this, however, is that it inserts the discourse back into assumptions about collective social responsibilities, assumptions that a succession of recent New Zealand governments have repudiated. An alternative proposition, interestingly in line with New Right philosophies about rationality and self-interest, is that caregivers, in light of reductivist and unresponsive services, should exercise their "choice" and refuse to care.

The empowerment model also seeks involvement by the community in the research process. Active participation in a research project involves a considerable amount of knowledge, or training to acquire that knowledge, and requires time for ongoing work. Gaining even some of this knowledge and developing work skills is useful for many and may well be invaluable if one is a member of a marginal ethnic community (albeit that expectations about participation by those in such communities may well be extremely complicated), but this does not mean that I can assume a simple transferability of a research model developed to respond to ethnic politics in the United States to a very different population whose daily responsibilities already required major commitments of time and energy. The problematic of community participation applies to its twin, empowerment, so that

> it makes little point to speak of ["empowerment"] in any abstract, transcultural sense. The meanings and implications are always dependent on the context of use, and on the structural location and continuing commitment of parties who are involved. This point tends to be overlooked . . . in academic discussions of ["empowerment"]. . . . It is often assumed that an abstract set of principles can be developed and applied across a range of settings irrespective of cultural practices, existing political structures and values, and the personal commitments and positions of those involved.
>
> *(Peterson and Lupton 1996:159; my substitutions)*

Is it legitimate to expect others to make that which is central to one's own working life a dominant part of their's? How does a refusal to participate site the refuser?[13] Further, developing an analysis requires specific skills if it is to engage successfully with powerful institutional discourses. Writing this is not to devalue the knowledge of individual participants about their specific situations and those factors that contribute to the maintenance of their problematic situation but to underscore the disciplinary, hierarchical (i.e., exclusory) functioning of the knowledge economy. Part of the strength of a research report is the richness and breadth of the associated research on which it draws, and the way it works with that writing—to interrogate it, rewrite it, reposition it. This raises important questions about use of data, about supporting evidence, about the type of research that will be accorded validity by the organization or institution whose practices and discourses the researcher/community is hoping to influence. These questions raise tensions between different modes of writing and complicate issues of the presentation of voice and of resourcing.

As someone who has published a book of transcripts of caregivers' experiences of caring (Opie 1991) as part of a number of research outputs associated with a particular project, my position about the political question of "voice" could appear to be ambivalent. The issue, it seems to me, cannot be usefully located within binary frameworks—this "lay" or that "research" voice is to be privileged. Rather, the issue is what voice is appropriate for what audience in light of the particular objectives of the research and the discursive positioning

of a particular research report. A publication foregrounding the "lay" voice
may have a particular resonance for a community; equally, presenting a differently structured report may have more resonance with a different audience. In
addition, there is always a danger that the text that does not provide an analysis and that focuses largely on individuals' experience may well be read in those
terms—the issues are seen in terms of the individual, and the wider political
and structural issues may get suppressed. The critical issue is what type or style
of document will best be heard by the particular audience(s) (lay, institutions,
and organizations) with which the writer(s) seek(s) to engage.

Questions about what type of report/writing will empower those with and
for whom one writes raises additional issues about resourcing and, for want of
a better phrase, "researcher stickability." Producing a range of different documents for different audiences is costly. In situations likely to be familiar to many
social scientists, where research budgets are tight but there is space for different
styles of reports addressing different audiences, should "committed" researchers,
for instance, be expected to forgo some of their salary in order to fund these different outputs; and are researchers who decide against this course of action "uncommitted"? It hardly needs be said that writing is time-consuming. In the
United States, untenured researchers on soft money constitute over 50 percent
of the staff in some universities (personal communication; see also Martin
1997). Following research grants in order to stay employed is likely to complicate the ability of many such researchers to continue a longer-term relationship
with a particular community. Nor, because they must move immediately from
one grant to another if they are to sustain their salaries, will researchers necessarily find sufficient time to develop the desirable range of outputs outside the
time frame of that specific research project. Conducting "empowering" research
would appear to throw up some unexpected ethical and structural problems.

Lincoln, moreover, appears to assume a close connection between "empowering research" and some mode of social change, thus raising interesting questions about the assumptions underlying the use of research findings and their
contribution to change. In New Zealand, a recent shift by the major funder
from a focus on outputs to one on outcomes has meant that those applying for
research funding must nominate end users, and these nominated users must
write in support of the proposal. Yet in the end researchers have little control
over whether or how their research findings are used. The uses to which the
nominated end users may put the research make up but one part of a complex
process within which discourses are maintained and challenged. A further problem about research take-up in New Zealand is that the "end user" of much social science research is properly government, but research critical of govern-

mental discourses has found it very difficult to get a hearing (*Drawing on the Evidence*, 1995). Given the complexity of changing discourses and most researchers' lack of political power, a significant research agenda may well be to introduce another voice from the margins as part of the processes by which dominant discourses are destabilized—in other words, it may be that the best we can ask for is to contribute *in the longer term* to a process of change.

The model of empowerment research writes of active, increasingly politicized and sophisticated participants. It privileges the local, vernacular voice, assuming that this passionate voice, along with the researcher's, will engage productively with the expert discourses embedded in institutional structures; as a consequence of the formers' assertion of the "truth," those who hold the determining power in the institutions will facilitate the insertion of that truth into the field of power. Such a position operates on the assumption that the articulation of a particular knowledge in itself is sufficient to achieve change. Temporally, the model is located in the immediate present, casting participants as both active agents and beneficiaries of change. The model removes the expert discourses from the field and assumes that institutions holding the determining power will facilitate the process of discursive change. Altogether, it offers too simplistic an account of what can be expected from research processes and outcomes.

In contrast, a discursive construction of caregivers and empowerment produces a more constrained body—one shaped by circumstance and difference affecting a desire to be involved in research and political processes. The issue of voice is critical, but it is not the *authenticity* of that voice which is the focus of attention, nor the passion of the researcher—dimensions which contribute to modernist notions about the validity of the research. In a desire for change, a critical issue for both the researcher and the researched is how voices operating on discursive margins can be best positioned and in what ways they should be written to effectively intersect with and disrupt the expert discourses. Neither the researcher nor the research participants can expect rewards/gratification for their efforts. They are faced instead with recognizing the inevitability of postponing (personal) gratification, in light of the complexity of achieving discursive change.

Empowerment Within the Field of Health

The health discourse developed in New Zealand over the last decade explicitly adopted "empowerment" of users as one of its policy platforms. Users were to have more "choice" and health authorities were encouraged to consult with their local communities about the development and operation of services

(Upton 1991). "Consultation" has also taken the garb of numerous surveys of consumer satisfaction, and many New Zealanders have responded repeatedly to a plethora of consultative documents about various aspects of health and welfare services.

Actual user empowerment through these processes, however, has been constrained. For example, the general practice in the document consultative process is to ask the public to respond to a series of set questions. The documents reflect priorities determined by the organization and/or government. The questions restrict discussion and evaluation of options because they operate within particular assumptions informing the text of the document. The quantity and quality of feedback about the results of the consultation has been variable. Pollit (1988) has criticized the rhetoric of consumer involvement in the context of the unavailability of quality information which consumers could access. One manager whom I interviewed spoke of service users being "surveyed out" and reluctant to participate in further surveys, and of the ease with which negative data could be massaged to achieve favorable evaluations to assist in the contracting processes. To complicate things further, consumer surveys appear to be problematic, partly because they position consumers as unreliable (Nocon and Qureshi 1996:36).

Interviewing caregivers constituted a mode, but I would also want to argue a different mode, of consultation. As governments' enthusiasm for New Right agendas continues unabated, I cannot claim that inserting caregivers' voices into the public discourse surrounding support services for older people has in itself achieved significant change in service provision, although there were other benefits to participants in the research. What I can claim is that the method (individual interviews) enabled the production of complex accounts of issues in service provision which are now available to inform research and policy on services and community care issues.

Discourses of empowerment therefore leave a variety of problems unattended. While valorizing the lay voice as challenging current hierarchies of knowledge/power may be theoretically attractive, the difficulty of actually dislodging professional and expert knowledge should not, as Fraser (1989) has also insisted, be underestimated, not least because the lay voice does not always have access to the evidence to which the "expert" gives credence. Embedded too within this discourse are assumptions about "community." At two or three points in this chapter I have referred to the fraught assumptions in social policy about "community" in relation to the provision of active support to caregivers—an issue that feminist researchers have raised repeatedly over the last decade—and the ease with which connections into that "community" are lost as a result of caregiving responsibilities. A point that needs to be made is that the discourse of participation and empowerment also writes a version of "community" which is grounded in locality, and which foregrounds its awareness of issues, its effectiveness in deciding what is needed, its responsibility, its ability to access necessary resources, and its solidarity. An alternative account, however, would foreground difference and asymmetry in relation to gender, socioeconomic positioning, ethnicity, age, and sexuality and would not assume an understanding or appreciation of difference. Rather than defining communities (whether this be in terms of identity, location, interest, and so on) as cohesive, the real possibilities of fragmentation and exclusion have to be admitted (Peterson and Lupton 1996).

Jottings for the Future

If an objective of this chapter has been to identify the material effects of discourse through an exploration of the ways in which discourses in health produce and shape multiple versions of the "same" body, so my intention has not been to allocate a truth value to a particular one or ones, to assert the rightness of this and the wrongness of that. Rather it has been to see how those "bodies" play out in the social, to identify points of exclusion within discourses and the material effect of those exclusions, and to recognize the partial and contradictory nature of all discourse. No single discourse can offer a final and complete account of the society in which it circulates. Each generates its own internal contradictions; such points of slippage allow alternative formulations of discourse. Adopting this position highlights the problems associated with remaining locked in binary conceptual structures and powerful knowledge economies which exclude alternative forms of knowledge that could significantly inform our understanding of the operations of our complex societies. This is not a plea for a return to the creation of grand narratives, an elision of difference, and too easy assumptions about the audibility of "voice" and "truth." I am arguing for the opposite: the engagement with difference and a willingness to explore the implications of discursive positions and the consequences of their construction of the social world.

On the local plane, this could involve a sensitivity to the problems associated with concepts of "community" and "empowerment," not in order to eliminate them as possible ways of approach but in order to work with them more precisely, more exactly, to place the different knowledges they generate against each other to see how these may move us on, to engage with the discursively generated contradictions and complications, not refuse them. If it is assumed that both managers and social workers share a common goal in the production of effective services to meet the "needs" of caregivers, rather than allocating the responsibility for decisions about service provision entirely with one group (currently managers but previously clinicians), those decisions could be arrived at in the course of discussions *between* clinicians, managers, and caregivers or their representatives, with careful attention to the implications of the bodies produced within each discursive domain. Calvino (1988) writes of the domination of six qualities for the next millennium: lightness, quickness, exactitude, visibility, multiplicity, and coherence. I want particularly to emphasize three: exactitude, visibility, and multiplicity.

Notes

1. Analysis of the data collected in the social work study indicated that social workers were differently positioned in relation to their practice, knowledge, and skills in their work with caregivers and people with a dementia. Workers I defined as "sophisticated" were those who understood good practice as involving attention to the emotional, not just the instrumental, needs of older people; whose knowledge-based practice demonstrated a capacity to work across these domains; and who resisted ageist discourses. They also actively wished to work with older people.

2. For two discussions about the epistemological problems of coding, with particular reference to qualitative data packages, see Coffey, Holbrook & Atkinson (1996) and Kelle (1997).

3. The concept of intertextuality is a key one in postmodern theory. In the way I am using it here, I mean that no one comes to a text "cold." Readers, coming from different social locations, cannot but bring different formal and experiential knowledge to readings of texts which will differently shape responses to those texts. A consequence of this is that there can be no single "definitive" reading of a particular text. All texts are open to multiple and different readings.

4. A number of texts on qualitative research, as well as qualitative software packages, comment on the importance of defining codes which will reflect the data which is then allocated to them. My experience with coding is that codes cannot adequately represent the complexity of the data which they are intended to "stand for." The code is merely a temporary construct, providing a first step in the development of the analysis.

5. For discussions from somewhat different perspectives of the restructuring process and its outcomes, see Boston et al. (1991), Holland and Boston (1990), and Kelsey (1995).

6. The restructuring of the health system is now widely acknowledged to have failed. While some substantial administrative changes were introduced in 1997, the New Right discourses driving the system remain.

7. This focus was reemphasized through the development during 1991 and 1992

of the Support Needs Assessment Protocol (SNAP), which came into use in 1993. Officials and others associated with SNAP stressed the identification of unmet needs as one desired outcome, along with empowerment of individual clients through the process of *their* elaboration of *their* needs, an emphasis unfortunately somewhat contradicted by the ever more dominant (sub)text of targeting and cost containment, and by the production of care packages which focused solely on responding to physical or instrumental needs. The SNAP form allocated a line and a half to the recording of "caregiver stress," so effectively excluding the nuanced assessment of stress necessary for the promised more responsive meeting of needs. Another issue raised by the focus on "stress" is the exclusion of a more complex writing of the caregiver's emotional positioning in his/her relationship to the care recipient (Opie 1994), a factor that bears closely on types of services that may be acceptable to the caregiver and on how services may be structured. In addition, the absence of space on the form to record the caregiver's input into the care situation meant that his/her input was suppressed while professional input into what policy described as a "partnership" was highlighted.

8. Since outputs were to drive funding allocations from 1993 onward, establishing high "current" levels of outputs was rendered all the more important because of the minimal historical and comparative data to inform funding decisions.

9. My observations of social workers interviewing caregivers and their relatives with a dementia pointed to a clear gender difference. The five sophisticated women workers tended not only to greet the caregivers warmly but also to greet the person with a dementia (at times with a kiss, if requested) and involve them in the conversation. Given the complicated politics of touching, making physical contact with their elderly female clientele carries more difficulties for the male workers, although other nonphysical forms of affirmation do not. The issue is wider, though, than to embrace or not to embrace. Symbolically, including and affirming the person with a dementia is also to affirm their identity—an affirmation that not only reinforces their presence but also reaffirms caregivers who must often go to great lengths to affirm the continuing identity and presence of their dementing relatives.

10. Only seven of the caregivers whose texts I analyzed received family support, and in some cases that support was not extensive. Nor did spousal caregivers always want to add to their children's concerns by involving them closely in some issues, because they saw them as already having major problems of their own. Only three out of the twenty-five had support from "the community" (for example, a local walking group had continued to visit and include one wife with a dementia in their outings for as long as possible).

11. This happened because, administratively, the person with the dementia was defined as "the consumer," i.e., the person to whom services were attached. With the person's death or admission into institutional care, the case was closed.

12. Raymond Williams traces the complex lineage of the word *community* since the fourteenth century, noting its "difficult interaction" due to its historical development where it refers to the "the sense of direct common concern" as well as "the ma-

terialisation of various forms of common organization," and he continues: "*Community* can be the warmly persuasive word to describe an existing set of relationships, or the warmly persuasive word to describe an alternative set of relationships. What is most important, perhaps, is that unlike all other terms of social organization . . . it seems never to be used unfavourably, and never to be given any positive opposing or distinguishing term" (Williams 1976:76; emphasis in original)

13. Minson has commented: "It is a mistake to automatically assume that limits on people's interests and preparedness to take responsibility are an obstacle to a totally politicized or actively involved 'community.' . . . Evidence of failures may be seen to indicate 'participants' successful resistance to imposed relations aimed at their 'liberation', as well as individuals' recognition of the personal and interpersonal demands of 'participation' and the limits of negotiation" (quoted in Peterson and Lupton 1996:162).

References

Beck, C. 1993. Qualitative research: The evaluation of its credibility, fittingness, and auditability. *Western Journal of Nursing* 15(2): 236–66.

Biggs, Simon. 1989. Professional helpers and resistances to work with older people. *Ageing and Society* 9: 43–60.

Boston, Jonathon, John Martin, June Pallot, and Pat Walsh (eds.). 1991. *Reshaping the state: New Zealand's bureaucratic revolution*. Auckland and New York: Oxford University Press.

Burchell, G., C. Gordon, and P. Miller (eds.). 1991. *The Foucault effect: Studies in governmentality*. London: Harvester.

Calvino, Italo. 1988. *Six memos for the next millennium*. Cambridge: Harvard University Press.

Castel, Robert. 1991. From dangerousness to risk. In G. Burchell, C. Gordon, and P. Miller (eds.), *The Foucault effect*, 281–98.

Coffey, Amanda, Beverley Holbrook, and Paul Atkinson. 1996. Qualitative data analysis: Technologies and representations. *Sociological Research Online* 1(1): <http://www.socresonline.org.uk/socresonline/1/1/4.html>.

Diamond, Irene and Lee Quinby. 1988. *Feminism and Foucault: Reflections on resistance*. Boston: Northwestern University Press.

Drawing on the evidence: Social science research and government policy. A report to the government through the Minister of Research, Science, and Technology. 1995. Wellington: Ministry of Research, Science, and Technology.

Fine, Michelle. 1997. Insider research: What counts as critical. Keynote paper presented at the conference, Reclaiming Voice: Ethnographic Inquiry and Qualitative Research in a Postmodern Age, University of California at Los Angeles, June 20–22.

Foucault, Michel. 1977. *Language, countermemory, practice: Selected essays and interviews by M. Foucault*. Edited by Donald Bouchard. Translated by Donald Bouchard and Sherry Simon. Oxford: Blackwell.

——. 1978. *The history of sexuality*, vol. 1, *An Introduction*. London: Penguin.

Fraser, Nancy. 1989. Struggle over needs: Outline of a socialist-feminist critical theory of late capitalist political culture. In *Unruly Practices: Power, discourse, and gender in contemporary social theory*, 161–90. Minneapolis: University of Minnesota Press.

Froggart, Alison. 1990. *Family work with elderly people*. London: Macmillan.

Fry, Roger. 1992. Major social theories of aging and their implications for counseling concepts and practice. *The Counseling Psychologist* 20(2): 246–329.

Gilmour, Jean. 1997. *Representations of dementia: A critical review of nursing literature*. Wellington: Wellington Polytechnic Press.

Gordon, Colin (ed.). *Power/knowledge: Selected interviews and other writings, 1972–1977. Michel Foucault*. Brighton, Eng.: Harvester Press.

Grosz, Elizabeth. 1994. *Volatile bodies: Towards a corporeal feminism*. Bloomington: Indiana University Press.

Hadley, Roger and Roger Clough. 1996. *Care in chaos: Frustration and challenge in community care*. London and New York: Cassell.

Holland, Martin and Jonathon Boston (eds.). 1990. *The fourth Labour government: Politics and policy in New Zealand*. Auckland, Melbourne, Oxford: Oxford University Press.

Hughes, Beverley. 1995. *Older people and community care: Critical theory and practice*. Buckingham (U.K.) and Philadelphia: Open University Press.

Kelle, U. 1997. Theory building in qualitative research and computer programs for the management of textual data. *Sociological Research Online* 2(2): <*http://www.socresonline.org.uk/socresonline/2/2/1.html*>.

Kelsey, Jane. 1995. *The New Zealand experiment: A world model of structural adjustment?* Auckland: Auckland University Press and Bridget Williams Books.

Kitwood, Tom. 1989. Brain, mind, and dementia: With particular reference to Alzheimer's disease. *Ageing and Society* 1: 1–15.

——. 1990. The dialectics of dementia: With particular reference to Alzheimer's disease. *Ageing and Society* 10: 177–96.

——. 1997. *Dementia reconsidered: The person comes first*. Buckingham (U.K.) and Philadelphia: Open University Press.

Kritzman, Lawrence (ed). 1988. *Michel Foucault: Politics, philosophy, culture: Interviews and other writings, 1977–1984*. London and New York: Routledge.

Lincoln, Yvonna. 1990. The making of a constructivist: A remembrance of transformations past. In E. Guba (ed.), *The paradigm dialog*, 67–88. London and Newbury Park, Calif.: Sage.

Lyman, Karen. 1993. *Day in, day out with Alzheimer's: Stress in caregiving relationships*. Philadelphia: Temple University Press.

Marino, Susan. 1991. Selected problems in working with the elderly. In Michael J. Holosko and Marvin D. Feit (eds.), *Social work practice with the elderly*, 47–74. Toronto: Canadian Scholar's Press.

Martin, Luther, Huck Gutman, and Patrick Luther (eds.). 1988. *Technologies of the self: A seminar with Michel Foucault*. Amherst: University of Massachusetts Press.

Martin, Randy (ed.). 1997. Academic labour (Special Issue). *Social Text* 51 (Summer).

McLean, Athena. 1995. Empowerment and the psychiatric consumer/ex-patient movement in the United States: Contradictions, crisis, and change. *Social Science and Medicine* 40(8): 1053–71.

Nocon, Andrew and Hazel Qureshi. 1996. *Outcomes of community care for users and carers: A social services perspective.* Buckingham (U.K.) and Philadelphia: Open University Press.

Opie, Anne. 1991. *Caring alone: Experiences of looking after the confused elderly at home.* Wellington: Daphne Brasell Associates.

——. 1992. *There's nobody there: Community care of confused older people.* Auckland: Oxford University Press; Philadelphia: University of Pennsylvania Press.

——. 1993. The discursive shaping of social work records: Organisational change, professionalism, and client "empowerment." *International Sociological Review,* n.s., 3: 167–89.

——. 1994. The instability of the caring body: Gender and caregivers of confused older people. *Qualitative Health Research* 4(1): 31–50.

——. 1995. *Beyond good intentions: Support work with older people.* Wellington: Institute of Policy Studies, Victoria University of Wellington.

——. 1998. "Nobody's asked me for my views": Users' empowerment by multidisciplinary health teams. *Qualitative Health Research* 8(2): 188–206.

Peterson, Alan and Deborah Lupton. 1996. *The new public health: Health and self in the age of risk.* Sydney: Allen and Unwin.

Pollit, Christopher. 1988. Bringing consumers into performance measurement: Concepts, consequences, and constraints. *Policy and Politics* 16(2): 77–87.

Reinharz, Shulamit. 1992. *Feminist methods in social science research.* New York and London: Oxford University Press.

Shipley, Jenny and Simon Upton. 1992. Support for independence: A discussion paper on the funding and delivery of disability support services. Wellington: Parliament Buildings.

Smale, Gerald and Graham Tuson. 1993. *Empowerment, assessment, care management, and the skilled worker.* National Institute for Social Work Practice and Development Exchange: London: HMSO.

Taylor, Ian (ed.). 1990. *The social effects of free market policies: An international text.* Hertfordshire: Harvester Wheatsheaf.

Upton, Simon. 1991. *Your health and the public health: A statement of government health policy.* Wellington: Parliament Buildings.

Williams, Raymond. 1976. *Keywords: A vocabulary of culture and society.* London: Fontana.

Young, Iris Marion. 1994. Punishment, treatment, empowerment: Three approaches to policy for pregnant adults. *Feminist Studies* 20(1): 33–58.

Contributors

Jane Aronson is Associate Professor in the School of Social Work at McMaster University. Her research focuses on long-term care as an arena for understanding how assumptions and practices concerned with women, caring work, and interpretations of need are reflected in health and social policies. Her current research explores the impacts of government cost-cutting and privatization on elderly women receiving home care.

Nancy Guberman and **Pierre Maheu** are professors of Social Work at the Université du Québec à Montréal. They have collaborated on numerous research projects in the areas of family caregiving, aging, and home care practice and are coauthors of three books, several book chapters, and many scientific articles on these subjects.

Amy Horowitz is currently the Senior Vice President for Research and Director of the Arlene R. Gordon Research Institute of Lighthouse International. She holds a D.S.W. from Columbia University. Dr. Horowitz serves on the editorial boards of *The Gerontologist*, the *Journal of Gerontological Social Worker*, and *Generations*. She is a Fellow and a Past Section Chair (Social Research, Policy, and Practice) of the Gerontological Society of America and a Past President of the State Society on Aging of New York. She has published widely on topics relating to family caregiving and adaptation to chronic disability in late life and is currently conducting a longitudinal study on the interrelationships between disability, depression, and rehabilitation among the elderly.

Sharon M. Keigher is Professor of Social Welfare at the University of Wisconsin-Milwaukee, where she teaches social work macropractice, gerontology, and health policy. She earned her Ph.D. (1985) in Social Service Administration from the University of

Chicago. She has published research on homelessness among the elderly, housing policies for older women, and financial supports for family and informal caregivers. Her current research on the "gray market" in home care is exploring the implications of direct payments on consumer control. She is author of *Housing Risks and Homelessness Among the Urban Elderly* (Haworth Press, 1991) and coauthor of *Wages for Caring: Compensating Families for Care of the Elderly* (Praeger, 1992). She is currently chair of the Social Research, Policy, and Practice section of the Gerontological Society of America and editor-in-chief of *Health and Social Work*.

Margaret MacAdam came to Baycrest Centre for Geriatric Care as Vice President, Social Services, with extensive experience managing, developing, and researching services for elderly people. Her doctorate comes from the Florence Heller School at Brandeis University. Before joining Baycrest she was Associate Research Professor at the Health Policy Institute at Brandeis. She is responsible for directing and evaluating the delivery of social services to elders served throughout Baycrest Centre. She is also Senior Vice President at the center, responsible for policy development and implementation of certain centerwide projects. Currently, Dr. MacAdam is working part-time for the Home Care Development Branch, Health Canada.

Anne Martin-Matthews is Director of the School of Family and Nutritional Sciences at the University of British Columbia. She completed her Ph.D. in sociology at McMaster University. She founded and was director for thirteen years of the Gerontology Research Centre at the University of Guelph, Ontario. She is currently editor-in-chief of the *Canadian Journal on Aging* and is a Fellow of the Gerontological Society of America. Her research and publications have focused largely on issues of family and aging, particularly on marital status transitions, formal and informal social support, and work/family balance. She is currently a coinvestigator of an SSHRC-funded Major Collaborative Research Initiative, based in economics at McMaster University and focusing on "Socioeconomic Dimensions of an Aging Population."

Sheila Neysmith is a professor with the Faculty of Social Work, University of Toronto. She received her doctorate from Columbia University. Her research and writing has focused on the effects of social policy on women as they age. She is coeditor of *Women's Caring: Feminist Perspectives on Social Welfare* (Oxford, 2d ed., 1998) and editor of *Restructuring Caring Labour: Power, Discourse, and Everyday Life* (Oxford, forthcoming). Her current research is a longitudinal study of the effects of policy changes on Ontario households.

Deborah O'Connor is an assistant professor at the University of British Columbia in the School of Social Work. She completed her D.S.W. in 1997 (Wilfred Laurier University). Her research and practice interests have focused primarily on working with cognitively vulnerable older adults and their families. She has an extensive background in clinical social work practice that she continues to develop through active participation in the practice community.

Anne Opie trained as a social worker in the U.K. and has practiced in the U.K., Australia, and New Zealand. She completed her Ph.D. on joint custody in 1988 and worked as a qualitative researcher in the areas of aging and health service delivery in New Zealand between 1989 and 1998. She has published extensively in these areas. Her most recent book, *Beyond Good Intentions: Support Work with Older People,* is a study of New Zealand social work services to caregivers and people with a dementia. Her recently completed research on teamwork as knowledge-based practice, provisionally titled *Thinking Teams Thinking Clients: Knowledge Work in Multidisciplinary Teams,* will be published by Columbia University Press in 1999. She is now working as Research Manager for the Legal Services Board in Wellington.

Index

Abel, E., 72, 92

access to income: autonomy and, 12; in widowhood, 36–37. *See also* economic issues; poverty

access to services: disability rates and, 101, 102; ethnocultural family caregiving and, 129, 147–48; widowhood and, 31. *See also* service delivery

activities of daily living (ADL), 8; age-related disability and, 99–100, 117; caregivers and, 165–66; disability movement and, 9–10; family caregivers and, 142; service delivery models and, 4; social workers and, 127; visual impairment and, 110

acute vs. long-term care mentality, 98, 108

ADL. *See* activities of daily living

adult day care centers, 145, 174

advocacy: geriatric rehabilitation and, 108; of health care providers, 57; in social work, 61–63, 64, 84

ageism, 47, 109; vs. ableism, 61;

"managing" narrative and, 59; social workers and, 62

agency: critical practice and, 19; lack of, 8; term, introduced, 10–11; widowhood and, 33–37. *See also* autonomy

aging theory: critical practice and, 18–19; prevailing knowledge and, 21; social change and, 29

aging with disabilities, 103–104, 117. *See also* geriatric rehabilitation

Albright, L., 112

Alt, P. M., 102

Amaral, P., 116

Ansello, E. F., 104

Antonucci, T., 162

Archbold, P. G., 141

Armstrong, H., 49

Armstrong, P., 49

Aronson, J. (Jane), 5, 14, 50, 51, 54, 55, 56, 57, 58, 74

assessment models, 195

assistive devices: disability rates and, 101; geriatric rehabilitation and, 108

Health and Welfare Canada, 84
health care: age-related disability and,
102, 104; aging women and, 4;
choice and, 11; ghettoization of,
128, 150; resources involved with,
5; restructuring of, 2–3, 155, 193,
208. *See also* service delivery
health care practitioners: busyness of,
50, 56–57, 191; community care
programs and, 6–7; health care
problems and, 4, 170. *See also*
caregivers; personal care workers
health insurance: as employee benefit,
7; for home care workers, 178
health maintenance organizations
(HMO), 16. *See also* managed
care
healthy behaviors, disability rates and,
100
hearing impairments, 103–104, 112
Hedstrom, N. J., 116
Helley, D., 143
help-seeking patterns of caregivers,
145–48
Hendershot, G. E., 101
Hertzman, Clyde, 5
hidden poor, 118
Hines, J., 112, 114
Hoch, C., 164, 168
Hoff, R. A., 116
Holbrook, Beverley, 208
Holden, K., 36, 37
Holland, Martin, 208
Holstein, Martha, 2
home care: bathing and, 10, 176–77;
vs. community-based care, 13;
consumer-directed, 182–85; in
ethnocultural families, 130, 145;
for older people, 47, 155–60;
service providers of, 81–82. *See
also* caregivers
Hooyman, Nancy R., 5, 142

Horowitz, A. (Amy), 105, 106, 111, 112,
113, 116, 141
Hochschild, A. R., 51
Hudson, C. M., 36
Hughes, B. (Beverley), 52, 55, 62, 63,
194
Hugman, R., 3
Hurd, M., 36
Hurst Rojiani, R., 57–58, 59
Husband, Charles, 14

identity: critical practice and, 19;
social work and, 64–65
identity politics, aging and, 9
image conflicts in care, 47–65
Income Security Programs, 32
independent living: disability movement and, 9–10; geriatric rehabilitation and, 108; movement, 61
individual experiences: ethnocultural
family caregiving and, 129–31;
spousal caregivers and, 73–83, 165,
167
information, caregivers and, 196–97
institutional completeness, described,
144
institutionalization as abandonment,
76
isolation: caregiving and, 91–93; social
need and, 42
Italian families: caregiving and, 129,
130, 133, 135, 145; help-seeking
behavior of, 146–47
Ivey, A. E., 128
Ivey, M. B., 128

Jack, R., 19
Jackson, B., 155
Jacob, A., 151
Jaggar, Alison, 8
Jagger, C., 106
Jarman-Rohde, Lily, 2

Critical issues for future
social work practice with